Power BI Machine Learning and OpenAI

Explore data through business intelligence, predictive analytics, and text generation

Greg Beaumont

BIRMINGHAM—MUMBAI

Power BI Machine Learning and OpenAI

Publishing Product Manager: Ali Abidi
Senior Editor: David Sugarman
Technical Editor: Sweety Pagaria
Copy Editor: Safis Editing
Project Coordinator: Farheen Fathima
Proofreader: Safis Editing
Indexer: Sejal Dsilva
Production Designer: Jyoti Chauhan
Marketing Coordinator: Shifa Ansari

First published: June 2023

Production reference:1290523

Published by Packt Publishing Ltd.
Livery Place
35 Livery Street
Birmingham
B3 2PB, UK.

ISBN 978-1-83763-615-0

www.packtpub.com

I would like to thank my wife and family for their continuous support, especially for their patience over the last seven months while I worked weekends to complete this book. I would also like to thank the mentors and colleagues I've worked with over the years, both at Microsoft and in the consulting profession, who went out of their way to be teachers and teammates. The US Federal Aviation Administration (FAA) deserves praise for their efforts in curating and providing the Wildlife Strike database used in this book as open data available to the public. Finally, I am grateful to the many customers I have worked with over the years who have challenged and inspired me to work harder, learn more, and re-think my perspectives about how their businesses intersect with technology.

Contributors

About the author

Greg Beaumont is a data architect at Microsoft, where he is tasked with solving complex problems and creating value for his customers. Focusing on the healthcare industry, Greg works closely with customers to plan enterprise analytics strategies, evaluate new tools and products, conduct training sessions and hackathons, and architect solutions that improve the quality of care and reduce costs. With years of experience in data architecture and a passion for innovation, Greg enjoys identifying and solving complex challenges. He strives to be a trusted advisor to his customers and is always seeking new ways to drive progress and help organizations thrive. He is a veteran of the Microsoft data speaker network and has worked with hundreds of customers on their data management and analytics strategies.

About the reviewers

Peter ter Braake started working as a developer in 1996 after studying physics in Utrecht, the Netherlands. Databases and business intelligence piqued his interest the most, leading to him specializing in SQL Server and its business intelligence components. He has worked with Power BI from the tool's very beginning. Peter started working as an independent contractor in 2008. This has enabled him to divide his time between teaching data-related classes, consulting with customers, and writing articles and books. Peter has also authored *Data Modeling for Azure Data Services*, Packt Publishing.

Inder Rana is a principal cloud architect for the Microsoft Azure cloud, specializing in data platforms including big data analytics and AI. With expertise in Azure services and a deep understanding of cloud architecture principles, Inder helps organizations leverage the power of Microsoft Azure to drive innovation and achieve their business goals. He is passionate about technology and strives to explain complex concepts in a simpler manner to help his clients understand and utilize technology in the right place for the right reasons.

Table of Contents

Part 2: Artificial Intelligence and Machine Learning Visuals and Publishing to the Power BI Service

5

6

7

Part 3: Machine Learning in Power BI

8

9

10

Iterating Power BI ML models 189

11

Applying Power BI ML Models 207

Part 4: Integrating OpenAI with Power BI

12

Use Cases for OpenAI 237

13

Using OpenAI and Azure OpenAI in Power BI Dataflows   251

14

Project Review and Looking Forward   267

Preface

Welcome! If you are interested in this book, you're most likely familiar with Power BI, **machine learning (ML)**, and OpenAI. Over the years, Power BI has evolved from a data visualization tool into a suite of user-friendly, end-to-end **software as a service (SaaS)** tools for data and analytics. I began writing this book with the goal of teaching Power BI professionals about the ML tool built into Power BI. Rather than write a technical manual, I decided to embrace the tradition of Microsoft's popular *Power BI Dashboard in a Day* course (found at `https://aka.ms/diad`) by writing the book as an end-to-end journey, starting with raw data and ending with ML, all within the SaaS Power BI toolset.

During the course of writing the book, an amazing new technology arrived on the scene called OpenAI. OpenAI can generate and summarize human language in amazing ways. The use case for this book was a perfect fit for adding OpenAI as a capstone to the journey.

This book will take you on a data adventure starting with real raw data from the **Federal Aviation Authority (FAA)**, reviewing requirements that mimic a real-world project, cleansing and curating the data using Power BI, making predictions using Power BI ML, and then integrating OpenAI into the use case. You can recreate the entire end-to-end solution by referencing the Packt GitHub site (`https://github.com/PacktPublishing/Unleashing-Your-Data-with-Power-BI-Machine-Learning-and-OpenAI/`) as you read the book.

Business Intelligence (BI), ML, and OpenAI use data in different ways requiring different data modeling techniques and preparation. In my experience, most Power BI professionals think about data differently from ML and AI professionals. When BI professionals first branch into ML, these differences can cause ML projects to fail. Through the example of a real data story, this book attempts to teach those differences in the context of a use case with similar challenges and requirements to those that you may face in the real world. The overarching theme is the intersection of these skill sets for real-world projects that seamlessly incorporate BI, ML, AI, and OpenAI.

If you are looking for a technical manual about Power BI ML or OpenAI, this book is not for you. This book will walk you through a hero's journey that builds up to ML and OpenAI as a capstone to the project. At the end of this book, beyond understanding how to use Power BI ML and OpenAI, you will understand how to *think about* and *understand* data projects in ways that can incorporate ML and OpenAI. Even if the tools in Power BI evolve to be different from the time this book was written, you should be able to apply these learned lessons to new tools and future challenges.

I also want to briefly discuss SaaS ML tools in this preface. I've often heard experienced ML professionals urge caution with regard to SaaS ML tools. I agree that ML as a discipline requires a different mindset and unique skillset from many other data tools. Many factors can lead to ML models returning misleading or biased results. ML projects that need to be highly accurate, or that could have harmful outcomes when wrong, should be handled by ML professionals using advanced ML tools.

That being said, a SaaS tool such as Power BI ML still has a powerful place with the right audience. Power BI professionals interested in learning about ML can skill up quickly by using Power BI ML. Rapid feature discovery, simple predictive use cases, and ad hoc hypothesis testing can all be achieved with a low bar to entry using Power BI ML. The ML models you will build in this book are intended to spark your interest in the subject, not provide a comprehensive course on building proper ML models. By the end of this book, a Power BI professional will understand the basics of why they might use ML, how data needs to be modeled for ML, and how ML can be used in the workflow of a data project. Hopefully, some of you are inspired to learn more about ML and graduate to more advanced ML tools and courses.

Regarding OpenAI, the final two chapters provide use cases for OpenAI that add value to the hands-on workshop with the affiliated GitHub workshop. Real FAA data is used to generate new descriptions and summarize events in your Power BI solution. The intent of this book is not for you to become OpenAI or ML experts, but rather to understand the intersection of BI, ML, AI, and OpenAI. It is my belief that as enterprise SaaS tools such as Power BI become easier to use, the intersection of these skills and tools is the future of our profession.

Who this book is for

This book is ideal for BI professionals who want to learn about Power BI ML and OpenAI in the context of a hands-on workshop using real-world data. A working knowledge of Power BI prior to reading this book will be helpful. Taking the *Power BI Dashboard in a Day* training is a great place to start, even if you follow the PDF document from the link at your own pace. ML professionals may also find value in this book from the perspective of the intersection of BI, ML, OpenAI, and AI. I would expect an ML professional to have a more advanced understanding of BI projects and the Power BI toolset after reading this book.

What this book covers

Chapter 1, Requirements, Data Modeling, and Planning, reviews the FAA Wildlife Strike data to be used in the book, browses the data in Power BI, reviews use cases for the data, and plans data architecture for future chapters.

Chapter 2, Preparing and Ingesting Data with Power Query, consists of data transformation and modeling to prep data for both a Power BI dataset and queries that will be used to build ML models. A foundation for exploring data in the context of BI while also prepping for ML is the underlying theme of the chapter.

Chapter 3, Exploring Data Using Power BI and Creating a Semantic Model, begins the process of designing a user-friendly BI dataset that can be the basis of reports. Naming conventions, table relationships, and custom measures will all be created so that you can begin doing analytics in Power BI to easily explore the FAA data to discover features for ML models.

Chapter 4, Model Data for Machine Learning in Power BI, will explore the data using Power BI to discover potential features that can be used to build ML models. Those features will then be added to queries in Power Query to form the basis of data that will be used with Power BI ML.

Chapter 5, Discovering Features Using Analytics and AI Visuals, leverages Power BI as an analytics and data visualization tool to rapidly explore the FAA data and discover new features for the ML queries. A variety of different measures and visualizations are used to provide variety for you.

Chapter 6, Discovering New Features Using R and Python Visuals, discovers additional features for the ML queries using the R and Python visuals in Power BI. R and Python visuals provide some advanced analytics capabilities that aren't easy with standard measures and visuals.

Chapter 7, Deploying Data Ingestion and Transformation Components to the Power BI Cloud Service, moves the content created in the previous six chapters to the Power BI cloud service. The Power BI dataflows, datasets, and reports are moved to the cloud for the remainder of the book and workshop.

Chapter 8, Building Machine Learning Models with Power BI, builds ML models in Power BI. The ML queries designed in the previous chapters are used to build three ML models for binary classification, general classification, and regression predictions.

Chapter 9, Evaluating Trained and Tested ML Models, reviews the three ML models that were built in Power BI. The testing results are reviewed and explained in the context of predictive capabilities.

Chapter 10, Iterating Power BI ML Models, discusses future plans for the ML models based on the findings of the previous chapter. Options include using the ML models, modifying the queries and rebuilding the models, and more.

Chapter 11, Applying Power BI ML Models, brings in new/more recent data from the FAA Wildlife Strike database and runs it through the ML models. Results are compared to the original testing results, and a process is put in place to score new data in the future.

Chapter 12, Use Cases for OpenAI, plans for the use of OpenAI with the project and workshop. Discussions about the intersection of BI and OpenAI lead to ideas for integrating OpenAI into your plans.

Chapter 13, Using OpenAI and Azure OpenAI in Power BI Dataflows, builds OpenAI API calls into the solution. Text generation and summarization are added directly to Power BI.

Chapter 14, Project Review and Looking Forward, discusses the key concepts from the book. Advice for applying the learnings from the book to your career and future plans is also reviewed.

To get the most out of this book

The Packt GitHub site affiliated with this book provides scripts and files for a comprehensive workshop to recreate everything in this book. The repository can be found at this link: `https://github.com/PacktPublishing/Unleashing-Your-Data-with-Power-BI-Machine-Learning-and-OpenAI/`. Basic Power BI tools that most Power BI professionals are already using, along with an OpenAI subscription, will facilitate the use of the GitHub repository.

Software/hardware covered in the book	Operating system requirements
Power BI Desktop – April 2023 or newer	Windows
Power BI cloud service	Web browser
Python – version compatible with Power BI Desktop	Windows
R – version compatible with Power BI Desktop	Windows
OpenAI	Web browser
Azure OpenAI (optional)	Web browser

From a licensing perspective, a workspace assigned to either Power BI Premium per User or Power BI Premium will be needed in the Power BI cloud service. Several chapters will also require a Power BI Pro license to follow along. For OpenAI, either an OpenAI or Azure subscription with access to OpenAI will be needed.

If you are using the digital version of this book, we advise you to type the code yourself or access the code from the book's GitHub repository (a link is available in the next section). Doing so will help you avoid any potential errors related to the copying and pasting of code.

Download the example code files

You can download the example code files for this book from GitHub at `https://github.com/PacktPublishing/Unleashing-Your-Data-with-Power-BI-Machine-Learning-and-OpenAI/`. If there's an update to the code, it will be updated in the GitHub repository.

We also have other code bundles from our rich catalog of books and videos available at `https://github.com/PacktPublishing/`. Check them out!

Conventions used

There are a number of text conventions used throughout this book.

`Code in text`: Indicates code words in text, database table names, folder names, filenames, file extensions, pathnames, dummy URLs, user input, and Twitter handles. Here is an example: "A calculated measure can be created for counting rows in the primary table of data with the following DAX expression: `Incidents = COUNTROWS('Strike Reports Fact')`."

A block of code is set as follows:

```
(if [Struck Engine 1] = true then 1 else 0) +
(if [Struck Engine 2] = true then 1 else 0) +
(if [Struck Engine 3] = true then 1 else 0) +
(if [Struck Engine 4] = true then 1 else 0)
```

Bold: Indicates a new term, an important word, or words that you see onscreen. For instance, words in menus or dialog boxes appear in **bold**. Here is an example: "Select **System info** from the **Administration** panel."

> **Tips or important notes**
> Appear like this.

Get in touch

Feedback from our readers is always welcome.

General feedback: If you have questions about any aspect of this book, email us at customercare@packtpub.com and mention the book title in the subject of your message.

Errata: Although we have taken every care to ensure the accuracy of our content, mistakes do happen. If you have found a mistake in this book, we would be grateful if you would report this to us. Please visit www.packtpub.com/support/errata and fill in the form.

Piracy: If you come across any illegal copies of our works in any form on the internet, we would be grateful if you would provide us with the location address or website name. Please contact us at copyright@packtpub.com with a link to the material.

If you are interested in becoming an author: If there is a topic that you have expertise in and you are interested in either writing or contributing to a book, please visit authors.packtpub.com.

Share Your Thoughts

Once you've read *Power BI Machine Learning and OpenAI*, we'd love to hear your thoughts! Scan the QR code below to go straight to the Amazon review page for this book and share your feedback.

https://packt.link/r/1-837-63615-X

Your review is important to us and the tech community and will help us make sure we're delivering excellent quality content.

Download a free PDF copy of this book

Thanks for purchasing this book!

Do you like to read on the go but are unable to carry your print books everywhere?

Is your eBook purchase not compatible with the device of your choice?

Don't worry, now with every Packt book you get a DRM-free PDF version of that book at no cost.

Read anywhere, any place, on any device. Search, copy, and paste code from your favorite technical books directly into your application.

The perks don't stop there, you can get exclusive access to discounts, newsletters, and great free content in your inbox daily

Follow these simple steps to get the benefits:

1. Scan the QR code or visit the link below

https://packt.link/free-ebook/9781837636150

2. Submit your proof of purchase
3. That's it! We'll send your free PDF and other benefits to your email directly

Part 1: Data Exploration and Preparation

Your journey starts with the ingestion and preparation of data using Power BI. After discussing data modeling for business intelligence and machine learning, you will learn how to connect to data for the use case, clean it up and check for errors, explore the data to ensure referential integrity, and then create a relational data model.

This part has the following chapters:

- *Chapter 1, Requirements, Data Modeling, and Planning*
- *Chapter 2, Preparing and Ingesting Data with Power Query*
- *Chapter 3, Exploring Data Using Power BI and Creating a Semantic Model*
- *Chapter 4, Model Data for Machine Learning in Power BI*

1

Requirements, Data Modeling, and Planning

You begin your journey by assessing the requirements and data for your project. The use case will be a fictional scenario, but everything will be built using real data from the **Federal Aviation Administration's (FAA) Wildlife Strike Database**. The data is real, the topic can be understood by anyone, and the findings within the data are interesting and fun. According to the FAA's website, about 47 animal strikes are reported daily by aircraft. These incidents can damage airplanes, potentially endanger passengers, and negatively impact wild animal (especially bird) populations.

For the use case, you have been assigned to provide your leadership with tools to do an interactive analysis of the FAA Wildlife Strike data, find insights about factors that influence the incidents, and also make predictions about future wildlife strike incidents and the associated costs. The primary goal of your project, predicting the future impact of FAA Wildlife Strikes, will require building some Power BI machine learning models.

Before uploading data to Power BI's **machine learning** (**ML**) tools, you'll need to create tables of data that will train the ML models. There is an old saying about data and analytics: *"Garbage in, garbage out."* **Software as a Service** (**SaaS**) machine learning tools are easy to use, but you still need to feed them good-quality curated data. Identifying the right training data and getting it into the right format are crucial steps in an ML project.

This project will encompass data exploration, data transformation, data analysis, and additional downstream data transformations before you begin working with Power BI ML tools. You are already an experienced **business intelligence** (**BI**) professional and Power BI user, and now you are ready to take your skills to the next level with ML in Power BI!

Power BI supports connections to source data in many different formats, ranging from relational databases to unstructured sources to big flat tables of raw data. Countless books have been written about the best ways to structure and model data for different use cases. Rather than dive into the specifics of data modeling, for this book, we will begin with two simple assumptions:

- Most of the time, a **star schema** design will provide the most efficient storage and query performance for business intelligence data models

- Basic ML models, such as the ones you will build in this book, are usually created with a **flattened table**

Just to be clear, not every solution will follow these assumptions. Rather, these assumptions are generalizations that can provide you with a starting point as you approach the design of a new data model. Quite often, there will not be a perfect answer, and the optimal design will be dictated by the types of queries and business logic that are generated by the end consumers of the data model.

If you've never heard the terms star schema and flattened data before, don't worry! The book will progress at a pace that is intended to help you learn and will also stay at a level that makes sense when you review the FAA data. Let's browse the FAA Wildlife Strike data and decide upon the best data modeling strategy for your new project!

In this chapter, we will take the following steps so that you can understand the data, think through how it will be used, and then formulate a preliminary plan for the data model:

- Reviewing the source data

- Reviewing the requirements for the solution

- Designing a preliminary data model

- Considerations for ML

Technical requirements

For this chapter, you will need the following:

- Power BI Desktop April 2023 or later (no licenses required)

- FAA Wildlife Strike data files from either the FAA website or the Packt GitHub repo: `https://github.com/PacktPublishing/Unleashing-Your-Data-with-Power-BI-Machine-Learning-and-OpenAI/tree/main/Chapter-01`

Reviewing the source data

You begin your journey by digging into the source data that you will be using for your project. Let's get started!

Accessing the data

The source data that you will be using for this book is real data from the United States **FAA**. The data contains reports filed when aircraft struck wildlife. There is a website providing details, documentation, updates, and access instructions at this URL: `https://wildlife.faa.gov/home`. The URL (and all URLs) will also be linked from the affiliated GitHub site at `https://github.com/PacktPublishing/Unleashing-Your-Data-with-Power-BI-Machine-Learning-and-OpenAI` in case changes are made after this book has been published.

If you'd prefer to follow along using the finished version of the content from this chapter rather than building it all step by step, you can download the PBIT version of the file at the Packt GitHub site folder for *Chapter 1*: `https://github.com/PacktPublishing/Unleashing-Your-Data-with-Power-BI-Machine-Learning-and-OpenAI/tree/main/Chapter-01`.

Within the FAA Wildlife Strike Database website, you can navigate to this link and run basic queries against the data and familiarize yourself with the content: `https://wildlife.faa.gov/search`. There are also two files linked from this page that you can reference while reviewing the source data.

At the time of this book's writing, the second heading on the web page is titled **Download the FAA Wildlife Strike Database**, and it has a link titled **Download** that allows you to download the entire historical database along with a reference file. You can download the files from the FAA site for the purposes of this book. There will also be a Power BI PBIT file containing the results of the efforts of this chapter at the GitHub repository. A PBIT file is a Power BI template that can be populated with the files that you download from the Packt GitHub site. If the FAA data ever becomes unavailable, you can still proceed with the contents from the GitHub site to recreate the contents of every chapter.

The files you will be using from the FAA are as follows:

- `wildlife.accdb`: This contains all of the historical FAA Wildlife Strike reports. You can also download a copy of the file that is identical to the book from the Packt GitHub site: `https://github.com/PacktPublishing/Unleashing-Your-Data-with-Power-BI-Machine-Learning-and-OpenAI/tree/main/Chapter-01`.

- `read_me.xls`: This contains descriptive information about the data in the `wildlife.accdb` database file. An `.xlsx` version of the file is available on the Packt GitHub site, too.

Exploring the FAA Wildlife Strike report data

The `wildlife.accdb` file is in an Access file format that can be opened with many different tools including Microsoft Access, Microsoft Excel, Power BI, and many more. For the purpose of this book, you will open it using **Power BI Desktop**. Power BI Desktop is available as a free download at this link: `https://powerbi.microsoft.com/en-us/downloads/`.

1. First, open up Power BI Desktop. Once it is open on your desktop, select the **Get data** drop-down menu from the ribbon and click on **More…** as shown in the following screenshot:

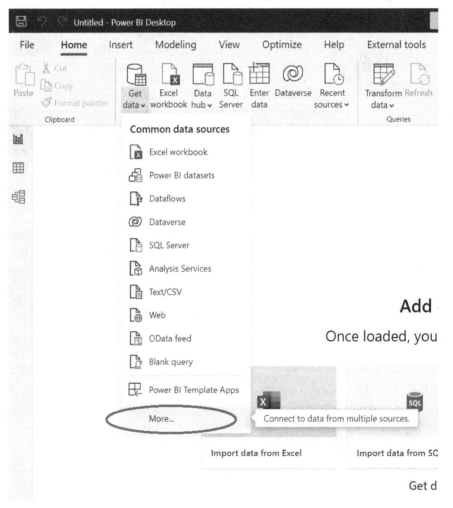

Figure 1.1 – Connecting to data with Power BI Desktop

2. Next, within the **Get data** window, select **Access database** and click **Connect**:

Figure 1.2 – Access database connector in Power BI

3. Select the **Access database** file that was downloaded and unzipped from the FAA Wildlife Strike Database, named **wildlife**:

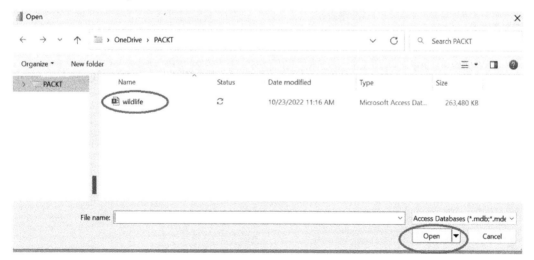

Figure 1.3 – The wildlife file shows up in Power BI

4. Select the **STRIKE_REPORTS** table and click **Transform Data**:

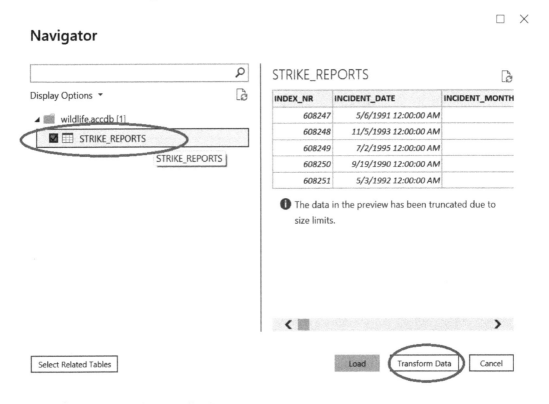

Figure 1.4 – Preview of the data before making transformations

5. The Power Query window will open in Power BI Desktop with a preview of the FAA Wildlife Strike data. On the ribbon, select the **View** header for **Data Preview**, and then check the boxes for **Column quality**, **Column distribution**, and **Column profile**. These features will provide some insights for the data preview, that helps you explore and understand the data:

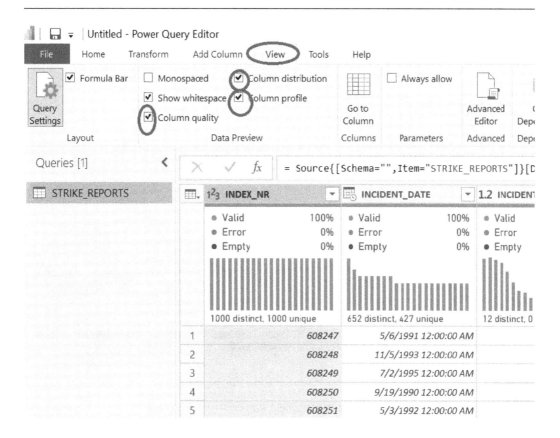

Figure 1.5 – Data Preview features in Power Query

In *Figure 1.5*, notice that the first column, **INDEX_NR**, is highlighted. You can see that none of the values are empty, none have errors, and in **Column statistics** at the bottom of *Figure 1.6*, every value is a unique integer. The name **INDEX_NR** gives it away, but this column is the unique identifier for each row of data.

Let's review another column in Power Query. Go ahead and highlight **TIME_OF_DAY**. As you can see in *Figure 1.6*, there are four distinct values and about 12% are blank. Blank values are an important consideration for this solution. Non-empty values include terms such as **Day**, **Dawn**, **Dusk**, and **Night**. What does an empty value mean? Was the field left blank by the person filing the report? Was it not entered properly into the system? You'll revisit this topic later in the book.

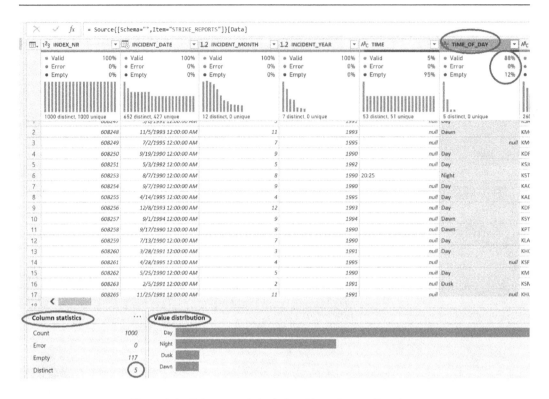

Figure 1.6 – Column statistics help with understanding data

Since there are over 100 columns in the FAA Wildlife Strike reports' data, we won't discuss all of them in this chapter. That being said, reviewing each and every column would be a great way to review the data for errors, empty fields, distribution of values, and more. For the purposes of this chapter, go ahead and open up the `read_me.xls` file that was included with the ZIP file from the FAA. The first sheet is **Column Name** and contains the names and descriptive data about the columns in the `wildlife.accdb` file. Most of the columns fall into one of the following categories:

- Date and time fields detailing the dates, times, and years for different events related to each report

- Descriptive information about the event such as height of contact, latitudes and longitudes, originating airports, and flight numbers

- Descriptive information about the aircraft such as ownership, aircraft type and manufacturer, number of engines, location of engines, and so on

- Estimates of the damage due to the strike such as costs, costs adjusted for inflation, damage location on the aircraft, and more

- Information about the wildlife struck by the aircraft including species, size, quantities hit, and so on

Once you've finished browsing the report data, close the `read_me.xlsx` document on your desktop, and then connect to it from Power BI per the following steps. The document version used in this book can be downloaded from the Packt GitHub site here: `https://github.com/PacktPublishing/Unleashing-Your-Data-with-Power-BI-Machine-Learning-and-OpenAI/tree/main/Chapter-01`.

1. Click on **Excel Workbook** in the left-hand panel:

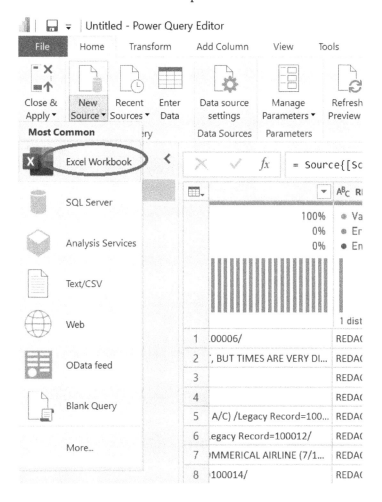

Figure 1.7 – Excel Workbook is a new source of data

2.   Select the **read_me** file from the browser and click **Open**:

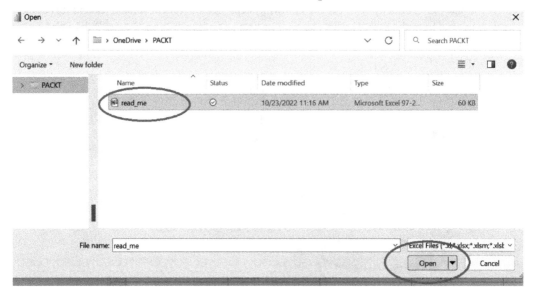

Figure 1.8 – Excel file ready to open in Power Query

3.   Tick the **Aircraft Type**, **Engine Codes**, and **Engine Position** boxes. Then, click **OK**.

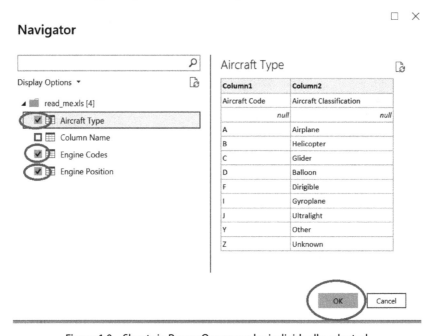

Figure 1.9 – Sheets in Power Query can be individually selected

After clicking **OK** and importing the three sheets, notice that **Aircraft Type**, **Engine Codes**, and **Engine Position** are now available in Power Query as three separate tables of data:

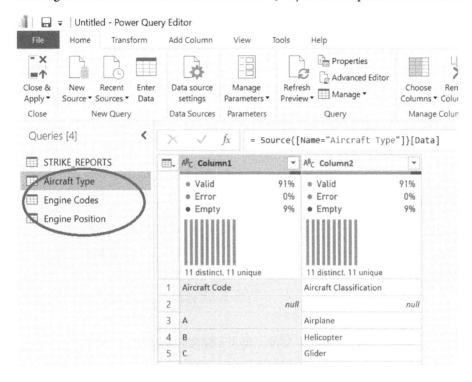

Figure 1.10 – Three new tables are previewed in Power Query

The three tables contain descriptive information about values that exist in the FAA Wildlife Strike reports' data:

- **Aircraft Type**: A table that maps the Aircraft Code to a description such as Airplane, Helicopter, or Glider
- **Engine Codes**: Information about engine manufacturer and model numbers
- **Engine Position**: Details about the location of an engine on the aircraft

For all three of these tables, you'll notice that there are some unnecessary rows and blank values. You will address these later in the book, so there is no need to make any modifications in Power Query at this time.

Once you've browsed the different columns from all the different tables in Power Query, click **Close & Apply** to import the data into Power BI and save it, per the following diagram:

Figure 1.11 – The Close & Apply button will import data into Power BI

Once the data is imported, you can save your Power BI Desktop file as a .pbix file. A copy of the PBIT file named *Chapter 1* Template.pbit, which can be populated with the data and then saved as a PBIX, can be found at this GitHub link: https://github.com/PacktPublishing/ Unleashing-Your-Data-with-Power-BI-Machine-Learning-and-OpenAI/tree/ main/Chapter-01.

Reviewing the requirements for the solution

Now that you've explored the FAA Wildlife Strike data, you have a better understanding of what data is available for your solution. The original assignment that you were given by your stakeholders was as follows:

- Provide leadership with tools to do interactive analysis of the FAA Wildlife Strike data
- Find insights about factors that influence the incidents
- Make predictions about future wildlife strike incidents

Those requirements sound pretty vague! Now that you have a better understanding of the available data, it's a good time to circle back with the stakeholders and clarify those requirements. You ask them questions such as the following:

- What types of interactive analysis do you want to do?

- Are you interested in the impact on endangered bird species?

- Maybe you'd like to view trends due to wildlife strikes and compare airports and regions?

- Perhaps you'd like to see the height and frequency of wildlife strikes at different times of the year?

- Would understanding correlations to factors such as aircraft size, time of day, season, geography, and height be useful?

- Are you interested in predicting specific risks or outcomes?

Entire books have been written about gathering requirements for data and analytics projects, and discussions on this particular topic could also be extensive. For the sake of keeping this book consumable, let's assume that your discussions with the stakeholders led to prioritizing the following deliverables for the project:

- **Analytic report**: Viewing trends over time such as number of incidents, location of incidents, height, and details such as types of aircraft and wildlife species

- **Predict damage**: When a strike is reported, make a prediction as to whether there will be a cost associated with any damage

- **Predict size**: When a strike is reported, make a prediction about the size of the wildlife that struck the aircraft

- **Predict height**: For wildlife strikes, predict the height of the incidents

Now, you review the notes you took about the FAA Wildlife Strike data during your data exploration efforts. In doing so, you can think about how the data might match up to the use cases. Based on the requirements and your initial exploration of the data, you decide that the FAA Wildlife Strike data from the `wildlife.accdb` file and the tables from the `read_me.xls` file (**Engine Codes**, **Aircraft Type**, and **Engine Position**) are appropriate content to include during the initial phases of your project.

Designing a preliminary data model

Earlier in this chapter, we made two simple assumptions about data modeling:

- Most of the time, a *star schema* design will provide the most efficient storage and query performance for business intelligence data models

- Basic ML models, such as the ones you can build in this book, are usually created with a *flattened table*

Now that you have a grasp of the underlying data and requirements, it is time to think about the data model for your FAA Wildlife Strike data solution. Logically, you can describe your tables of data as follows:

- **STRIKE_REPORTS** (from `wildlife.accdb`): Each row represents a report that was filed. The table of data contains both descriptive values (date, location, and type) along with values that can be summed up and averaged (height and costs).

- **Engine Codes** (from `read-me.xls`): This contains information about the aircraft engines that can be tied to **STRIKE_REPORTS**.

- **Aircraft Type** (from `read-me.xls`): This contains information about the aircraft that can be tied to **STRIKE_REPORTS**.

- **Engine Position** (from `read-me.xls`): This contains information about the aircraft engine positions that can be tied to **STRIKE_REPORTS**.

At this point, you are faced with some data model choices. No matter what decision you make, some people might question your architecture, since there is no perfect design. Depending on how end users will use the data, the data model design may change. This book will demonstrate some of the differences in data model designs for ML models versus traditional BI designs. At a high level, there are three basic approaches you can take in Power BI:

- **Flatten**: You can flatten all the data onto a single table by joining **Engine Codes**, **Aircraft Type**, and **Engine Position** onto **STRIKE_REPORTS**.

- **Star schema**: You can build out a true star schema with **STRIKE_REPORTS** as a fact table and **Engine Codes**, **Aircraft Type**, and **Engine Position** as dimension tables. Some additional data from **STRIKE_REPORTS** would also be broken out into separate dimension tables. For example, **AIRPORT_ID**, **AIRPORT**, **STATE**, and **FAAREGION** could be separate dimension tables.

- **Hybrid design**: You can build out a hybrid design using both a flattened and star schema design pattern for the sake of practicality and ease of use.

Let's look at each of these in turn.

Flattening the data

Flattening the FAA Wildlife Strike reports' data would require joining the **Engine Codes**, **Aircraft Type**, and **Engine Position** tables onto the **STRIKE_REPORTS** table so that everything is on one big flat table of data. The result would be something that looks like this:

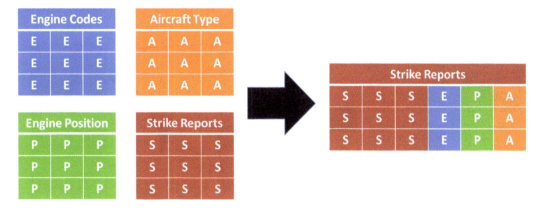

Figure 1.12 – Tables on the left are combined to form a single table on the right

The following table contains some, but not all, of the pros and cons of a flattened table of data:

Pros	Cons
• Simplicity • No joins needed for code • Commonly used by data scientists • Can compress well with columnar databases • No relational data models for business users	• Repetitive data can lead to an inefficient storage footprint • Limitations for queries with advanced logic • Less flexibility for future change and evolution of solution • Complex logical queries can be less efficient

Figure 1.13 – Pros and cons of a flattened table for BI

Next, let's look at the star schema.

Star schema

A true star schema built to best practices would include relationships between **Engine Codes**, **Aircraft Type**, and **Engine Position** with the **STRIKE_REPORTS** table. It would also break off parts of the **STRIKE_REPORTS** table into smaller dimension tables. The following figure is a representation of the approach for a true star schema. There may be more dimension tables that would need to be broken off of the **STRIKE_REPORTS** table in addition to **Location** and **Species**, but this is an example of how it might look:

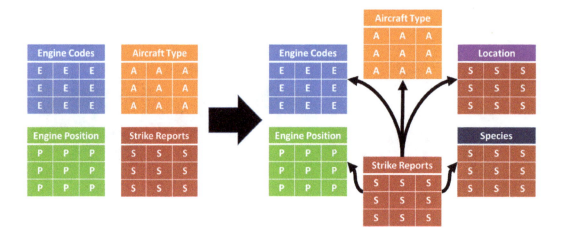

Figure 1.14 – Tables on the left are combined into a star schema,
and some data is split off into new dimension tables

The following table contains some, but not all, of the pros and cons of a true star schema design:

Pros	Cons
• Tables often line up with business logic • Balance of minimal data duplication and efficient queries • Usually expandable if the scope of the solution grows and new data is introduced • Traditionally considered the gold standard for BI data models	• With modern tools, the benefits of reducing data duplication are less impactful versus older tools • Complicated ETL • Machine learning models are usually trained with flat tables of data • Don't always scale well with very large data volumes having tens of billions of rows

Figure 1.15 – Pros and cons of a star schema for BI

Hybrid design

For the FAA Wildlife Strike data, combining aspects of a flattened design and a star schema is also an option. At the time of this book's writing, the entire **STRIKE_REPORTS** table is fewer than 300,000 rows and has fewer than 100 columns. Only two columns contain verbose free text, so data volume is not an issue when using Power BI. For this particular use case, the differences in data storage requirements between flattened and star schema data models are minimal. With data volumes of this small size, you can design the data model to meet the needs of the solution without some of the performance concerns that would be introduced for data sources with tens of millions of rows or hundreds of columns containing free text fields. Columns of data left on a transaction table that will be used as categories are technically called **degenerate dimensions**. A hybrid design could look something like the following example:

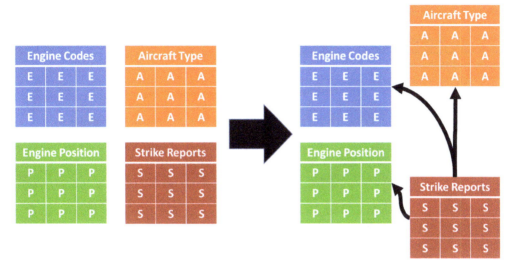

Figure 1.16 – Tables from the left are enhanced and combined into a star
schema with some descriptive data still in the fact table

The following table contains some, but not all, of the pros and cons of a hybrid design:

Pros	Cons
• Rapid prototyping • Less logic in the data transformation layer • Flexible design	• Possibly less performant than a star schema for traditional BI • Additional logical complexity for users versus a big flat table • Data will still need to be flattened out for machine learning • Not perfect for either BI or ML, but a compromise between the two

Figure 1.17 – Pros and cons of a hybrid design and considerations for additional data

Before finalizing a preliminary logical design for your FAA Wildlife Strike solution, take a step back to think about the data and the requirements. You can review the expected deliverables from earlier in the chapter, including an analytic report and predictions of damage, size, and height.

In addition to the FAA Wildlife Strike data you've been using, what other data might be useful for the solution? Also, what is the effort to get the data? Here are a few examples that you could research:

Additional Data Sources	Level of Effort
Date-based table of aggregations such as Month, Quarter, Season, and Holidays	Easy
Time-based table of aggregations such as hour, AM/PM, and so on	Easy
Data for flights that didn't have a wildlife strike could provide a baseline for the percentage of flights with strikes	Difficult
Weather data that could be mapped to the date and time of wildlife strikes	Difficult
Additional data about wildlife species such as weight ranges, habitat ranges, and so on	Difficult

Figure 1.18 – Additional potential data sources for the solution

Additional flight, weather, and wildlife data could provide greater analytic and predictive value for the solution. However, adding those sources would require quite a bit of effort that exceeds the scope of your project and the length of this book. If the initial project goes well, you can circle back to these options for future enhancements.

There may be value in adding a Time table to the solution, so open up Power Query and take another look at the **TIME** column. Notice that 95% of the entries are empty:

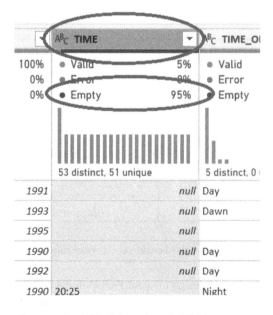

Figure 1.19 – 95% of the values for TIME are empty

Due to a lack of complete data, you decide to leave a Time table out of the initial build.

How about a Date table so that you can roll up data by week, month, quarter, year, holidays, weekends, and more? Looking at the **INCIDENT_DATE** column in Power Query, it is populated for every entry in the preview:

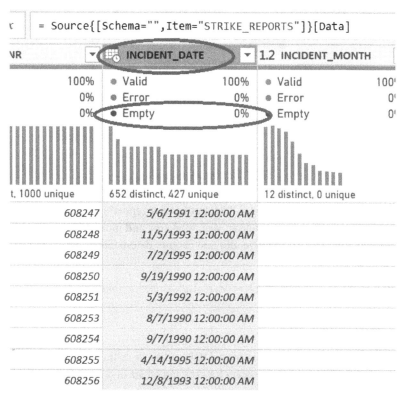

Figure 1.20 – INCIDENT_DATE is fully populated with date values

INCIDENT_DATE can be used as a key for connecting to a Date table containing many different date-based aggregations. You decide to pull in a Date table for the architecture. The resulting preliminary data model will now look as follows:

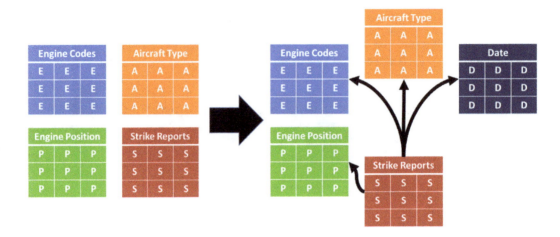

Figure 1.21 – A Date table is added to the preliminary data model

The Date table was not present in the source data, but in your reporting model, it will allow you to slice and dice data by day, week, month, quarter, year, weekend, and more. When you explore data in future chapters, it will add new ways to dive into and explore date-based trends. The Date table will be added in *Chapter 2*.

In the final section of the chapter, we'll look at what else we need to take into account for ML.

Considerations for ML

Now that you've created a preliminary data model that will serve as the basis for analytic reporting in Power BI, you start thinking about a process for creating tables of data to be used with Power BI machine learning. You will need to create a single table of flattened data for each machine learning model that you train, test, and deploy.

Creating tables of data to train a machine learning model entails treating each column as a feature of the algorithm that you will be training and then using to make predictions. For example, if you wanted to create a machine learning algorithm that predicts whether something is an insect, the **features** (ML terminology for columns on a single table) might be [Six Legs Y/N?], [Life Form Y/N?], [Count of Eyes], and [Weight], and then a column that will be predicted, such as [Insect Y/N?]. Each row would represent something that is being evaluated for a prediction to answer the question, "Is this an insect?"

You decide to take the following approach, in the following order, so that you can do everything within Power BI:

1. Data exploration and initial data model creation in Power BI Desktop Power Query.

2. Analytic report created in Power BI.

3. Feature discovery in Power BI.

4. Create training data sets in Power Query.

5. Move training data sets to Power BI dataflows.

6. Train, test, deploy a Power BI machine learning model in Power BI dataflows.

This process is shown in *Figure 1.22*.

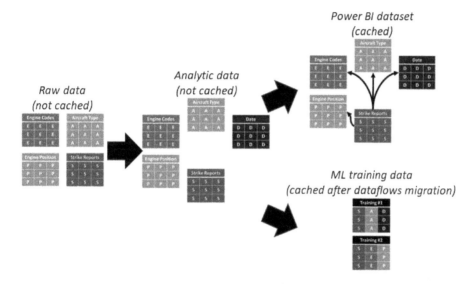

Figure 1.22 – All of the ETL (extract, transform, load) will happen
in Power BI Power Query and Power BI dataflows

Power BI ML offers three different types of predictive model types. Those types, as defined in the Power BI service, are as follows:

- A **binary prediction** model predicts whether an outcome will be achieved. Effectively, a prediction of "Yes" or "No" is returned.

- **General classification** models predict more than two possible outcomes such as *A*, *B*, *C*, or *D*.

- A **regression** model will predict a numeric value along a spectrum of possible values. For example, it will predict the costs of an event based on similar past events.

As part of your preliminary planning, you consider how these options could map to the deliverables that were prioritized by your stakeholders:

- **Analytic report**: This deliverable will be a Power BI analytic report and could use some Power BI AI features, but it will not be a Power BI ML model. The analytic report will help you explore and identify the right data for Power BI machine learning models.

- **Predict damage**: Predicting whether or not damage will result from a wildlife strike is a good match for a binary prediction model since the answer will have two possible outcomes: yes or no.

- **Predict size**: Predicting the size of the wildlife that struck an aircraft based upon factors such as damage cost, damage location, height, time of year, and airport location will probably have multiple values that can be predicted such as *Large*, *Medium*, and *Small*. This requirement could be a good fit for a general classification model.

- **Predict height**: This deliverable predicts the height at which wildlife strikes will happen and provides that prediction as a numeric value representing height above ground level in feet. It is likely a good fit for a regression model, which predicts numeric values.

There is no way of knowing with certainty whether the FAA Wildlife Strike data will support these specific use cases, but you won't know until you try! Discovery is a key part of the process. First, you must identify features in the data that might have predictive value, and then train and test the machine learning models in Power BI. Only then will you know what types of predictions might be possible for your project.

Summary

In this chapter, you explored the data available for your project and reviewed subsequent options for mapping data to the requirements of your stakeholders. You reviewed data architecture options to meet both business intelligence and ML requirements in Power BI and decided upon a hybrid approach that blends a star schema design with flattened data. You also formulated a plan to explore, analyze, design, build, and deploy your solution. Finally, you decided upon three use cases for predictive ML models in Power BI.

In the next chapter, you will ingest and prep data from the FAA Wildlife Strike database using Power Query within Power BI. You'll deep dive into data characteristics, decide what is needed for your design, and build out a flexible foundation that will support both the current project and future iterations and changes. Your approach in Power Query will support both business intelligence analytics in Power BI and predictive analytics in Power BI ML.

2

Preparing and Ingesting Data with Power Query

In *Chapter 1* of this book, you kicked off a project to design a solution that will help track and predict height and outcomes related to aircraft striking wildlife. You gathered requirements from the project stakeholders, took a deep dive into the FAA Wildlife Strike data, mapped the requirements to the available data, and put together a preliminary data model design, which will be the foundation of your reports and predictive analytics using Power BI ML models.

Creating tables of data that will be used for ML requires a clear understanding of the FAA Wildlife Strike data and an architecture that allows you to discover features in the data. In this chapter, you will embark upon a journey to prepare queries for the data that you explored in *Chapter 1*, model that data for Power BI using your preliminary data model as a guide, and create curated queries, which will be the basis of both datasets and ML training datasets in Power BI.

Technical requirements

This chapter builds on the work that was begun in *Chapter 1*. All of the data can be found at `https://github.com/PacktPublishing/Unleashing-Your-Data-with-Power-BI-Machine-Learning-and-OpenAI/tree/main/Chapter-02`.

For this chapter, you will need the following:

- Power BI Desktop April 2023 or later (no licenses required)
- FAA Wildlife Strike data files from either the FAA website or the Packt GitHub site at GitHub: `https://github.com/PacktPublishing/Unleashing-Your-Data-with-Power-BI-Machine-Learning-and-OpenAI/tree/main/Chapter-02`

If you'd prefer to follow along using the finished version of the content from this chapter rather than building it all step by step, you can download the completed PBIT version of the file at the Packt GitHub site folder for *Chapter 2*: `https://github.com/PacktPublishing/Unleashing-Your-Data-with-Power-BI-Machine-Learning-and-OpenAI/tree/main/Chapter-02`.

Preparing the primary table of data

You have decided to start the process of building out the design for your dataset by modeling the primary table of data from the FAA Wildlife Strike database. You start by opening the `Chapter 1.pbix` Power BI Desktop file that was created in *Chapter 1*. You can also download a clean copy of the file from the Packt GitHub site for this book at this link as a PBIT file, which can be populated as a PBIX using the data downloaded in *Chapter 1*: `https://github.com/PacktPublishing/Unleashing-Your-Data-with-Power-BI-Machine-Learning-and-OpenAI/tree/main/Chapter-01`.

Open Power Query within Power BI, and you will see the four tables of data that constitute the raw data from the FAA:

- **STRIKE_REPORTS**
- **Aircraft Type**
- **Engine Codes**
- **Engine Position**

Review the preliminary data model that you created in *Chapter 1*. For the first step, you will organize the existing queries of the raw data into a folder, which can be referenced as you create modified queries for your data model:

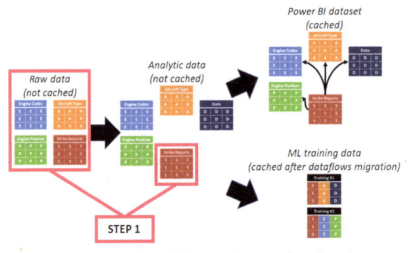

Figure 2.1 – Power Query folders contain stages of transformations

Next, you need to do something about the raw data. Power Query allows you to organize queries into groups, which function as logical groupings, much like a folder within SharePoint or OneDrive.

Within Power Query, the terms "query" and "table" are used interchangeably depending on the context. For the remainder of the book, the term "query" will be used when referring to data that is not cached or logic being created to generate a table, while "table" will refer to data that has been cached in either Power BI datasets or dataflows in the Power BI service.

Grouping the raw data

You create a group for the raw data queries, which can be referenced as a view of the original data later in the project. In examples of data lakes or data lakehouse architectures, you will often see bronze/silver/gold or raw, curated, optimized layers, which serve as both reference points within the transformation process that happens to data and for data that might have been referred to as staging tables in older data warehousing terminology. While Power BI Power Query and dataflows are different from data lakehouse architectures, grouping your queries and tables into separate stages can help with understanding the logic and also with expanding future iterations of the solution. No matter what happens downstream with the data, a Power BI developer can return to the **Raw data** folder to see the data as it appears in the source:

1. In the **Queries** panel on the left side of the page, right-click and select **New Group….** Name the new group Raw Data, and add the following description: Raw FAA Wildlife Strike Data Tables.

2. Right-click on each of the four queries, and move each of them into the new group, **Raw Data**.

3. Right-click on each of the four queries and *disable* **Enable load**. Why bother with this step? By disabling **Enable load**, these queries will be simple previews of the source data, which do not get loaded into your dataset and consume storage space.

The group is a logical container that exists for the purpose of organizing your queries. The queries represent the raw data as it exists from the source, and can be referenced by new queries that you create in Power Query. As your data model and ML use cases evolve over time, you can iteratively reference the source data in an unaltered form to evaluate changes and create new training data for future ML models. The left side portion of **Step 1** in *Figure 2.1* is now complete! Your **Queries** panel in Power Query should now look as follows:

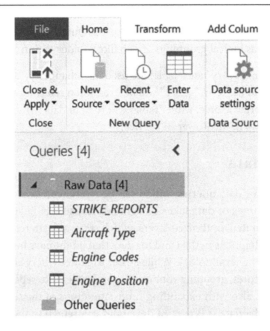

Figure 2.2 – Queries representing the unaltered raw data

Next, you need to design the table.

Designing a curated table of the primary STRIKE_REPORTS data

You're now ready to start building curated tables of data, which can be used first to populate a Power BI dataset and then later to populate tables of data for ML. In the days before Power BI, when every bit of data took up precious space and running a query was a great time for a coffee break, architects would often build out their dimension tables before populating simple fact tables, which consisted of integer keys with numeric fields used for calculated measures.

If you are building a Power BI dataset with tens of millions of rows or more, taking care to follow best practices with large volumes of data is still a good idea. For this solution with fewer than 300,000 rows of FAA Wildlife Strike data, the decision was made in *Chapter 1* to build a hybrid design for the sake of practicality and ease of use, which contains elements of both a star schema and flattened data design. With a hybrid approach, you decide to start your efforts with the primary **STRIKE_REPORTS** data table, which is mostly a fact table but also has descriptive text columns – these could've been broken out into dimensions but will be used as degenerate dimensions.

Evaluating the data for the **STRIKE_REPORTS** table is going to be a tedious, repetitious, and lengthy effort. You realize that this portion of your effort will probably be one of the least enjoyable parts of this book, but you also know that soldiering through it will result in better data, which leads to a more productive analytics and ML journey.

You decide to break up the evaluation of the **STRIKE_REPORTS** table into seven steps so that you can comprehend the data and take a few breaks:

1. Evaluate dimension tables for necessary key values.

2. Evaluate the date and time columns in the **STRIKE_REPORTS** table.

3. Evaluate geographical and location columns in the **STRIKE_REPORTS** table.

4. Evaluate aircraft and operator description columns in the **STRIKE_REPORTS** table.

5. Evaluate the species and animal columns in the **STRIKE_REPORTS** table.

6. Evaluate the weather, flight details, and strike damage columns in the **STRIKE_REPORTS** table.

7. Look at the other columns from the **STRIKE_REPORTS** table.

Next, you will go through each step in detail.

Evaluating dimension tables for necessary key values

Before you begin curating the **STRIKE_REPORTS** table, you review the other (dimension) tables that will be part of your solution. You'll need to identify the primary key column for each of these tables. When working through the **STRIKE_REPORTS** table, you'll need to make sure a foreign key exists to map that table to the other tables:

- **Aircraft Type**: For this table, you can see that **Aircraft Code** is a unique letter for each option in the table. These values match up to values in the **AC_CLASS** column in **STRIKE_REPORTS**. You'll want to keep **AC_CLASS** for your curated table as a foreign key to the **Aircraft Type** table.

- **Engine Codes**: This table is a little bit tricky. You'll need to use both the **Manufacturer Code** and **Model Code** columns to identify a unique row. This is called a compound key. Per the **read_me.xls** file, the **AMA** and **AMO** columns from **STRIKE_REPORTS** map to these columns.

- **Engine Position**: **Engine Code** is a simple integer column that identifies each unique row of the table. However, it maps to four columns in the **STRIKE_REPORTS** table per the definitions on the read_me.xls definitions list. **ENG_1_POS**, **ENG_2_POS**, **ENG_3_POS**, and **ENG_4_POS** are all foreign keys for the **Engine Position** table. This scenario will present some interesting architectural options that you will need to consider.

- **Date table**: As of right now, you do not have a **Date** table in your Raw Data folder. Per your preliminary data model, you'll need a **Date** table to do aggregations at the week, month, quarter, and year levels. You will add a **Date** table later in this chapter, but you'll also need to evaluate the columns in the **STRIKE_REPORTS** table for suitable foreign keys.

Evaluating the date and time columns on the STRIKE_REPORTS table

Those who've worked long enough in business intelligence and analytics know that a **Date** table is the cornerstone of many analytical solutions. Time tables are often important too, but due to missing data, you already decided to skip a **Time** table for your first round of development. Details about the data can be found in the **Column Name** sheet of the `read_me.xls` file and also in the **STRIKE_REPORTS** query preview within the `Raw Data` folder of Power Query. You take notes on the following criteria for each column of data:

- **Column name**: The name of the column in the **STRIKE_REPORTS** table.

- **Initial data type**: What is the data type either detected in the **Microsoft Access** file or auto-detected by Power BI?

- **Notes**: Your notes about each column.

- **Keep?**: Yes/no for whether you keep this column. You'll be able to add it back in the future if you change your mind.

- **New data type**: What should the data type be for the new curated version of the table?

- **Key**: Is this a foreign key column? If so, what table will it integrate?

- **Reporting name**: A user-friendly name for the column that will look good on reports, reflect the language of report users, and work well with tools such as Power BI Natural Language Query.

Column name	Initial data type	Note	Keep?	New data type	Key?	Reporting name
INCIDENT_DATE	Date/Time	This is the date that a wildlife strike happened. The time component of the data is not used.	Yes	**Date**	Yes – to the **Date** table	Incident date
INCIDENT_MONTH	**Decimal**	This column is not needed since it exists within **INCIDENT_DATE**, which will link to the Date table containing month values.	No			

Column name	Initial data type	Note	Keep?	New data type	Key?	Reporting name
INCIDENT_YEAR	Decimal	This column is not needed since it exists within **INCIDENT_ DATE**, which will link to the **Date** table containing year values.	No			
TIME	Text	This column has missing data, but you may reconsider it in the future.	No			
TIME_OF_DAY	Text	This column is more frequently populated than **TIME** and might be valuable.	Yes	Text	No	Time of day
LUPDATE	Date/Time	Information about when the report was updated doesn't need to be part of your initial effort.	No			

Figure 2.3 – A table of columns from STRIKE_REPORTS related to date and time

Next, you need to work on the location columns.

Evaluating the geographical and location columns in the STRIKE_REPORTS table

Geographical and location columns will provide information about where wildlife strikes happened in parts of the world covered by the FAA. These types of information could potentially be valuable for differentiating trends, patterns, and frequency that differ based on local climates and wildlife populations.

Once again, you take a deep dive into the **STRIKE_REPORTS** data and list out the columns that are geographical or refer to location:

Column name	Initial data type	Notes	Keep?	New data type	Key?	Reporting name
AIRPORT_ID	Text	A unique identifier for an airport.	Yes	Text	No	Airport ID
AIRPORT	Text	Name of an airport.	Yes	Text	No	Airport name
STATE	Text	Abbreviation for a state.	Yes	Text	No	State
ENROUTE_STATE	Text	Abbreviation for the destination state.	Yes	Text	No	State
FAAREGION	Text	The FAA region listed in the report.	Yes	Text	No	FAA region
RUNWAY	Text	The runway for the flight.	Yes	Text	No	Runway
LOCATION	Text	Free text comments about the location. You decide to leave it out for your first round of development since it is 96% empty.	No	Text	No	
LATITUDE	Decimal	The latitude listed in the report.	Yes	Decimal	No	Latitude
LONGITUDE	Decimal	The longitude listed in the report	Yes	Decimal	No	Longitude

Figure 2.4 – A table of columns from STRIKE_REPORTS related to geography and location

Note that in a true star schema design, a **Geography** table is often a separate dimension. Again, you are proceeding with a hybrid approach so that you minimize the complexity of your first round of development. You could always break off a geography dimension in future iterations of development.

Evaluating the aircraft and operator description columns in the STRIKE_REPORTS table

Information about the aircraft and aircraft operators is also in the **STRIKE_REPORTS** table from the FAA Wildlife Strike data. You perform a similar analysis of these columns:

Column name	Initial data type	Notes	Keep?	New data type	Key?	Reporting name
OPID	Text	The ID of the operator.	Yes	Text	No	Operator ID
OPERATOR	Text	The name of the operator.	Yes	Text	No	Operator
REG	Text	Aircraft registration number.	No			
AIRCRAFT	Text	Aircraft description.	Yes	Text	No	Aircraft
AMA	Text	Aircraft manufacturer code.	Yes	Text	Yes – **Engine Codes**	AMA
AMO	Text	Aircraft model code.	Yes	Text	Yes – **Engine Codes**	AMO
EMA	Text	The latitude listed in the report.	Yes	Text	No	EMA
EMO	Text	The longitude listed in the report.	Yes	Text	No	EMO
AC_CLASS	Text	Aircraft class.	Yes	Text	Yes – **Aircraft Type**	Aircraft class code
AC_MASS	Text	Aircraft mass key; also contains a few text entries of NULL. You'll need to add some descriptions down the line.	Yes	Text	No	Aircraft mass code

Column name	Initial data type	Notes	Keep?	New data type	Key?	Reporting name
TYPE_ENG	Text	The type of engine key; will also need descriptions added.	Yes	Text	No	Engine type code
NUM_ENGS	Text	Some of the entries are NULL (text) while others are integers or empty. You decide to keep it as a text value for now, but will reconsider while designing the dataset.	Yes	Text	No	Number of Engines
ENG_1_POS	Text	These four columns for Engine Position also contain some NULL text entries and will be kept as text for now.	Yes	Text	Yes –**Engine Position**	Engine 1 position code
ENG_2_POS	Text		Yes	Text	Yes – **Engine Position**	Engine 2 position code
ENG_3_POS	Text		Yes	Text	Yes – **Engine Position**	Engine 3 position code
ENG_4_POS	Text		Yes	Text	Yes –**Engine Position**	Engine 4 position code

Figure 2.5 – A table of columns from STRIKE_REPORTS related to aircraft and operator descriptions

Next, you will look at the columns recording the animals involved.

Evaluating the species and animal columns in the STRIKE_REPORTS table

Information about different species of wildlife that struck aircraft, how large they were, and the results of the impact might also be beneficial in predicting costs and damages associated with wildlife strikes. You take a look at columns of data related to wildlife:

Column name	Initial data type	Notes	Keep?	New data type	Key?	Reporting name
BIRD_BAND_NUMBER	Text	Mostly empty	No			
SPECIES_ID	Text	ID of species	Yes	Text	No	Species ID
SPECIES	Text	Species name	Yes	Text	No	Species

Column name	Initial data type	Notes	Keep?	New data type	Key?	Reporting name
REMAINS_COLLECTED	True/False	Not needed for the project	No		No	
REMAINS_SENT	True/False	Not needed for the project	No			
WARNED	Text	Was there a warning?	Yes	Text	No	Warned
NUM_SEEN	Text	The number of animals seen	Yes	Text	No	Number seen
NUM_STRUCK	Text	The number of animals struck	Yes	Text	No	Number struck
SIZE	Text	The size of the animals	Yes	Text	No	Size

Figure 2.6 – A table of columns from STRIKE_REPORTS related to species and animal descriptions

You will look at a few more columns in the next section.

Evaluating the weather, flight details, and strike damage columns in the STRIKE_REPORTS table

Information about the state of the flight such as the height and speed of the aircraft could also be interesting and useful data. You also take a look at information related to damage, costs, and injuries from the wildlife strikes:

Column name	Initial data type	Notes	Keep?	New data type	Key?	Reporting name
PHASE_OF_FLIGHT	Text	Note phases, such as takeoff and cruising	Yes	Text	No	Phase of flight
HEIGHT	Decimal	The height of the aircraft at the time of impact	Yes	Integer	No	Height
SPEED	Decimal	Speed of the aircraft at the time of impact	Yes	Integer	No	Speed

Column name	Initial data type	Notes	Keep?	New data type	Key?	Reporting name
DISTANCE	Decimal	Distance from the airport	Yes	Decimal	No	Distance
SKY	Text	Visibility notes	Yes	Text	No	Sky
PRECIPITATION	Text	Notes about rain, snow, and so on	Yes	Text	No	Precipitation
AOS	Decimal	The amount of time for which the aircraft is out of service	Yes	Decimal	No	AOS
COST_REPAIRS	Fixed Decimal Number	Cost of repairs	Yes	Fixed Decimal Number	No	Cost of repairs
COST_OTHER	Fixed Decimal Number	Other costs	Yes	Fixed Decimal Number	No	Other costs
COST_REPAIRS_INFL_ADJ	Fixed Decimal Number	Costs (inflation-adjusted)	Yes	Fixed Decimal Number	No	Cost of repairs (adjusted)
COST_OTHER_INFL_ADJ	Fixed Decimal Number	Other costs (inflation-adjusted)	Yes	Fixed Decimal Number	No	Other costs (adjusted)
DAMAGE_LEVEL	Text	Level of damage	Yes	Text	No	Damage level
OTHER_SPECIFY	Text	96% empty and free text so skip it for now	No			
EFFECT	Text	Effect on the flight	Yes	Text	No	Effect on flight
EFFECT_OTHER	Text	Other effects, 98% empty	No			
REMARKS	Text	Various remarks about the incident	Yes	Text	No	Remarks
NR_INJURIES	Decimal	Number of injuries	Yes	Integer	No	Number of injuries
NR_FATALITIES	Decimal	Number of fatalities	Yes	Integer	No	Number of fatalities
COMMENTS	Text	Comments in free text	No			

Figure 2.7 – A table of columns from STRIKE_REPORTS related to weather, flight, and damage descriptions

You also find 34 **True/False** columns related to the strikes and related damage. **True/False** columns are often straightforward to evaluate for use with ML, so you decide to include these columns. Most of them start with **ING** (ingested), **DAM** (damage), or **STR** (struck):

Additional True/False columns included				
INGESTED_OTHER	STR_NOSE	STR_ENG2	STR_ENG3	STR_ENG4
INDICATED_DAMAGE	DAM_NOSE	DAM_ENG2	DAM_ENG3	DAM_ENG4
DAM_OTHER	STR_ENG1	ING_ENG2	ING_ENG3	ING_ENG4
STR_RAD	DAM_ENG1	STR_WING_ROT	STR_LG	STR_LGHTS
DAM_RAD	ING_ENG1	DAM_WING_ROT	DAM_LG	DAM_LGHTS
STR_WINDSHLD	STR_PROP	STR_FUSE	STR_TAIL	STR_OTHER
DAM_WINDSHLD	DAM_PROP	DAM_FUSE	DAM_TAIL	

Figure 2.8 – True/false columns that flag specific events for a wildlife strike in the STRIKE_REPORTS table

Other columns from the STRIKE_REPORTS table

You decide to leave out the other columns from the curated **STRIKE_REPORTS** table because you doubt they will add value to your initial round of analysis. Unnecessary columns will also bloat the metadata browsing experience for end users, and increase the size of the dataset with unnecessary storage. The following columns can always be added later if they are needed: **INDEX_NR**, **REPORTED_NAME**, **REPORTED_TITLE**, **SOURCE**, **PERSON**, and **TRANSFER**.

You've decided on what columns to keep, the data types, and user-friendly names for the columns. Now, you can move on to building out the curated layer, which will serve as the foundation for your Power BI dataset and your ML models in Power BI.

Building a curated table of the primary STRIKE_REPORTS data

You can now start building out a curated version of the STRIKE_REPORTS metadata and query logic in Power Query. You will follow these steps:

1. Reference the raw table to create a new query.

2. Keep only the columns that you need.

3. Make data type changes.

4. Make column name changes.

Let's begin.

Referencing the raw table to create a new query

You will put your new query into a new group in Power Query called **Curated Reporting Queries**:

1. Create a new group in Power Query called **Curated Reporting Queries** using the same methods by which you created the **Raw Data** group.

2. Right-click on the **STRIKE_REPORTS** query in the **Raw Data** group and select the option for **Reference**. Your new query will reference the unaltered source query from the `wildlife.accdb` source. This way, you can make changes to the metadata and query logic while still having an unaltered view of the source in Power Query.

3. Right-click the **STRIKE_REPORTS (2)** table and move the query to **Curated Reporting Queries**.

4. In the right-hand panel, in **Query Settings**, rename the query from **STRIKE_REPORTS (2)** to `Strike Reports`. This way, your table will have a clean and user-friendly name.

Your **Queries** panel in Power Query should now look like this:

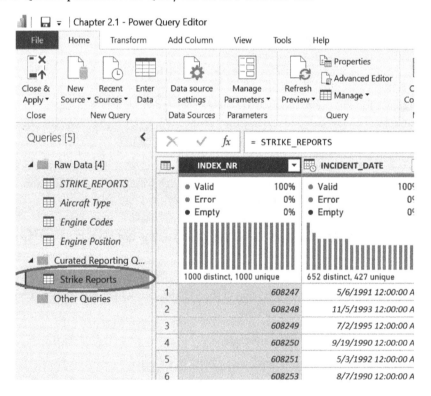

Figure 2.9 – A curated table of data, which will be used for datasets and ML queries

Next, you need to get rid of unnecessary columns.

Keeping only the columns that you need

Now that you've started your new query, you can select the columns that you want to keep. Based on the seven batches of evaluations that you've completed, you can remove unnecessary columns. On the ribbon of Power Query, under the **Home** tab, in the **Manage Columns** section, you can select **Choose Columns**. You are able to unselect the following columns:

INCIDENT_NR	EFFECT_OTHER	SOURCE
INCIDENT_MONTH	COMMENTS	PERSON
INCIDENT_YEAR	REMAINS_COLLECTED	LUPDATE
LOCATION	REMAINS_SENT	TRANSFER
REG	REPORTED_NAME	BIRD_BAND_NUMBER
OTHER_SPECIFY	REPORTED_TITLE	TIME

Figure 2.10 – Columns to remove from the Strike Reports query

Now, your query only contains the columns that you plan to use for your analysis.

Data type changes

Based upon your evaluation of the **STRIKE_REPORTS** data, you decided to change a few of the data types for columns. On the ribbon of Power Query, under the **Transform** tab, in the **any columns** section, you can select **Data Type** for each of the columns that you highlight:

Column	Existing data type	New data type	Reason
INCIDENT_DATE	Date/Time	Date	The **Time** portion is not used; also makes a good foreign key as a **Date** type.
HEIGHT	Decimal	Integer	All of the values are either blank or integers.
SPEED	Decimal	Integer	All of the values are either blank or integers.
NR_INJURIES	Decimal	Integer	Not measured in decimals.
NR_FATALITIES	Decimal	Integer	Not measured in decimals.

Figure 2.11 – Changing data types in the query to prepare them for datasets and ML queries

Column name changes

Good-quality metadata has several benefits for analytics, especially when end users are not acquainted with the source data naming conventions. In addition to discoverability with search tools, good naming conventions will also make tools such as Power BI Q&A more intuitive and valuable. Based upon your evaluations, you make the following changes to column names by right-clicking on each column and selecting **Rename…**:

Column name	Reporting name	Column name	Reporting name
INCIDENT_DATE	Incident date	COST_OTHER_INFL_ADJ	Other costs (adjusted)
TIME_OF_DAY	Time of day	DAMAGE_LEVEL	Damage level
AIRPORT_ID	Airport ID	EFFECT	Effect on flight
AIRPORT	Airport name	REMARKS	Remarks
STATE	State	NR_INJURIES	Number of injuries
ENROUTE_STATE	Enroute state	NR_FATALITIES	Number of fatalities
FAAREGION	FAA region	INGESTED_OTHER	Ingested other
RUNWAY	Runway	INDICATED_DAMAGE	Indicated damage
LATITUDE	Latitude	STR_RAD	Struck random
LONGITUDE	Longitude	DAM_RAD	Damaged random
OPID	Operator ID	STR_WINDSHLD	Struck windshield
OPERATOR	Operator	DAM_WINDSHLD	Damaged windshield
AIRCRAFT	Aircraft	STR_NOSE	Struck nose
AMA	AMA	DAM_NOSE	Damaged nose
AMO	AMO	STR_ENG1	Struck engine 1
EMA	EMA	DAM_ENG1	Damaged engine 1
EMO	EMO	ING_ENG1	Ingested engine 1
AC_CLASS	Aircraft class code	STR_PROP	Struck propeller
AC_MASS	Aircraft mass code	DAM_PROP	Damaged propeller
TYPE_ENG	Engine type code	STR_ENG2	Struck engine 2
NUM_ENGS	Number of engines	DAM_ENG2	Damaged engine 2
ENG_1_POS	Engine 1 position code	ING_ENG2	Ingested engine 2
ENG_2_POS	Engine 2 position code	STR_WING_ROT	Struck wing or rotor
ENG_3_POS	Engine 3 position code	DAM_WING_ROT	Damaged wing or rotor

Column name	Reporting name	Column name	Reporting name
ENG_4_POS	Engine 4 position code	STR_FUSE	Struck fuselage
SPECIES_ID	Species ID	DAM_FUSE	Damaged fuselage
SPECIES	Species	STR_ENG3	Struck engine 3
WARNED	Warned	DAM_ENG3	Damaged engine 3
NUM_SEEN	Number seen	ING_ENG3	Ingested engine 3
NUM_STRUCK	Number struck	STR_LG	Struck landing gear
SIZE	Size	DAM_LG	Damaged landing gear
PHASE_OF_FLIGHT	Phase of flight	STR_TAIL	Struck tail
HEIGHT	Height	DAM_TAIL	Damaged tail
SPEED	Speed	STR_ENG4	Struck engine 4
DISTANCE	Distance	DAM_ENG4	Damaged engine 4
SKY	Sky	ING_ENG4	Ingested engine 4
PRECIPITATION	Precipitation	STR_LGHTS	Struck lights
AOS	AOS	DAM_LGHTS	Damaged lights
COST_REPAIRS	Cost of repairs	STR_OTHER	Struck other
COST_OTHER	Other costs	DAM_OTHER	Damaged other
COST_REPAIRS_INFL_ADJ	Cost of repairs (adjusted)		

Figure 2.12 – Name changes for the Wildlife Strike query

Now that you've renamed the columns that you will use for the Strike Reports query, you can move on to populating curated versions of the other tables of descriptive data.

Building curated versions of the Aircraft Type, Engine Codes, and Engine Position queries

Next, you will create queries for new versions of the reference (dimension) tables in the **Curated Reporting Queries** group of Power Query. Before starting these tasks, you also consider the **Date** table. The **Date** table will be an essential part of the Power BI dataset but is an architectural component that does not exist within the dataset. Therefore, it will be added to the dataset layer in a downstream group later in this chapter. You have moved on to another phase of the effort:

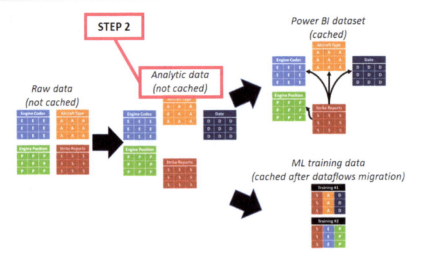

Figure 2.13 – Moving on to the reference table queries for analytic data

For each of the three tables, **Aircraft Type**, **Engine Codes**, and **Engine Position**, in the **Raw Data** group, right-click it, select **Reference**, move the resulting queries to the **Curated Reporting Queries** group, and then rename it to include **Info** at the end of its name so that they have unique names. Your Power Query queries should look like this:

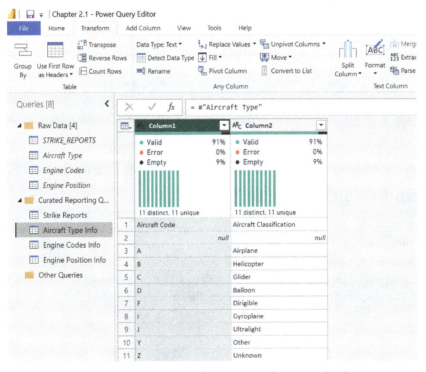

Figure 2.14 – New queries for the curated reporting level

Now, you can proceed to clean up and modify each of the queries so that they are suitable for building dimension tables and ML queries. For these steps, as an experienced Power BI user, you likely have extensive experience in cleaning up tables of data, which you can leverage to quickly make changes. That "Power BI Dashboard in a Day" class that you took with a Microsoft partner was very helpful!

The Aircraft Type Info query

You notice in the **Aircraft Type Info** table that Power BI shows the column names as the first row, and there is an empty row. On the ribbon of Power Query, under the **Transform** tab, in the **Table** section, you can select **Use First Row as Header**. Next, left-click the carat next to the **Aircraft Code** column and unselect **(null)**. Now, your **Aircraft Type Info** table should look like this:

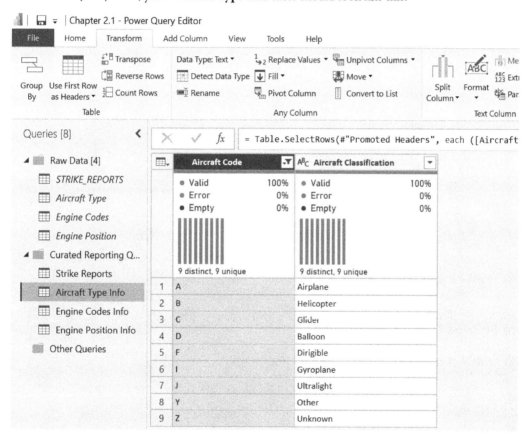

Figure 2.15 – Column names added to Aircraft Type Info

Next, you need to query the engine position.

The Engine Position Info query

Engine Position Info requires exactly the same transformative steps as **Aircraft Type Info**. Sometimes, the headers will be promoted automatically, which differs slightly depending on your version of Power BI. You repeat the steps from the previous section, and your table should look as follows:

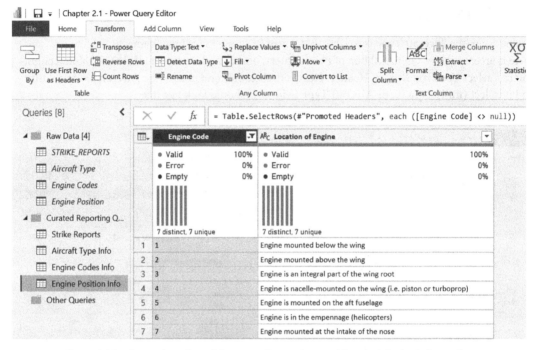

Figure 2.16 – Curated version of the query for engine position descriptive information

Next, you need to query the engine codes.

The Engine Codes Info query

The **Engine Codes Info** query needs a little bit more work:

1. Select the dropdown from the upper left of the query view and remove the top two rows.

2. Select **Use the First Row as Header**.

3. Highlight **Column5** and **Column6** and then **Remove Columns**.

4. Highlight the **Manufacturer Code** and **Engine Manufacturer** columns. Right-click and select **Fill** and **Down**.

5. Left-click the caret for **Model Code** and unselect (**null**).

Your **Engine Codes Info** query should look like this:

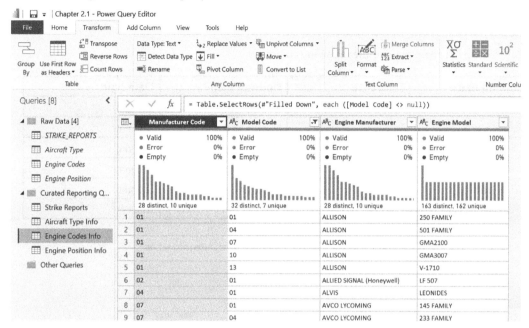

Figure 2.17 – A curated query for information about the engines on planes involved with wildlife strikes

Let's build a curated query next!

Building a curated query to populate a Date table

Date aggregations are an important component of both Power BI and business intelligence tools as a whole. Understanding and recalculating trends at the level of weeks, months, quarters, and years adds robust analytical capabilities. Date tables can even be used to slice and dice data by weekends, holidays, fiscal calendars, and more. Power BI even has the capability to specify a table as a **Date** table to enable special time intelligence capabilities.

A `.csv` file of **Date** data is available at the Packt GitHub site link: `https://github.com/PacktPublishing/Unleashing-Your-Data-with-Power-BI-Machine-Learning-and-OpenAI/tree/main/Chapter-02`. Follow these steps to bring it into Power Query:

1. Copy `https://raw.githubusercontent.com/PacktPublishing/Unleashing-Your-Data-with-Power-BI-Machine-Learning-and-OpenAI/main/Chapter-02/date.csv`.

2. In Power Query, select **New Source** and then **Web**. Paste in the URL and hit **OK**.

3. When the preview shows, select **OK**.

4. Rename the query Date Info and move it to the **Curated Reporting Queries** group in Power Query.

5. Select **Use First Rows as Headers**.

6. Change the data type for the following columns:

Column name	Data type	Column name	Data type
Date	Date	Month Num	Integer
Day Num Week	Integer	Month Year Order	Integer
Day of Year	Integer	Month Day Num	Integer
Week Num	Integer	Quarter Num	Integer
Week Ending	Date	Quarter Year Order	Integer
Week Year Order	Integer	Year	Integer

Figure 2.18 – Data type changes for the Date Info table

Your query for a **Date** table should now look like this:

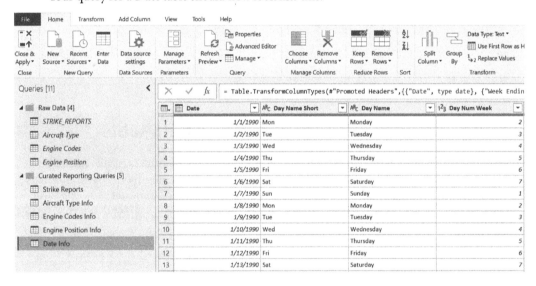

Figure 2.19 – The Date data is now available in Power Query to create a Date table in a Power BI dataset

You've now successfully built out a layer of curated queries for your Power BI dataset and ML queries. The queries aren't yet ready to be used for datasets, as they will still need foreign and primary key values, along with housekeeping tasks to deal with any potential data issues. You're now ready to start taking steps for building out your Power BI dataset!

Summary

In this chapter, you created queries coming from the FAA Wildlife Strike data, which will be used as the basis for both Power BI datasets and ML training datasets. Throughout the chapter, you removed unnecessary columns, cleaned up the column names, and formatted the queries so that they can be used as tables of data.

In the next chapter, you will explore the data in these queries and create a semantic model in a Power BI dataset, which relates all of the data together for the purpose of creating a Power BI report – this will kickstart analytics on the FAA Wildlife Strike data.

3

Exploring Data Using Power BI and Creating a Semantic Model

Chapter 2 was a tedious process of combing through the FAA Wildlife Strike raw data, identifying the columns of data that you want to carry forward for analysis, and then setting up queries that will transform the data and metadata for the purpose of analysis and ML with Power BI. However, it was important work.

Now, you are ready to create a **semantic** model layer using a Power BI dataset and then set the foundation for the data that you will use to train ML models in Power BI. If you aren't familiar with a semantic layer, it is a description commonly used in business intelligence solutions to describe a layer that translates data descriptions into common business terms and logic. For example, a source column named `columnname` or `column_name` might be displayed to users as **Column Name** via the semantic layer. Also, the logic for runtime calculations such as **Year to Date Cumulative Sales** often exists in the semantic layer. In the Microsoft Power BI ecosystem, the semantic layer exists within the Power BI dataset.

The Power BI dataset will consist of all of the data created by the queries in *Chapter 2* but with the addition of custom columns, relationships between tables, and calculated measures that will help you aggregate columns for the purpose of doing mathematical operations for your analytics. Going back to the *Reviewing the requirements for the solution* section of *Chapter 1*, this will be the basis for the **Analytical Report** that you have been tasked to deliver.

Once you've built out your Power BI dataset with some basic calculated measures, you will start building the basis for the data that will be used for ML in Power BI. This will be the basis for the **Predict Damage**, **Predict Size**, and **Predict Height** ML models that are requirements from the *Reviewing the requirements for the solution* section of *Chapter 1*.

Technical requirements

For this chapter, you will need the following:

- Power BI Desktop April 2023 or later (no licenses required)
- FAA Wildlife Strike data files from either the FAA website or the Packt GitHub site at this link: `https://github.com/PacktPublishing/Unleashing-Your-Data-with-Power-BI-Machine-Learning-and-OpenAI/`.

Designing relationships between tables

In a Power BI dataset, relationships between tables determine how queries that involve data from both tables are generated. If you've taken an introductory class on Power BI, such as *Dashboard in a Day*, learning about relationships is a foundational skill for Power BI development. Back in *Chapter 2*, you determined that the tables have the following key values to establish relationships:

- **Date Table**: The `Date` column matches up to the `Incident Date` column on the `Strike Reports` table
- **Aircraft Type Info**: `Aircraft Code` matches up with `Aircraft Class Code` on the `Strike Reports` table
- **Engine Codes Info**: `Manufacturer Code` and `Model Code` are compound keys matching up with `AMA` and `AMO` from the `Strike Reports` table
- **Engine Position Info**: `Engine Code` maps to four columns on the `Strike Reports` table – `Engine 1 Position Code`, `Engine 2 Position Code`, `Engine 3 Position Code`, and `Engine 4 Position Code`

Let's go ahead and make sure that proper key values exist for all of these tables!

You can pick up where you left off with your PBIX file from *Chapter 2*, or you can follow along using the finished version of the content from this chapter. You can download the PBIT version of the file from the Packt GitHub site folder for *Chapter 3*: `https://github.com/PacktPublishing/Unleashing-Your-Data-with-Power-BI-Machine-Learning-and-OpenAI/tree/main/Chapter-03`.

Date table

You've already created a **Date** table named **Date Info**, which has a field named **Date** containing every unique **Date** value between 1990-2024. Within Power Query, you'll see within **Column Statistics** that there are no blank values and every value is unique and does not repeat. **Date** is the primary key of the **Date** table.

For the **Strike Reports** table, **Incident Date** is the foreign key value that will map to the **Date** table. The column represents the date that a wildlife strike was reported to have happened. The column is also fully populated with valid data.

Since the **Date** table contains a valid primary key, and **Incident Date** on the **Strike Reports** table is a valid **Date** field, you do not need to do any additional transformations. The columns are ready for a relationship in the dataset!

Aircraft Type Info

On the **Aircraft Type Info** table, you see a text column named **Aircraft Code**. Each row contains a unique letter that identifies the row. **Aircraft Classification** is another column that provides a description of the type of aircraft. If working with extremely large data volumes, integer key values are a best practice. However, since the total data volume is a manageable size, you're fine using the character text values as a primary key for the **Aircraft Type** table.

The **Strike Reports** table contains a corresponding column named **Aircraft Class Code**. You left-click the caret next to the column name and select **Load More** to see all the possible unique values in the table. You notice that there are values registering as both **(null)**, which is actually blank, and the four-letter value **NULL**, which is a text entry:

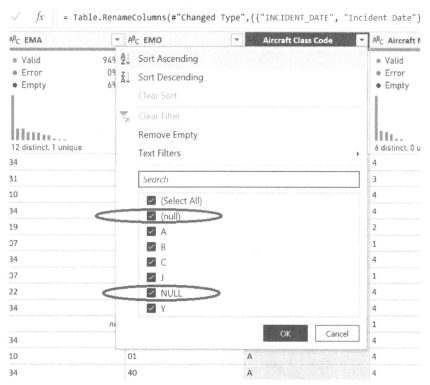

Figure 3.1 – A screenshot showing (null) and NULL text values

The **NULL** text value does not exist in the Aircraft Type Info query. It differs from **(null)** because **NULL** contains actual text while **(null)** is an empty value. If you filter the column for either **(null)** or the **NULL** text value, you notice that the rows containing those values appear to have differences. Most of the blank **(null)** values are on rows where wildlife was struck by unknown flights and many columns are blank, while some of the **NULL** text values contain **Flight** numbers.

When you build out data for use with Power BI ML, you will want to remove or replace all blank values since ML models usually need a design that does not have null values. Power BI datasets still work with null foreign key values, but that approach is not ideal. You decide to add two new rows to the Aircraft Type Info query, one for the **NULL** text value and one for blank values that show up as **(null)**. You will also need to replace the blank values in the Strike Reports query. Here are the steps you need to perform:

1. Right-click the **Aircraft Class Code** column and select **Replace Values…**, then type in `null` for **Value to Find** and `blank` for **Replace With**. Now, all of the empty values will contain the word `blank`.

2. On the **Home** ribbon of Power Query, select **Enter Data**. Name the new table **Aircraft Type Added Data**. Create two columns, **Aircraft Code** and **Aircraft Classification**.

3. Enter `blank` for both columns in row 1 and `NULL` for both columns in row 2. Your table should look like this before hitting **OK**:

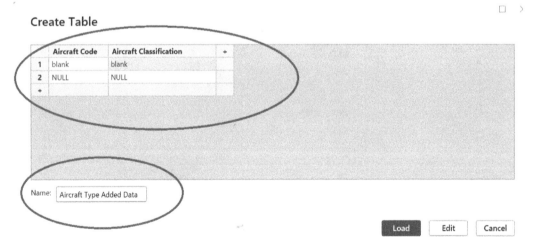

Figure 3.2 – New data for Aircraft Type to account for blanks and the text value NULL

4. Right-click the new query in the **Queries** pane, and move it to the **Raw Data** group. Right-click it again, and uncheck **Enable Load**. Power Query should now look like this:

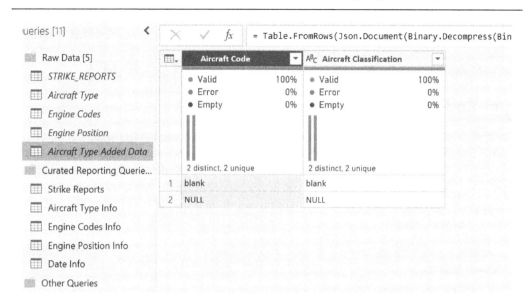

Figure 3.3 – New data added to the Raw Data group that will not be loaded to the dataset

5. Left-click on the **Aircraft Type Info** query. On the Power Query ribbon, under **Home | Combine**, select **Append Queries | Append Queries**. Append the **Aircraft Type Added Data** query. Your **Aircraft Type Info** query should now look like this:

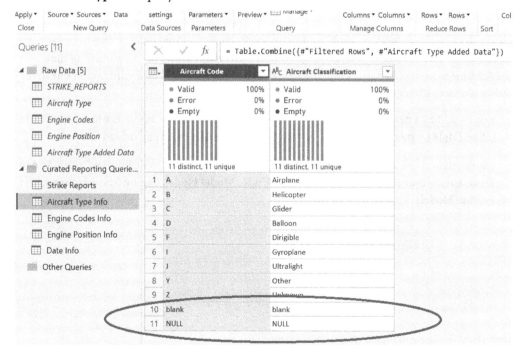

Figure 3.4 – New rows added to Aircraft Type Info query

Now, both the **Strike Reports** query and the **Aircraft Type Info** query will have referential integrity, meaning that when you populate the dataset, every key value on the **Strike Reports** table will be a value that finds a match on the **Aircraft Type Info** table. The **Aircraft Type Info** query is ready to go!

Engine Codes Info

As noted previously, you've already determined that **Manufacturer Code** and **Model Code** are compound keys matching up with **AMA** and **AMO** from the **Strike Reports** query. For the **Engine Codes Info** query, you observe that a combination of **Manufacturer Code** and **Model Code** results in a unique row definition. On the **Strike Reports** query, you browse the values in the **AMA** and **AMO** columns to find that there are blank **(null)** values in both columns and some invalid values that will not match up with the **Engine Codes Info** query. You evaluate a few options for handling these discrepancies:

- Account for all of the incomplete and non-matching values by adding new rows to the **Engine Codes Info** query.

- Break off the **Engine Manufacturing** data into a separate query, which will be a new dimension.

- Add a new row to the **Engine Codes Info** table for unmatched values, called `Incomplete or Missing`. A new foreign key will be added to the **Engine Codes Info** query for incomplete or missing compound key values.

While the first and second options would follow best practices, you decide to move ahead with option three (put all of the incomplete entries and mismatched values into a single bucket) for your first round of development. If you determine later that better matches will improve your results in a meaningful way, you can always circle back in future rounds of development. Options one and two would require significant effort, and right now, you doubt that the benefits would justify the investment of time. You have a deadline to meet! Changing the architecture in the future will still be a valid option due to the flexibility of Power Query and Power BI.

First, begin by adding a new row to the **Engine Codes Info** query. Create a new query in the **Raw Data** group called **Engine Codes Added Data**, just as you did with **Aircraft Type Added Data**:

1. On the ribbon of Power Query, select **Enter Data**. Name the new table **Engine Codes Added Data**. Create four columns: **Manufacturer Code**, **Model Code**, **Engine Manufacturer**, and **Engine Model**.

2. Enter `Incomplete or Missing` for all four columns in row 1. Your table should look like this before hitting **OK**:

Create Table   □   ✕

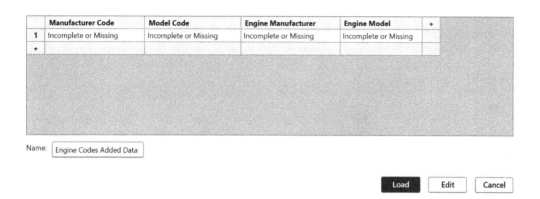

Figure 3.5 – Incomplete or missing key values can be bucketed in the report for Engine Codes

3. Right-click the new query in the **Queries** pane, and move it to the **Raw Data** group. Right-click it again, and uncheck **Enable Load**.

4. Left-click on the **Engine Codes Info** query. On the Power Query ribbon, under **Home | Combine**, select **Append Queries | Append Queries**. Append the **Engine Codes Added Data** query. Your **Engine Codes Info** query now contains the additional row of data. Power Query should now look like this (notice that **Incomplete or Missing** is now in the table):

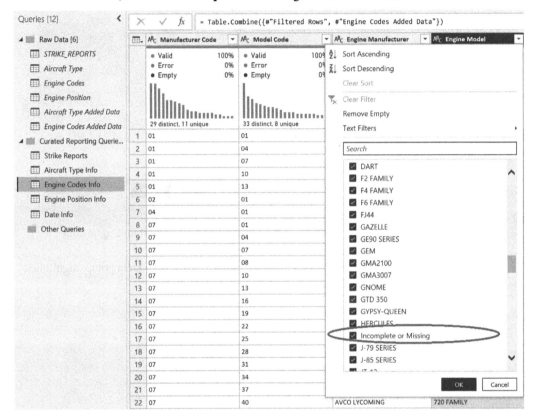

Figure 3.6 – The Engine Codes Info query now has a bucket for missing and incomplete key values

5. Power BI datasets require a single key column, and do not support compound keys. You'll need to add a single primary key to the **Engine Codes Info** query. On the Power Query ribbon, select **Add Column | General | Index Column | From 1**. Rename the new **Index** column to **Engine Codes Info Key**. The **Engine Codes Info** query now looks like this:

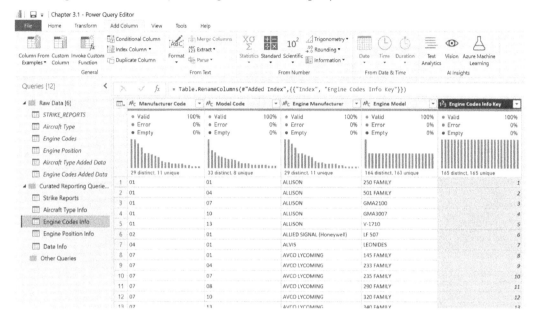

Figure 3.7 – Integer primary key value added to the Engine Codes Info query

6. Now, you will add a corresponding foreign key to the **Strike Reports** query. While on the **Strike Reports** query in Power Query, select **Home | Combine | Merge Queries | Merge Queries**. Select **Engine Codes Info** as the second table. Click on **EMA** on the **Strike Reports** table and **Manufacturer Code** on the **Engine Codes Info** table. You'll see that greater than 50% of the rows found a match:

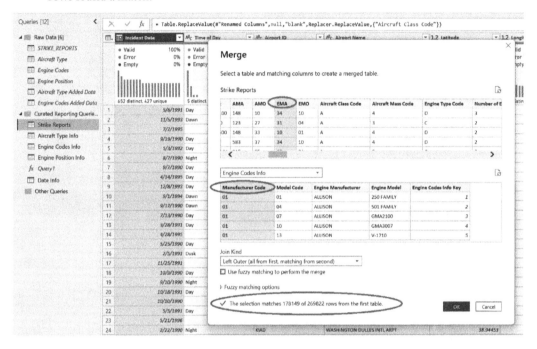

Figure 3.8 – Not all of the EMA values from Strike Reports found a match on the Engine Codes Info query

7. Since the table matches up via a compound key, **EMA** and **EMO** to **Manufacturer Code** and **Model Code**, you press Ctrl and click **EMO** on the **Strike Reports** table and **Model Code** for the **Engine Codes Info** table. You lose a few matches versus the **Manufacturer** keys alone, which would justify breaking off the **Manufacturer** information into a separate dimension table. However, since the difference is small, you decide to add breaking out **Manufacturer** as a separate dimension to the backlog for future rounds of development. If you don't get any matches, check to ensure that the **EMA** and **EMO** columns in both tables are text values since data types need to be the same. Proceeding with the current plan will still give you a fairly similar match rate:

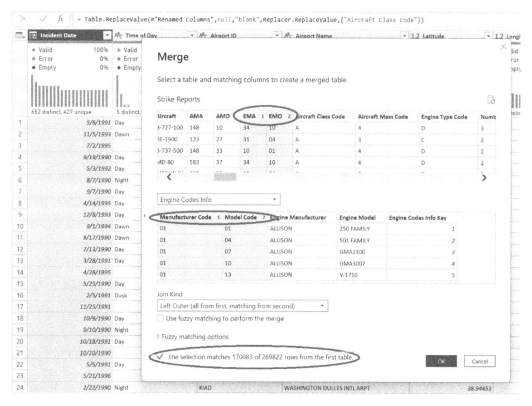

Figure 3.9 – A compound key can tie together Strike Reports and
Engine Codes Info but not every row finds a match

8. Click **OK**. You'll see a new column was added to **Strike Reports** named **Engine Codes Info**. Click the caret and select only **Engine Codes Info Key**:

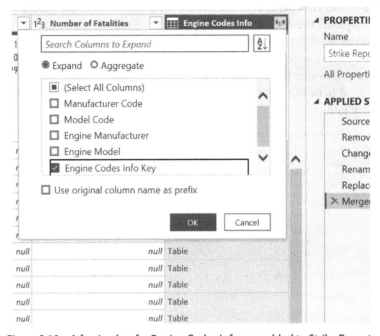

Figure 3.10 – A foreign key for Engine Codes Info was added to Strike Reports

9. Click **OK**. You now have a single foreign key value, **Engine Codes Info Key**, for the **Engine Codes Info** table in your dataset.

Let's move on to the next step.

Engine Position Info

You previously determined that **Engine Code** on the **Engine Position Info** table was a primary key for the table, and all four of the columns (**Engine 1 Position Code**, **Engine 2 Position Code**, **Engine 3 Position Code**, and **Engine 4 Position Code**) from the **Wildlife Strikes** query were foreign keys referencing the engine position. You revisit the preliminary data model, which includes **Engine Position Info** as a dimension table referencing **Strike Reports** as a fact table. Since there is not a single foreign key on the **Engine Position Info** table referencing a single primary key on the **Strike Reports** table, a dimensional design can be handled in a few different ways, such as the following:

- A separate fact table having a separate row for each engine position.

- Change the granularity of the existing fact table to have a separate row for each engine position.

- Add a separate copy of **Engine Position Info** for each of the four foreign key columns on the **Strike Reports** table.

- Add inactive relationships between the **Engine Position Info** and **Strike Reports** table that can be switched out interactively using the DAX expression language.

The first option might be a valid choice if significant analytics were to be performed on the engine positions and you were building a complex star schema design. The second and third options would work from a logical perspective but would add unnecessary complexity and bloat to your design. Remember, you will be performing analytics for the purpose of building predictive models using ML in Power BI. Keeping the columns on the **Strike Reports** table in the current format will work well for building queries to be used for ML purposes. You know that Power BI ML works best with simple flattened tables of data, with each of those four columns as a potential feature of the data. You decide to proceed with the fourth option since it works best for your ML use case and will not add bloat or unnecessary complexity to your design.

You take a look at the data within the **Engine 1 Position Code**, **Engine 2 Position Code**, **Engine 3 Position Code**, and **Engine 4 Position Code** columns of the **Strike Reports** table. All four columns are similar to the **Aircraft Class Code** column that you previously reviewed in having both (**null**) entries, which are actually blank, and the four-letter **NULL** value, which is a text entry. You handle this scenario in a similar manner by adding two new rows to the **Engine Position Info** query for **blank** and **NULL** entries:

1. Right-click each of the **Engine 1 Position Code**, **Engine 2 Position Code**, **Engine 3 Position Code**, and **Engine 4 Position Code** columns and select **Replace Values…**, then type in null for **Value to Find** and blank for **Replace With**. Now, all of the empty values will contain the word **blank**.

2. On the ribbon of Power Query, select **Enter Data**. Name the new table **Engine Position Added Data**. Create two columns, **Engine Code** and **Location of Engine**.

3. Enter blank for both columns in row 1 and NULL for both columns in row 2.

4. Right-click the new query in the **Queries** pane, and move it to the **Raw Data** group. Right-click it again, and uncheck **Enable Load**. Power Query should now look like this:

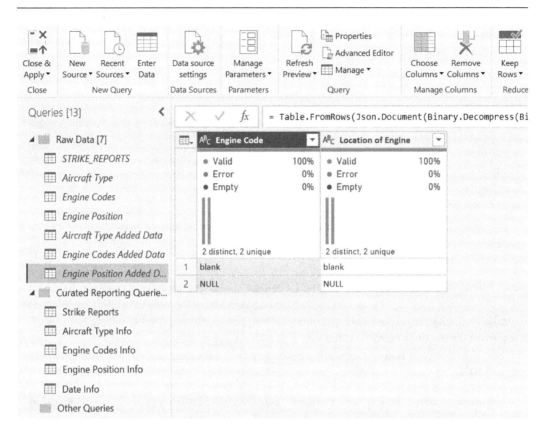

Figure 3.11 – New data to account for blank and NULL text values in Engine Position

5.   Left-click on the **Engine Position Info** query. On the Power Query ribbon, under **Home |
     Combine select Append Queries | Append Queries**, append the **Engine Position Added
     Data** query. Your **Engine Position Info** query should now look like this:

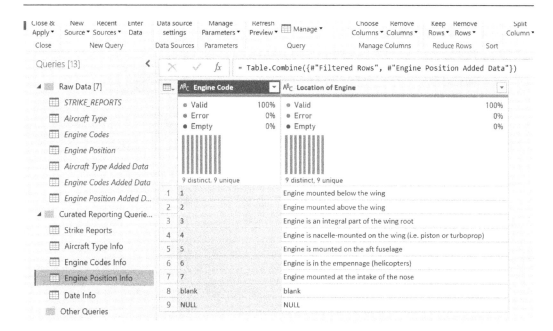

Figure 3.12 – Engine Position Info can now match for blank rows and the NULL text value

You are sure to note that although it is a best practice to use integer values for primary and foreign keys, Power BI has the flexibility and performance to handle text values as key columns in this solution. Replacing all of the key values on these tables with integer values would introduce unnecessary complexity at this point in your efforts.

At this point, you are ready to start building your Power BI dataset!

Building a Power BI dataset

You review the preliminary data model design from your earlier efforts, and note that you have approached a fork for which the relational analytic data that will populate the Power BI dataset will likely have differences from the flattened data used for ML in Power BI:

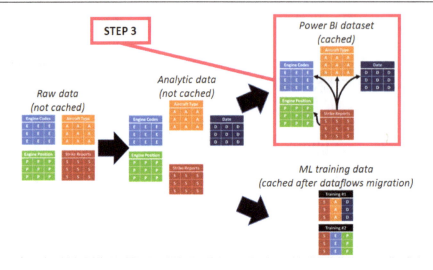

Figure 3.13 – You will now populate Power Query queries for the Power BI dataset

In order to keep your work both organized and optimized for future changes, you decide to create a new group in Power Query that will contain the tables for the Power BI dataset. You take note that when working with extremely large data volumes or a complex data model, avoiding complexity within Power Query is often a best practice. However, with your data volumes, complexity, and overall use case, it makes sense to have separate groups for different segments of the project:

1.   Create a new group within **Queries** called **Curated Dataset Tables**.

2.   Right-click each of the **Strike Reports, Aircraft Type Info, Engine Codes Info, Engine Position Info**, and **Date** queries, and select **Reference**.

3.   Move each of those new queries into the **Curated Dataset Tables** group.

4.   Rename the queries for readability to **Strike reports Fact, Aircraft Type Dim, Engine Codes Dim, Engine Position Dim**, and **Date Dim**.

5.   Within the **Curated Reporting Queries** group, right-click each query and uncheck **Enable Load**. These queries do not need to be imported and cached within Power BI.

Power Query should now look like this:

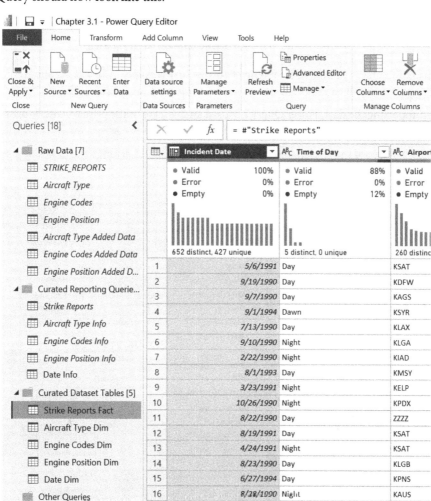

Figure 3.14 – Queries that will be populated as tables in the Power BI dataset

Now, it is time for your dataset to blast off! First, you will go through the following steps to build your Power BI dataset:

1. Import and process the **Wildlife Strike** data queries from Power Query.
2. Create relationships between fact and dimension tables.
3. Clean up the metadata and adjust the settings.

Importing and processing the Wildlife Strike data queries from Power Query

You run the full queries and import the **Wildlife Strike** data for your dataset:

1. In the Power Query ribbon, select **Home** | **Close** | **Close & Apply** | **Close & Apply**. Your dataset will populate with data imported using the Power Query transformations.

2. After importing the data, Power Query is closed and you are in the primary interface of Power BI Desktop.

3. On the left side of the application, click the **Model** view and arrange the tables in a manner that is easy to read:

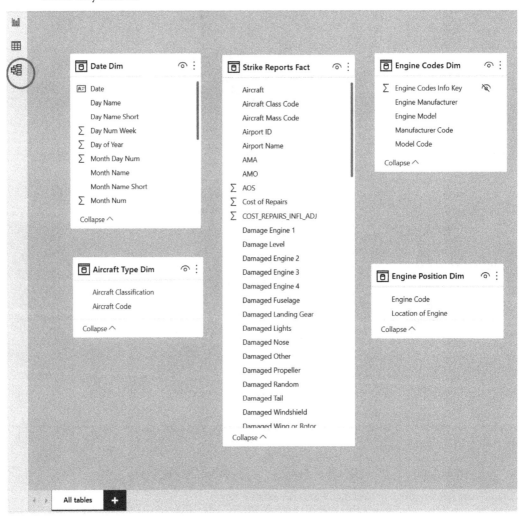

Figure 3.15 – Arrange the dataset tables in the Model view

Creating relationships between fact and dimension tables

Next, you'll create relationships between the tables of data. On the **Date Dim** table, drag the **Date** column and drop it on the **Incident Date** column of the **Strike Reports Fact** table. Power BI will appear as follows:

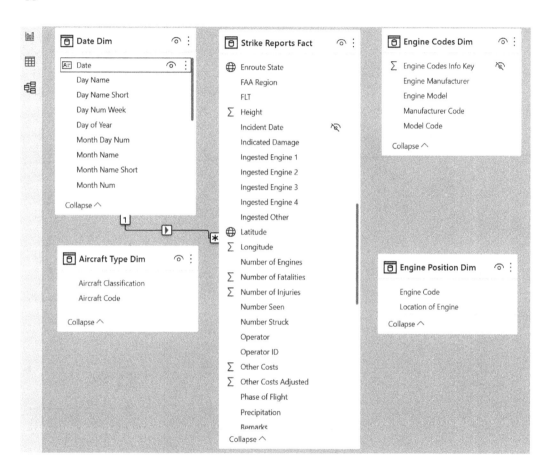

Figure 3.16 – A relationship has been created between Strike Reports Fact and Date Dim

Double-click on the relationship line to reveal that the relationship was determined to be a many-to-one with a cross-filter direction of **Single**. The arrow on the relationship line indicates that the **Date Dim** table can filter the **Strike Reports Fact** table, but not the other way around. The **Make this relationship active** box is also checked:

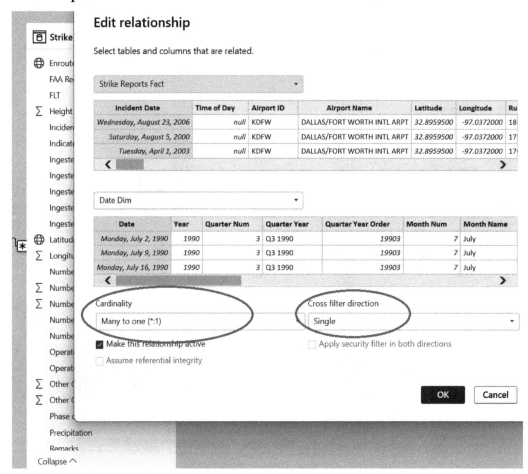

Figure 3.17 – The cardinality and filter direction are set to Many to one and Single

Repeat the process by dragging and dropping the remaining columns to the **Strike Reports Fact** table:

Source Table (Column)	Destination Table (Column)	Cardinality	Cross – filter direction	Make this relationship active
Strike Reports Fact (Aircraft Class Code)	Aircraft Type Dim (Aircraft Code)	Many to one (fact to dimension)	Single (dimension to fact)	Yes
Strike Reports Fact (Engine Codes Info Key)	Engine Codes Dim (Engine Codes Info Key)	Many to one (fact to dimension)	Single (dimension to fact)	Yes
Strike Reports Fact (Engine 1 Position Code)	Engine Position Dim (Engine Code)	Many to one (fact to dimension)	Single (dimension to fact)	Yes
Strike Reports Fact (Engine 2 Position Code)	Engine Position Dim (Engine Code)	Many to one (fact to dimension)	Single (dimension to fact)	No
Strike Reports Fact (Engine 2 Position Code)	Engine Position Dim (Engine Code)	Many to one (fact to dimension)	Single (dimension to fact)	No
Strike Report Fact (Engine 2 Position Code)	Engine Position Dim (Engine Code)	Many to one (fact to dimension)	Single (dimension to fact)	No

Figure 3.18 – Relationship settings between the Strike Reports Fact table and dimension tables

Your Power BI model view should now look like this:

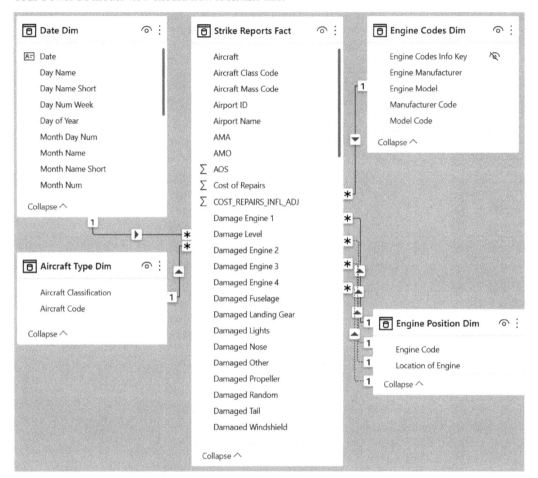

Figure 3.19 – Completed relational design for the Power BI dataset

The relationships between tables are now defined and complete.

Cleaning up the metadata and adjusting settings

Next, you move on to clean up the metadata so that the end users of the analytic reports can easily understand the content of the dataset. This process will involve the following tasks:

- Hiding unnecessary columns
- Adjusting **Summarization** and **Data Category** settings
- Adjusting settings for the **Date Dim** table

Hiding unnecessary columns

Columns that serve as a foreign key or surrogate primary key remain part of the browsable solution for report developers and viewers by default. You hide the visibility of these columns since they are part of the dataset for relationships but do not have a practical use in reporting. In the **Fields** panel on the right-hand side of the screen, right-click on these columns and select **Hide in report view**:

Table (Column) to Hide
Engine Codes Dim (Engine Codes Info Key)
Strike Reports Fact (Engine Codes Info Key)
Strike Reports Fact (Incident Date)
Strike Reports Fact (Aircraft Class Code)

Figure 3.20 – Columns that aren't needed in the reports are hidden

Adjusting Summarization, Data Category, Format, and Sort by settings

Power BI provides settings for columns of data that impact how the data is displayed and aggregated in reports. The **Summarization** setting determines whether numeric values will add/average/min/max or whether they are not intended to be used for math. The **Don't Summarize** setting will ensure that numeric values do not get summarized by default. **Data Category** settings will determine how data is displayed within the context of maps, URLs, and so on when added to reports. When you highlight a column, **Summarization** and **Data Category** are on the Power BI data view ribbon at **Column Tools | Properties**. **Format** is also configured on the ribbon, and determines the display characteristics on the page such as decimal points. **Sort by** determines a column to sort another column, such as using numeric values 1-12 to sort the months January through February on a data visualization. You use the following settings for columns in this solution:

Table (Column)	Summarization	Data Category	Format	Sort by
Strike Reports Fact (Latitude)	Don't Summarize	Latitude	Decimal number with 7 places	
Strike Reports Fact (Longitude)	Don't Summarize	Longitude	Decimal number with 7 places	
Strike Reports Fact (State)	Don't Summarize	State or Province	Text	
Strike Reports Fact (Enroute State)	Don't Summarize	State or Province	Text	

Table (Column)	Summarization	Data Category	Format	Sort by
Date (Quarter Year)	Don't Summarize		Text	Date (Quarter Num)
Date (Month Name)	Don't Summarize		Text	Date (Month Num)
Date (Month Name Short)	Don't Summarize		Text	Date (Month Num)
Date (Month Year)	Don't Summarize		Text	Date (Month Year Order)
Date (Week Year)	Don't Summarize		Text	Date (Week Year Order)
Date (Day Name)	Don't Summarize		Text	Date (Day Num Week)
Date (Day Name Short)	Don't Summarize		Text	Date (Day Num Week)

Figure 3.21 – Categories, summarization, format, and sort settings for columns

As you build out your analytical report and determine suitable features for ML in Power BI, you may modify more settings and add to this list.

Adjusting settings for the Date Dim table

Specifying the **Date Dim** table as an official date table will unlock capabilities in Power BI such as **Time Intelligence**. Marking the **Date Dim** table as an official date table can be accomplished by navigating to **Table Tools | Calendars | Mark as date table** in the **Data** view and selecting **Date** as the official date column for the solution.

Having built out the foundation of the relational model in the Power BI dataset, you can move on to build runtime calculations. You've got the data model set up the way you need it, but adding some logic to the semantic layer for mathematical operations will empower you to dive deeper with analytics.

Adding measures to your Power BI dataset

As a final activity for this chapter, you will add a few basic measures to the Power BI dataset. Measures are not stored on the tables of data but rather during runtime on reports. These measures will be used to do mathematics such as total number of reports, average damage cost amounts, average height of contact calculations, and more. For now, you choose a few basic measures that will give you a starting point for analysis. In future chapters, you can add more measures as you discover new perspectives within the data.

Measures can be added using the DAX expression language, which is a key skill for Power BI. Most of the formulas will be fairly simple for anyone who is familiar with writing formulas in Excel.

Add the following measures in the **Data** view of Power BI while the **Strike Reports Fact** table is highlighted:

Name	DAX formula	Description
Incidents	`Incidents = COUNTROWS('Strike Reports Fact')`	This formula will calculate a count of the total incidents that were reported
Average Speed	`Average Speed = AVERAGE([Speed])`	An average speed for incidents at the time of impact
Average Height	`Average Height = AVERAGE([Height])`	An average height for incidents at the time of impact
Total Cost of Repairs	`Total Cost of Repairs = SUM([Cost of Repairs])`	A sum of all repair costs
Average Cost of Repairs	`Average Cost of Repairs = SUM([Cost of Repairs])`	An average of all repair costs
Incidents with Costs	`Incidents with Costs = CALCULATE([Incidents],FILTER('Strike Reports Fact',[Cost of Repairs] > 0)`	A count of incidents that resulted in costs incurred
Percentage Incidents with Costs	`Percentage Incidents with Costs = DIVIDE([Incidents with Costs],[Incidents])`	A percentage of incidents that resulted in costs incurred

Figure 3.22 – Calculated measures and the corresponding DAX expressions

As you progress in your exploration of the data, you will probably add more measures to your list. The measures listed in the preceding table are a good start before moving to your next phase of analysis.

Summary

In this chapter, you designed key values for tables in a Power BI dataset, created a Power BI dataset, and added measures to the Power BI dataset. You have progressed from exploring and understanding raw data to working with a multidimensional dataset in Power BI that contains runtime measures. You now have the basic foundation for analytics and building an analytics report.

In the next chapter, you will build an analytical report that dives into the data and uncovers features that you will earmark for machine learning in Power BI. As you enrich the analytical report and discover new features, you will also begin to build out the datasets in Power Query that will be used to train and test using Power BI ML.

4

Model Data for Machine Learning in Power BI

In *Chapter 3* of this book, you prepped FAA Wildlife Strike data for a Power BI dataset, built a relational dataset that will function as a foundation for analytics, and then configured basic settings in that dataset so that you could take a deep dive into the data and discover features for ML in Power BI.

As you begin discovering features in the data for your ML models, you will need a process for adding those features to queries that can be used for training and testing those models in Power BI. In this chapter, you will build out an analytic report in Power BI as you explore the dataset for features suitable for ML in Power BI. When features are discovered, you will create queries within Power Query that will eventually serve the purpose of training and testing your ML models.

Technical requirements

For this chapter, you will need the following:

- Power BI Desktop April 2023 or later (no licenses required)
- FAA Wildlife Strike data files from either the FAA website or the Packt GitHub site: `https://github.com/PacktPublishing/Unleashing-Your-Data-with-Power-BI-Machine-Learning-and-OpenAI`

Choosing features via data exploration

Your project is to be implemented completely within Power BI, without using external tools. Power BI ML is a **software as a service** (**SaaS**) tool that does not require the setup of an infrastructure or advanced coding skills. Traditionally, most ML projects are implemented using highly specialized tools that require strong coding skills with languages such as R and Python. By implementing the entire project in Power BI, you will be able to complete it in a short timeline, build all of the components with SaaS tools and minimal coding, and then manage deployment, scalability, and future changes using a single suite of tools.

The data architecture techniques in this chapter are tailored to analysts and business intelligence developers, and the process will be a great way to learn the basics of finding and modeling features for ML. Experienced ML architects who are fluent in R or Python might handle the process differently, but you need to proceed with tools that are within your skill set. Using Power BI tools including Power Query, datasets, dataflows, and ML will enable you to complete the project with little code effort, all within Power BI.

When you run potential features through Power BI ML, the tool will help identify the features that have strong predictive value. Some of the features that you add to tables may turn out to have little predictive value, but running them through the Power BI ML tool will help identify the value of features.

Adding Power Query tables to your architecture for ML training and testing

Revisiting your preliminary data architecture, you will be populating the ML training data tables in Power Query with features that you discover while creating an analytical report in Power BI using your dataset:

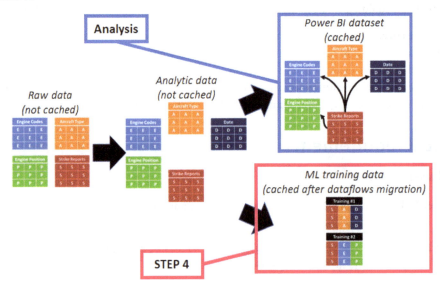

Figure 4.1 – ML training data will be discovered during analysis in Power BI

You decide to review the deliverables that will fulfil the stakeholder requirements, as discussed in *Chapter 1*:

- **Analytic Report**: This will be created as part of the analysis process using your Power BI dataset

- **Predict Damage, Predict Size, Predict Height**: You will need three separate tables of training data for each of these three machine learning models

As you build out your analytic report and discover new features that can be used for predictions, you will iteratively build out your training data tables in Power Query for use with ML. You are building an architecture that can be updated and modified for future versions of the project, too:

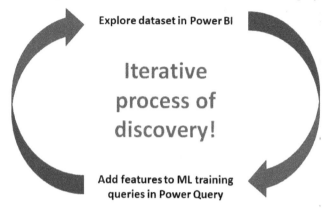

Figure 4.2 – Data exploration and feature discovery is an iterative process

You can resume where you left off with your PBIX file from *Chapter 3*, or you can follow along using the finished version of the content from this chapter. You can download the PBIT version of the file from the Packt GitHub site folder for *Chapter 4*: `https://github.com/PacktPublishing/Unleashing-Your-Data-with-Power-BI-Machine-Learning-and-OpenAI/tree/main/Chapter-04`.

First, you'll need to create a group of new queries to make tables that can be modified during this iterative process:

1. Create a new group in Power Query called `ML Queries`.
2. Right-click the **Strike Reports** query in the **Curated Reporting Queries** group, and select **Reference**.
3. Rename the new query `Predict Damage`.
4. Right-click the new query and unselect **Enable Load**.
5. Right-click the new query and move it to the new **ML Queries** group.
6. Repeat these steps two more times, but rename the queries `Predict Size` and `Predict Height`.

Your Power Query groups should now look like this:

Figure 4.3 – You now have a separate group for ML Queries

Are you scratching your head and wondering why all three queries are identical? Reviewing the iterative process from *Figure 4.2*, you'll see that each of these queries will be modified as you discover new features in the data using Power BI. Through this process, each query will be whittled down and customized to represent a unique set of features that relate to the intended prediction. Before beginning feature discovery via analytics, you think through the likely granularity of each query for your ML models. Effectively, you want to define what an individual row of data represents:

- **Predict Damage**: The *yes*/*no* binary prediction for damage will be applied to an individual reported wildlife strike. The question asked will be *"Based upon the circumstances of the strike, how likely is there to be damage to the aircraft?"* Each row will be a unique wildlife strike report flight.

- **Predict Size**: Predicting the size of the wildlife that struck the aircraft is your second deliverable. This prediction could be useful in identifying the size of an animal that struck an aircraft if there was no visual confirmation or remains recovered. This prediction will also be at the level of a unique wildlife strike report flight.

- **Predict Height**: Ideally, you'd like to predict the height of different wildlife that hit an aircraft. Data about the time of year, location, and species could be used to predict the height. Predicting the height of an individual event would also keep the grain of the table identical to the source database.

The next stage is building the report.

Building an analytic report to discover and choose initial features for the Predict Damage ML model

At the bottom of your blank Power BI report, change the name of the page to `Predict Damage`. This page will be part of your analytic report. You first ask the question "*What constitutes a yes/no answer to indicate whether a wildlife strike caused damage?*" Referring to the `read_me.xls` documentation, you find a column named **Indicated Damage**, which is on the **Strike Reports** table, and provides a *True/False* value. This column will serve as the column you are predicting in the Predict Damage binary ML model.

You follow these steps to dive into the data:

1. From the **Fields** list, drag **Incidents** onto the canvas.

2. Create a new calculated measure to calculate the percentage of incidents that had damage:

   ```
   Indicated Damage % = DIVIDE(CALCULATE([Incidents],FILTER('Strike
   Reports Fact',[Indicated Damage] = TRUE)),[Incidents])
   ```

3. Format **Indicated Damage %** as a percentage.

4. Drag **Indicated Damage %** onto the table with **Incidents**.

5. Change the table to a matrix.

6. Drag **Aircraft Type Dim[Aircraft Classification]** onto rows.

Your matrix should appear as follows:

Aircraft Classification	Incidents	Indicated Damage %
Airplane	189,667	9.4%
blank	19,375	0.0%
Glider	6	66.7%
Helicopter	4,065	20.1%
NULL	56,703	0.4%
Other	1	
Ultralight	5	
Total	**269,822**	**7.0%**

Figure 4.4 – Animal strikes with reported damage by aircraft classification

You notice that the vast majority of wildlife strike reports are for airplanes, and 9.4% of the reports indicated damage. Helicopters also have several thousand reports, but you decide to whittle the data down to airplanes since those are the most common passenger aircraft and do not introduce flight path complexities such as hovering:

7. Drag **Aircraft Type Dim[Aircraft Classification]** into **Filters on this page** of the Power BI filter pane.

8. Filter for **Airplane** and leave the other options unchecked.

Move the matrix to the left side of the canvas, and create a new chart to view incidents and damage by year.

9. Choose **Line and stacked column chart** from the **Visualizations** column.

10. Put **Strike Report Fact[Incidents]** on the column *y* axis.

11. Put **Strike Report Fact[Indicated Damage %]** on the line *y* axis.

12. Put **Date Dim[Year]** on the *x* axis.

You notice an interesting trend on the chart. The number of reported incidents increased over time until the COVID-related disruptions of 2020. At the same time, the percentage of strikes that caused damage went down and appear to have leveled off around 2014.

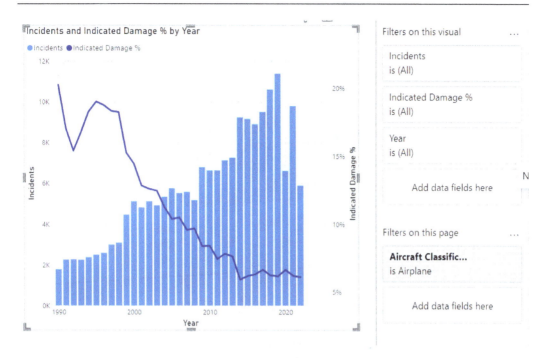

Figure 4.5 – Incidents and incidents with damage by year

Why did these trends develop? You don't know the answers, but the following are among the possible causes:

- Improved surveillance and deterrence of wildlife by air traffic control over time
- Better compliance with filling out reports when there wasn't any damage
- Improvements in aircraft technology
- Changes in quantities of flights, times of flights, and times at various altitudes

For the time being, you decide to focus on data starting in the year 2014 since older data likely has different trends. Is this the perfect starting point? Advanced analytic techniques might unveil the perfect start date for your data, but for your first round of analytics in Power BI, you settle on 2014 as the starting point. Drag **Date Dim[Year]** into **Filters on this page** of the Power BI filter pane and filter to greater than or equal to 2014.

Using common sense, it would seem that larger wildlife could be more likely to cause damage versus small animals. Copy and paste the matrix on the left side of the page showing **Aircraft Classification**, and replace **Aircraft Classification** with **Strike Report Fact[Size]**. Your report should look as follows:

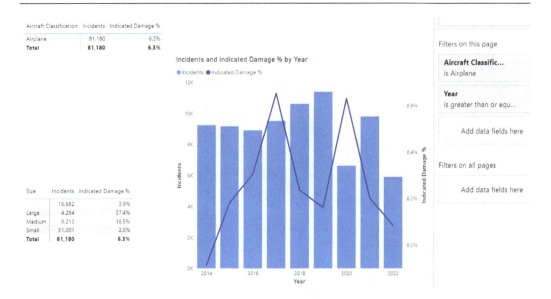

Figure 4.6 – Viewing incidents and damage with filter criteria applied

You notice that increasing the size of the wildlife appears to result in a larger percentage of incidents with damage. Several incidents also left the size field blank, which will need to be fixed if you use that field for ML. Basic ML tools generally require non-blank values in the data that is used for training and testing. Power BI ML has built-in featurization tools that will account for blank values, but handling blank values is a good idea before building ML models.

For your first iteration of the **Predict Damage** data for ML in Power BI, you've isolated the following features. You will add more features in future chapters of the book, but this is a good start to test your architectural design in Power Query:

- A row represents an individual reported event.

- **Strike Report Fact[Indicated Damage]** is the field you will be training the machine learning model to predict.

- You will use rows that have **Aircraft Classification** of `Airplane`.

- You will use data with **Incident Date** on or after January 1, 2014.

- You will also use **Strike Report Fact[Size]** as a feature for the machine learning model. You'll need to replace the blank values with a value such as text reading `blank`.

Building an analytic report to discover and choose initial features for the Predict Size ML model

Now you move on to find a few features to be used in predicting the size of the wildlife that struck an aircraft. Predicting the size of the animal or animals could be helpful in understanding what may have hit an aircraft at a certain altitude, location, and in a certain season. When the species is unknown, size could be a valuable factor in determining future risks and also for identifying possible collisions with endangered or protected wildlife.

You've already included size as a predictive factor for your damage prediction ML model, but there will inevitably be scenarios where the animal was not seen or found. The Predict Size algorithm will predict whether a strike happened with wildlife that is large, medium, or small:

1. You start by duplicating the **Predict Damage** page, and change the name to `Predict Size`. You will reuse the content that has already been created.

2. First, you decide to keep the **Aircraft Classification** filter set to `Airplane` so that your machine learning models will apply to the same types of use cases for your project. You modify the line and stacked column chart as follows:

- Remove **Indicated Damage %** from the chart

- Add **Strike Reports Fact[Size]** to the column legend

- In the filter pane, clear the filter on **Date[Year]**

   You notice that blank (empty) values for **Size** start showing up in the year 2010:

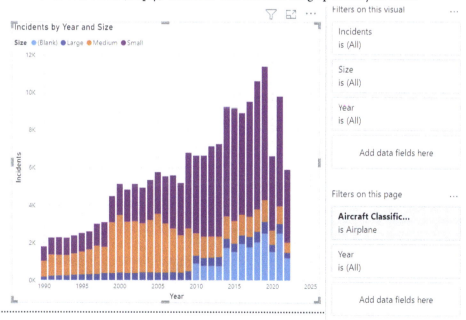

Figure 4.7 – Blank values start showing up in 2010

3. You add **Strike Reports Fact[Size]** to the filter pane for **Filters on this page** and remove the blank values from the report. While blank values for **Size** were included with your previous query for predicting damage, blank values do not provide value for this model since you are trying to predict the outcome of the **Strike Reports Fact[Size]** field. The **Predict Damage ML** model will be beneficial for evaluating the likelihood of damage from a strike, while the **Predict Size ML** model will predict the size of the wildlife strike when other factors are known.

You notice that even with the blank values removed for **Size**, there was some sort of change in 2010. Fewer medium-sized strikes were reported, and more small strikes were reported:

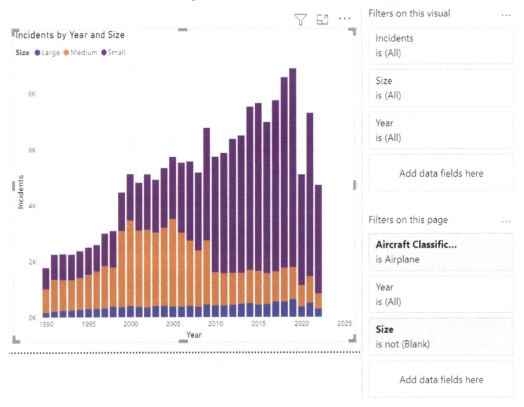

Figure 4.8 – Distribution of reported sizes appears to change in 2010

You decide to include data starting in the year 2010 by filtering **Date[Year]** in the filter pane. Make the change in **Filters on this page** with **Year** added as a filter.

On the **Predict Damage** report page, you already observed that the likelihood of damage increases as the size of the strike increases. Therefore, you decide to keep **Strike Reports Fact[Indicated Damage]** as a feature for predicting size.

You are aware that birds, which are often the culprits in these wildlife strikes, migrate over the course of the year. You remove **Date[Year]** from the *x* axis of the line and stacked column chart, and replace it with **Date[Month Num]**. Notice that the frequency and distribution of strikes and the size of strikes change throughout the year:

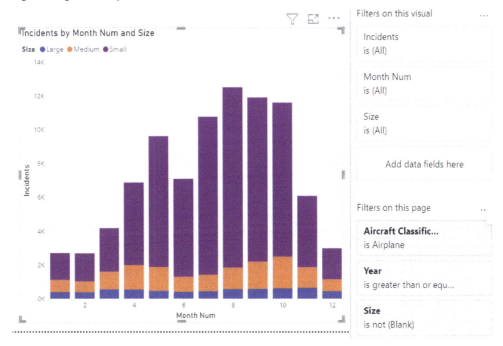

Figure 4.9 – Frequency and distribution appear to change by month when all years are aggregated

You decide to add the month number as a feature to your query for data to train and test the Predict Size ML model. Is month of year a better level of aggregation than day of year, week of year, or quarter of year? You might revisit this question in future iterations of the solution, but for now, you decide to proceed since a deep dive would require extra time and effort that could impact your deadline.

Logically, larger-sized wildlife strikes could cause more severe or expensive damage. The **Strike Reports Fact** table contains four columns with cost data including **Cost of Repairs**, **Other Costs**, **Cost of Repair Adjusted**, and **Other Costs Adjusted**. The adjusted columns are indexed for inflation, so you decide to use those values. You decide to combine those columns into a single column. In order to combine them, you go back to Power Query and create a new column on the **Strike Reports** query of the **Curated Reporting Queries** group:

1. Click on the **Strike Reports** query of the **Curated Reporting Queries** group.
2. On the Power Query ribbon and select **Add Column | General | Custom Column**.
3. Name the new column `Total Costs Adjusted`.

4. Enter the following as the M expression that adds the columns together:

```
= if [Cost of Repairs Adjusted] = null then [Other Costs
Adjusted]
else if [Other Costs Adjusted] = null then [Cost of Repairs
Adjusted]
else [Cost of Repairs Adjusted] + [Other Costs Adjusted]
```

The conditional statements exist to ensure that rows with one null value don't get skipped.

5. Change the data type to **Fixed Decimal Number**.

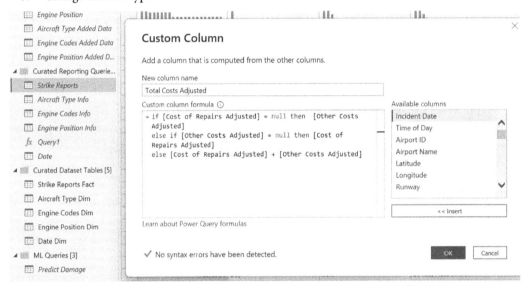

Figure 4.10 – Add a custom column for total costs

Since you referenced the **Strike Reports** query in your other downstream queries, the new column will also propagate to those queries! Next time you reprocess your Power BI dataset, a column for **Total Adjusted Costs** will appear on the **Strike Reports** Fact table. Click **Close & Apply** in Power Query to update your dataset. Once processed, you decide to add three new DAX expressions to the **Strike Reports** Fact table of the dataset for sum (total charges for all rows selected), average (an average of all rows selected), and median (the middle value of all rows selected to eliminate the impact of extremely large and rare cost events):

- `Total Costs Inflation Adjusted = SUM([Total Costs Adjusted])`
- `Cost per Strike Avg = AVERAGE([Total Costs Inflation Adjusted])`
- `Cost per Strike Median = MEDIAN([Total Costs Adjusted])`

Finally, thinking about climate and geography, you realize that the species of animals at different times of the year will be different in the Pacific Northwest, versus the deep South, versus New England. Certain species will inhabit different parts of the country, and some species migrate to new geographies at different times of the year. For example, flamingos will never fly through Minnesota. For the first iteration of your project, you decide to filter the data down to the top 15 airports that experience wildlife strikes:

1. Copy and paste the matrix visual with **Size**, **Incidents**, and **Indicated Damage %**.

2. Move **Size** from rows to columns.

3. Add **Strike Reports Fact[Airport ID]** to the rows.

4. Sort by **Total Incidents**.

5. Choose the top 15 airports based on total strikes. Exclude ZZZZ since this is not a valid airport code and was most likely used when the airport was unknown. Notice that the locations provide some geographical diversity, too:

Airport ID	Airport City
KDEN	Denver, CO
KMEM	Memphis, TN
KDFW	Dallas, TX
KSMF	Sacramento, CA
KCLT	Charlotte, NC
KORD	Chicago, IL
KPHL	Philadelphia, PA
KSDF	Louisville, KY
KMCO	Orlando, FL
KLGA	Queens, NY
KATL	Atlanta, GA
KJFK	Queens, NY
KIAH	Houston, TX
KAUS	Austin, TX
KBNA	Nashville, TN

Figure 4.11 – Top 15 airports by incident count

You've now identified the feature that you will be predicting, along with the features used to score the machine learning model in Power BI:

- A row represents an individual reported event
- **Strike Report Fact[Size]** is the field you will be training the machine learning model to predict – Large, Medium, or Small strike size
- You will use rows that have an **Aircraft Classification** of Airplane
- You will use data with an incident date on or after January 1, 2010
- Blank values will be removed from **Strike Report Fact[Size]**
- You will include the **Strike Reports Fact[Indicated Damage]** flag as a feature
- You will filter down to the top 15 airports by wildlife strike volume
- You will include the month of the year as a feature

Building an analytic report to discover and choose initial features for the Predict Height ML model

Your third ML model in Power BI is planned to predict the height of a wildlife strike on an aircraft. The regression model will predict a numeric value in feet above the ground. You plan to predict height at the level of an individual flight, and if those results have low accuracy, then you will roll incidents up to an aggregate level.

First, on your Power BI report, duplicate the **Predict Damage** page and rename it to Predict Height. **Height** is a single column in the table of data. You'll want to filter out rows for which the height is missing.

You create new DAX expressions to analyze **Height**, in addition to **Average Height**, which was created in *Chapter 3*:

- Median Height = MEDIAN([Height])
- Max Height = MAX([Height])
- Min Height = MIN([Height])

Now you begin analyzing the data:

1. On the line and stacked column chart, remove **Indicated Damage %** from the line *y* axis and replace it with both **Strike Reports Fact[Average Height]** and **Strike Reports Fact[Median Height]**.
2. Clear the **Date[Year]** filter on the filter panel for **Filters on this page**.
3. Leave the **Airplane Classification** filter as Airplane.

4. On the filter panel, add **Height** and set it to **is not blank**.

5. Ensure that **Secondary y-axis** is turned on for the visual.

Your chart should look as follows:

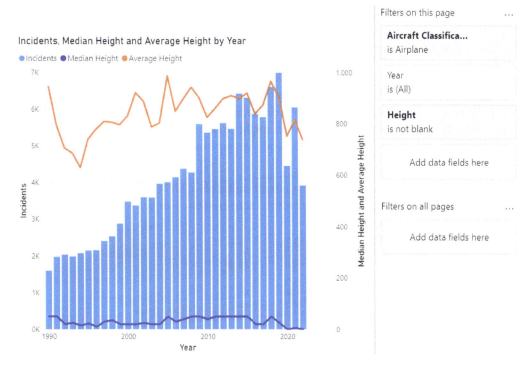

Figure 4.12 – Average and median height over time

You decide to reapply a filter to the **Year** for the whole page for 2010 and later, so that the date range is in line with **Predict Size**.

On the matrix containing **Size**, **Incidents**, and **Indicated Damage %**, follow the following steps:

1. Remove **Indicated Damage %**.

2. Add **Strike Reports Fact[Average Height]**, **Strike Reports Fact[Median Height]**, **Strike Reports Fact[Max Height]**, and **Strike Reports Fact[Min Height]** to the values of the matrix.

3. Add **Strike Reports Fact[Height]** to the filter pane under **Filters on all pages** and set it to **is not blank**.

   Notice that there is a slight uptrend as **Size** increases for the median and a more significant uptrend for the average:

Size	Incidents	Average Height	Median Height	Max Height	Min Height
	9,601	1,298.9	200	31,300	0
Large	5,255	1,083.6	100	29,000	0
Medium	11,584	1,261.7	200	22,000	0
Small	47,818	663.4	10	25,000	0
Total	**74,258**	**868.7**	**30**	**31,300**	**0**

Figure 4.13 – Height average, median, max, and min by size of wildlife strike

At this level of summarization, there does not appear to be a great deal of difference between size and height. Since there are many different species that get grouped into size categorizations, this feature might not be highly valuable. For example, a single small bird might be classified as `Small` while a big flock of the same birds might be classified as `Large`. You will keep **Size** on the table of data for predicting height, and then see how it fairs when you run it through Power BI ML.

4. Copy and paste the matrix visual that you built, and replace **Strike Reports Fact[Size]** with **Strike Reports Fact[Species]**. You see a much more dramatic change:

Species	Incidents	Average Height	Median Height	Max Height	Min Height
Unknown bird - small	19,941	1,034.3	200	25,000	0
Unknown bird	9,405	1,295.3	200	31,300	0
Unknown bird - medium	5,666	2,060.5	1,000	22,000	0
Barn swallow	3,234	54.9	0	21,000	0
Mourning dove	2,401	79.3	0	10,000	0
Killdeer	1,654	43.8	0	9,500	0
American kestrel	1,578	43.0	0	6,000	0
Horned lark	1,572	54.8	0	15,000	0
European starling	1,442	68.5	0	4,100	0
Unknown bird - large	1,341	2,473.1	1,500	29,000	0
Gulls	1,174	404.4	50	11,500	0
Red-tailed hawk	1,111	146.1	0	8,500	0
Cliff swallow	921	94.9	0	4,800	0
Sparrows	901	213.7	0	10,000	0
Rock pigeon	853	141.0	0	6,000	0
Eastern meadowlark	792	36.1	0	4,300	0
Chimney swift	563	851.5	300	13,000	0
Swallows	554	60.0	0	3,000	0
Canada goose	549	805.1	100	15,000	0
Perching birds (y)	506	1,251.2	200	20,000	0
American robin	504	2,004.6	1,000	16,000	0
Western meadowlark	499	107.9	0	7,000	0
Tree swallow	487	131.8	0	10,000	0
Turkey vulture	480	900.1	500	13,000	0
Ring-billed gull	437	127.2	0	4,000	0
Hawks	375	446.2	5	8,000	0
Bank swallow	347	136.9	0	10,000	0
Barn owl	344	39.0	0	3,000	0
Herring gull	333	167.7	0	7,000	0

Filters

Search

Filters on this visual

Average Height
is (All)

Incidents
is (All)

Max Height
is (All)

Median Height
is (All)

Min Height
is (All)

Species
is (All)

Add data fields here

Filters on this page

Aircraft Classification
is Airplane

Year
is greater than or equal to 2010

Height
is not blank

< Back to report

Figure 4.14 – Height metrics by species

Average, median, and max heights differ greatly by species. Ground-dwelling species, which most likely were struck on the runway, are also on the list and consistently have heights of zero feet. For example, if you filter **Species** to Swine (pigs), you can see there were four incidents that happened at a height of zero. Common sense tells you that this is expected, and you do not need to test the hypothesis "Pigs don't fly." In all seriousness, you may want to filter down the list to species that can be airborne, and also eliminate catch-all buckets such as Unknown bird - small. Specific species that actually fly could potentially be a strong predictive factor.

5. Copy and paste the matrix visual again, and replace **Size** with **Date[Month Num]**. You also see a pattern by month:

Month Num	Incidents	Average Height	Median Height	Max Height	Min Height
1	2,395	451.4	35	11,500	0
2	2,304	558.3	30	14,000	0
3	3,504	972.7	100	25,000	0
4	5,668	1,276.1	200	20,000	0
5	7,699	1,175.8	100	21,000	0
6	6,149	353.0	0	31,300	0
7	9,498	332.1	0	22,000	0
8	10,924	626.4	0	25,000	0
9	9,621	1,223.9	100	21,000	0
10	8,955	1,375.8	400	23,000	0
11	4,860	1,006.0	125	18,000	0
12	2,681	481.3	20	11,500	0
Total	**74,258**	**868.7**	**30**	**31,300**	**0**

Figure 4.15 – Height metrics by month of the year

Month Num could be a valuable feature for predicting height. Some bird species migrate to different geographies and occupy different heights, depending on the time of year. Adding in the **Airport ID** field as a feature and filtering to the top 15 airports listed under the **Predict Size** portion of this chapter (*Building an analytic report to discover and choose initial features for the Predict Size ML model*) could also enhance the value of **Month Num**.

At this point, you decide to move on to the next step of your project and start building out the foundations for ML training and testing data in Power Query. For the **Predict Height** query you have decided the following:

- Height will be predicted by the regression model
- Data will be filtered to start in 2010
- **Aircraft Classification** will be set to `Airplane`
- **Size** of wildlife strikes will be a feature
- **Species** will be a feature
- The top 15 airports will be a filter criterion for predicting height

You've now discovered enough potential features to return to Power Query and begin building out some queries that will be the basis of the data used to train and test your ML models.

Creating flattened tables in Power Query for ML in Power BI

Now that you've done some analysis and discovered features that you'd like to include for your first round of ML models, you return to Power Query and get to work. You review your notes from the previous sections of this chapter and begin with the **Predict Damage** table in the **ML Queries** group.

Modifying the Predict Damage table in Power Query

Since a row will represent an individual event that is predicted, you do not need to do any groupings with the data. You will be selecting columns and filtering down the rows to a set of data that is better suited to the task:

1. Highlight the **Predict Damage** table in the **ML Queries** group.
2. The aircraft class code for airplane is A, so filter the **Aircraft Class Code** column to A.
3. Filter the **Incident Date** column to be on or after `1/1/2014`.
4. On the Power Query ribbon, select **Home | Manage Columns | Choose Columns** and keep the **Size** and **Indicated Damage** columns.
5. On the **Size** column, replace the `null` value with `empty` so that you do not have blank values.

Are you confused that there are only two columns? Don't worry! As you progress through future chapters, more features will be added to the table. This example was kept simple to reinforce the methodology of building up your tables of features slowly as you progress through the discovery process. Your table should look as follows:

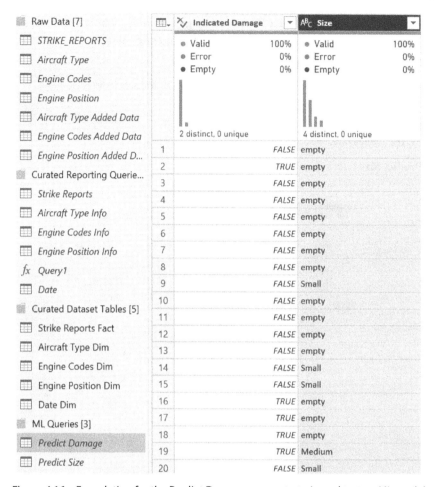

Figure 4.16 – Foundation for the Predict Damages query to train and test an ML model

Next, we'll do the same with the **Predict Size** table.

Modifying the Predict Size table in Power Query

Repeat the same process for the **Predict Size** query in the Power Query **ML Queries** group:

1. Highlight the **Predict Size** table in the **ML Queries** group.

2. The aircraft class code for airplane is A, so filter the **Aircraft Class Code** column to A.

3. Filter the **Incident Date** column to be on or after 1/1/2010.

4. Filter down to the top 15 airports you noted during the analysis. For the **Airport ID** column, select the values KDEN, KMEM, KDFW, KSMF, KCLT, KORD, KPHL, KSDF, KMCO, KLGA, KATL, KJFK, KIAH, KAUS, and KBNA.

5. On the Power Query ribbon, select **Home | Manage Columns | Choose Columns** and keep the **Size**, **Indicated Damage**, **Airport ID**, and **Incident Date** columns.

6. Uncheck **(null)** values for **Size**.

7. Add a custom column named **Month Number** using the following M code:

```
= Date.Month([Incident Date])
```

8. Remove **Incident Date**.

Your **Predict Size** query should now look like this:

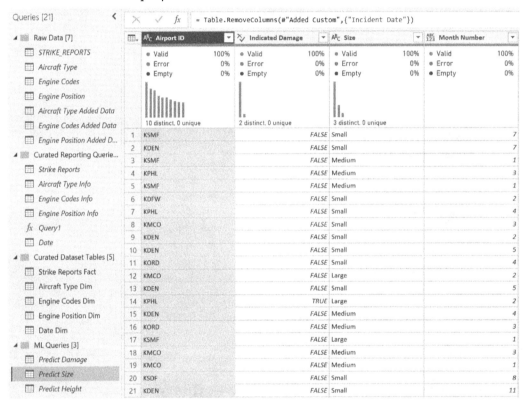

Figure 4.17 – Foundation for the Predict Size query to train and test a machine learning model

Finally, we'll do this for the **Predict Height** table.

Modifying the Predict Height table in Power Query

The **Predict Height** table in Power Query will also follow the same process of whittling down the breadth of columns and volume of rows:

1. Highlight the **Predict Height** table in the **ML Queries** group.

2. The aircraft class code for airplane is A, so filter the **Aircraft Class Code** column to A.

3. Filter the **Incident Date** column to be on or after 1/1/2010.

4. On the Power Query ribbon, select **Home | Manage Columns | Choose Columns** and keep the **Size**, **Species**, **Airport ID**, **Incident Date**, and **Height** columns.

5. Replace null values with empty for the **Size** column.

6. Filter down to the top 15 airports you noted during the analysis. For the **Airport ID** column, select the values KDEN, KMEM, KDFW, KSMF, KCLT, KORD, KPHL, KSDF, KMCO, KLGA, KATL, KJFK, KIAH, KAUS, and KBNA.

7. Filter **Height** to remove the null values.

8. Add a custom column named **Month Number** using the following M code:

   ```
   = Date.Month([Incident Date])
   ```

9. Remove **Incident Date**.

   Your **Predict Height** table should now look like this:

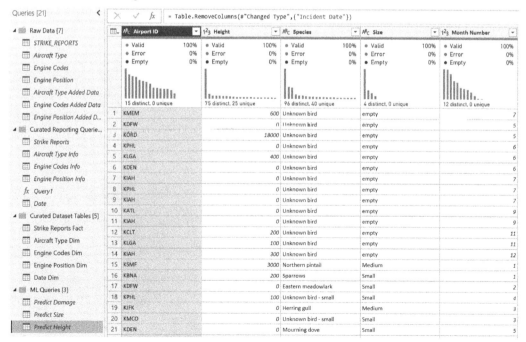

Figure 4.18 – Foundation for the Predict Height query to train and test a machine learning model

Your ML queries have now been modified to include new potential features discovered in this chapter.

Summary

This chapter began building the foundation of your ML adventure in Power BI. You created a group of queries in Power Query that will be the basis for training and testing your binary, general classification, and regression ML models. You began building out an analytical report while discovering features in the data that might be valuable for predictive analytics in ML. Finally, you added those features to new queries in Power Query. You're ready to add new features to your queries that will attempt to predict whether damage occurred, the size of the wildlife involved in a strike, and the height of wildlife strikes.

In the next chapter, you will dive deeper into the Power BI dataset to discover new predictive features. You'll leverage some of the Power BI AI capabilities to uncover new insights and potentially new features for use with ML. Finally, you will add your new findings to the queries that will be used to train and test your ML models in Power BI.

Part 2: Artificial Intelligence and Machine Learning Visuals and Publishing to the Power BI Service

In the next few chapters, you will be enriching the training dataset with new features discovered through data visuals and exploration.

This part includes the following chapters:

5

Discovering Features Using Analytics and AI Visuals

In *Chapter 4*, you discovered features within the FAA Wildlife Strike data to be tested with Power BI ML to see whether they are good predictive features, built out queries in Power Query to structure those features into tables, and completed the foundation of your high-level data architecture. You are ready to take a deep dive into analytics and prep for ML in Power BI.

In this chapter, you will continue to build out your Power BI analytical reports as you explore data and discover trends. You will also try a few of the Power BI AI visuals to see if you can uncover additional features that could be added to your machine learning efforts. At the end of this chapter, you will have a more complete analytical report and more robust data to build, train, and test your Power BI ML models.

Technical requirements

For this chapter, you'll need the following:

- Power BI Desktop April 2023 or later (no licenses required)
- FAA Wildlife Strike data files from either the FAA website or the Packt GitHub site at this link: https://github.com/PacktPublishing/Unleashing-Your-Data-with-Power-BI-Machine-Learning-and-OpenAI

Identifying features in Power BI using a report

Now that you've built out the base queries for Predict Damage, Predict Size, and Predict Height, you can add additional features to evaluate in each of the queries that will be used for Power BI ML. Features to evaluate the ML models will be added to each ML query. Building the ML models in Power BI will allow you to narrow down the list of features to those that are most useful. In order to make the chapter easy to read, you can take a look at potential new features one by one as they pertain to the three queries for Power BI ML. When training and testing your ML models in Power BI, the predictive value of each feature will be evaluated when you build the ML models. Therefore, if a feature is in question, you're better off keeping it in the query and then removing it later on if it turns out to provide little value.

Note that if you don't want to build all of these Power BI report pages as part of your journey through this book, the completed PBIT template is available at this link: `https://github.com/PacktPublishing/Unleashing-Your-Data-with-Power-BI-Machine-Learning-and-OpenAI/tree/main/Chapter-05`.

Number Struck

Number Struck is a column of data that represents five options for the number of animals involved for each wildlife strike incident: **1**, **2-10**, **11-100**, **More than 100**, or the text value **NULL**. You copy and paste the **Line and stacked column chart** on the **Predict Damage** page, and replace **Year** with **Number Struck** on the *x* axis. The text value **NULL** likely contains incidents that represent all four of the other categories. Aside from **Null**, as the **Number Struck** value increases, the likelihood of damage also appears to increase and could represent a correlation between the number of animals struck and the likelihood of damage. The number of incidents also increases as the number of animals struck increases:

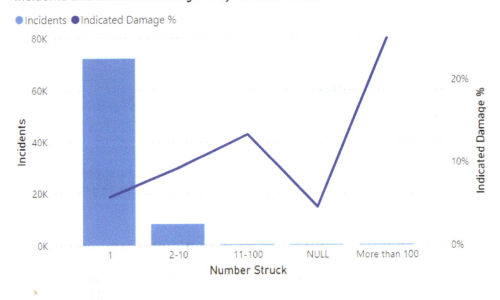

Figure 5.1 – Damage likelihood increases with Number Struck

Now take a look at how **Number Struck** relates to the **Predict Size** use case. Remember, **Size** refers to the size of the animals striking the aircraft. Copy and paste the **Line and stacked column chart** on that page, replace **Month Num** with **Number Struck**, and change the chart to a **100% Stacked column chart**. You discover an unexpected distribution in the **NULL** column. Many of those incidents were classified as **Large** in size. You don't know the reasons for this finding, but here are a few possibilities:

- If one large animal struck the aircraft, it is possible that the **Number Struck** field was sometimes skipped.

- If the strike wasn't witnessed maybe **NULL** actually means unknown.

- Strike damage discovered after a flight might be assumed to be a large animal, but the number was not known.

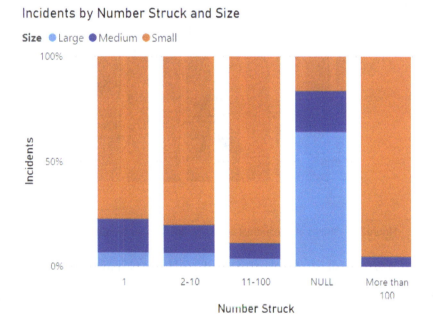

Figure 5.2 – The size of wildlife strike is distributed differently when broken down by Number Struck

Finally, you take a look at the **Predict Height** page to see if **Number Struck** has some interesting patterns. You copy and paste the **Line and stacked column chart** on the **Predict Damage** page to the **Predict Height** page, and replace **Year** with **Number Struck** on the *x* axis. Add **Average Height** and **Median Height** to the *y* axis. Incidents with smaller numbers of animals appear to happen at higher heights:

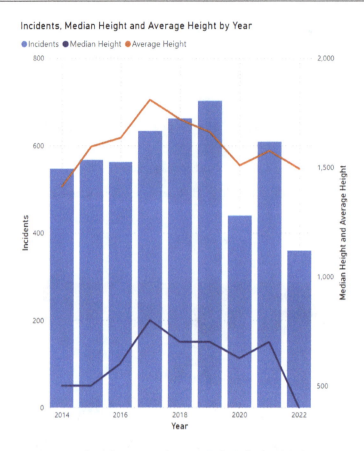

Figure 5.3 – Strikes of one animal appear to have higher height metrics

Your efforts with analytics validate that Number Struck could possibly provide value to all three ML feature sets. Later in this chapter, you will add it to the queries.

Aircraft Mass Code

Based upon the read_me.xls documentation, the Aircraft Mass Code values indicate the following mass values for the aircraft involved in a wildlife strike:

- **1**: 2,250 kg or less
- **2**: 2,251–5,700 kg
- **3**: 5,701–27,000 kg
- **4**: 27,001–272,000 kg
- **5**: above 272,000 kg

The text value NULL is not in the documentation, but most likely indicates that the size of the aircraft was unknown. You create a similar **100% Stacked column chart** for **Aircraft Mass Code** as you did for **Number Struck** above for the **Predict Damage** page. You can see from *Figure 5.4* that smaller aircraft appear to have higher damage percentages versus larger aircraft, which would make sense from a common sense perspective.

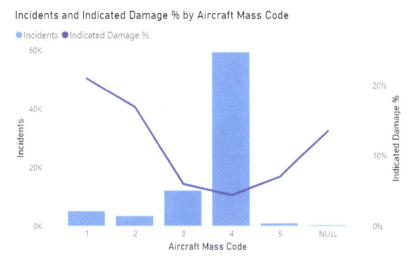

Figure 5.4 – Smaller aircraft appear to have higher rates of damage

Now you can take a look at **Aircraft Mass Code** for **Predict Size** by copying and pasting the **100% Stacked column chart** and replacing **Number Struck** with **Aircraft Mass Code**. The differences are noticeable but do not stand out:

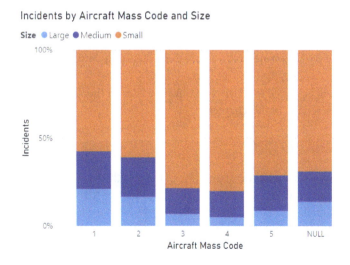

Figure 5.5 – Slight differences in Size due to Aircraft Mass Code

Repeat the same process for **Aircraft Mass Code** on the **Predict Height** page using a **Line and stacked column chart**. **Average Height** and **Median Height** are the lines on the *y* axis:

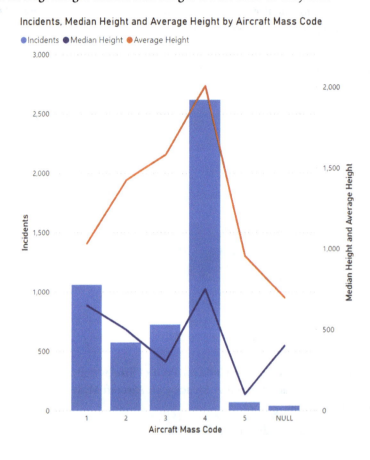

Figure 5.6 – Height metrics appear to trend up slightly with larger aircraft

Aircraft Mass Code will be added to all three ML queries later, in the *Adding new features to the ML queries in Power Query* section of this chapter.

Month Num (Number)

Month Num, which is the numerical representation of the month, was added to the **Predict Size ML** query in the last chapter. You decide to evaluate it for the other two ML queries, starting with Predict Damage. On the **Predict Damage** page, do the following:

1. Highlight the existing **Incidents and Indicated Damage % by Year** chart.

2. Drag **Month Num** to **Visualizations | X-axis**, underneath **Year**.

3.   You can now drill down into the **Incidents and Indicated Damage % by Year** chart and view **Month Num** on the *x* axis.

Notice that damage likelihood seems to decrease during the summer months (June through September in North America):

Incidents and Indicated Damage % by Month Num

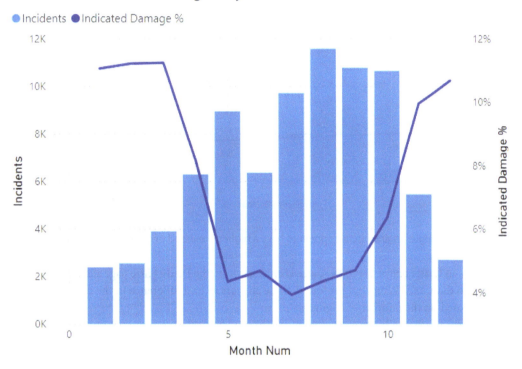

Figure 5.7 – Damage likelihood appears to fluctuate seasonally

You'll be adding **Month Num** as a feature to the **Predict Damage** ML query at the end of this chapter.

Number of Engines

As with the previous examples, you take a look at **Number of Engines** for the other two ML queries, starting with **Predict Damage**. Copy and paste a **Line and stacked column chart**, and then add **Number of Engines** to the *x* axis. It appears that single-engine aircraft have a higher likelihood of reporting damage after a strike:

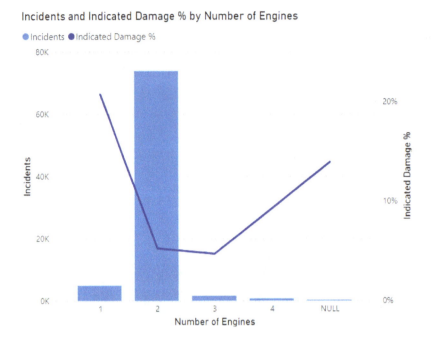

Figure 5.8 – Single-engine aircraft appear to have a higher likelihood of damage after a strike

Now you copy and paste one of the 100% stacked bar charts from the **Predict Size** page and put **Number of Engines** on the *x* axis. While not profound, there appears to be a difference in the distribution of animal size based on the number of engines:

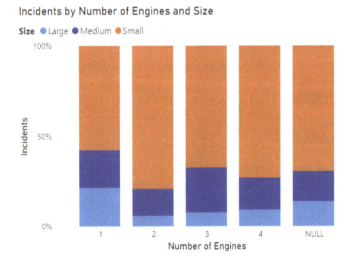

Figure 5.9 – Slight changes in animal size distribution based on the number of engines

You note that there are additional variables in determining the size of the strike, per the `read_me.xls` documentation. This categorization is a subjective value and factors such as pilot experience, geographical cultural differences, and more could lead to variability. In particular, this chart makes you wonder whether private pilots might describe wildlife strikes differently than experienced professional pilots who work for large airlines and fly large aircraft with multiple engines. Maybe that's research that a data scientist could undertake another day. Nonetheless, you will be adding **Number of Engines** to both the **Predict Damage** and **Predict Size** ML queries.

Percentage of engines struck, ingested wildlife, and were damaged

While **Number of Engines** is a column in the source database, you'll need to do some work to find out how many engines were struck, ingested wildlife, and were damaged by the strike. Taking into consideration **Number of Engines**, having two engines struck could also be a very different scenario for a two-engine aircraft versus a four-engine aircraft. **Number of Engines** will be a feature in your ML queries, but separate features for the percentage of engines that were struck, ingested wildlife, and were damaged could also be interesting.

The **Strike Reports Fact** table has four True/False columns that indicate engine strikes named **Struck Engine 1**, **Struck Engine 2**, **Struck Engine 3**, and **Struck Engine 4**. Calculating the percentage of engines struck requires adding up how many of those columns are `TRUE`, and then dividing that number by **Number of Engines**. Open up Power Query and follow these steps to add a new column for **Number of Engines Struck**:

1. Highlight **Strike Reports** in the **Curated Reporting Queries** group.

2. Add a new custom column from the Power Query ribbon and name it **Number of Engines Struck**.

3. Add the following M code:

```
(if [Struck Engine 1] = true then 1 else 0) +
(if [Struck Engine 2] = true then 1 else 0) +
(if [Struck Engine 3] = true then 1 else 0) +
(if [Struck Engine 4] = true then 1 else 0)
```

4. Once your screen looks like the following screenshot, click **OK**:

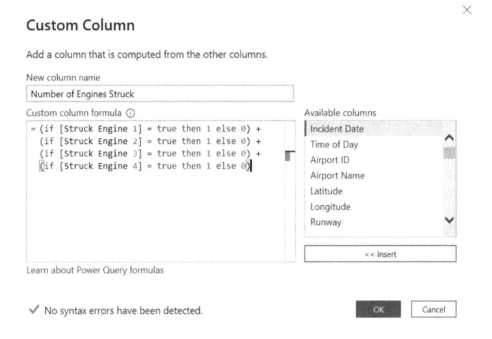

Figure 5.10 – New column to count the number of engines that were struck for each wildlife strike

Now create another column to calculate the percentage of engines struck for each event.

5. Highlight **Strike Reports** in the **Curated Reporting Queries** group.

6. Add a new custom column from the Power Query ribbon and name it **Percentage of Engines Struck**.

7. Add the following M code (note that **Number of Engines** is a text field because some values are a text value of NULL instead of a number, so a conversion is made):

```
if [Number of Engines] = "NULL" then 0 else
Value.Divide([Number of Engines Struck],Number.From([Number of
Engines]))
```

Your Strike Reports query should now look like this:

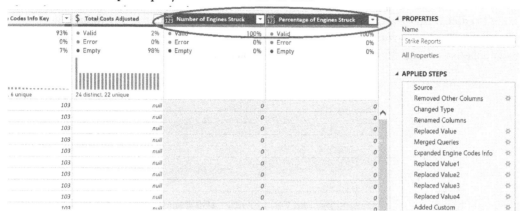

Figure 5.11 – Two new columns added to the curated query will propagate
to the layers for a Power BI dataset and ML queries

Change the data type of **Number for Engines Struck** to **Integer**, and **Percentage of Engines Struck**
to **Percentage**.

Adding new columns for Number of Engines Ingested, Percentage of Engines Ingested, Number of
Engines Damaged, and Percentage of Engines Damaged will follow the exact same pattern:

- Use **Ingested Engine 1**, **Ingested Engine 2**, **Ingested Engine 3**, and **Ingested Engine 4** for
  Number of Engines Ingested and **Percentage of Engines Ingested**.

- Use **Damaged Engine 1**, **Damaged Engine 2**, **Damaged Engine 3**, and **Damaged Engine 4**
  for **Number of Engines Damaged** and **Percentage of Engines Damaged**.

Here's a snapshot of all six new columns in the Strikes Report query:

Number of Engines Struck		Percentage of Engines Struck		Number of Engines Ingested		Percentage of Engines Ingested		Number of Engines Damaged		Percentage of Engines Damaged	
• Valid	100%	• Valid	100%	• Valid	100%	• Valid	100%	• Valid	100%	• Valid	100%
• Error	0%	• Error	0%	• Error	0%	• Error	0%	• Error	0%	• Error	0%
• Empty	0%	• Empty	0%	• Empty	0%	• Empty	0%	• Empty	0%	• Empty	0%
4 distinct, 1 unique		6 distinct, 1 unique		1 distinct, 0 unique		1 distinct, 0 unique		3 distinct, 1 unique			
0		0		0		0		0		0	
0		0		0		0		0		0	
0		0		0		0		0		0	
0		0		0		0		0		0	
0		0		0		0		0		0	
0		0		0		0		0		0	
0		0		0		0		0		0	
0		0		0		0		0		0	
0		0		0		0		0		0	

Figure 5.12 – Six new columns to analyze the number and percentage
of engines struck, ingested, and damaged

Now you can click **Close and Apply** and refresh the dataset with the new columns.

For the **Predict Damage** page, you add a new Matrix visual with **Number of Engines** on rows, **Percentage of Engines Struck** on columns, and **Indicated Damage %** in values. The likelihood of damage appears to change depending on the number of total engines and the number of engines struck:

Number of Engines	0.00	0.33	0.50	0.75	1.00	Total
1	20.7%					**20.7%**
2	5.1%		21.8%		16.7%	**5.3%**
3	4.6%	66.7%				**4.7%**
4	9.2%			100.0%		**9.3%**
NULL	13.9%					**13.9%**
Total	**6.1%**	**66.7%**	**21.8%**	**100.0%**	**14.8%**	**6.3%**

Figure 5.13 – Damage likelihood changes based on the total number
of engines and the percentage of engines struck

You decide to add all of these new features to the **Predict Size** and **Predict Height** ML queries so that you can test them out. You will leave **Number of Engines Damaged** and **Percentage of Engines Damaged** off the **Predict Damage** ML query since TRUE means that damage was already observed.

Identifying additional features using the key influencers visual in Power BI

Power BI has a built-in AI visual called **key influencers** that can be used to discover interesting patterns in data. You will now take a look at some additional columns from the FAA Wildlife Strikes data and explore how they influence the likelihood of damage and the size of the animals.

Start by duplicating the **Predict Damage** page and renaming the copied version to **Predict Damage Key Influencers**. By adding a duplicate page, you preserve the filters in the **Filter** panel. Delete all of the visuals on the page. In the **Visualizations** pane, add the **Key influencers** visual to the page. Now follow these steps:

1. With the **Key influencers** visual highlighted, add the **Indicated Damage** field to **Analyze**.

2. Add the **Phase of Flight**, **Precipitation**, **Sky**, and **Effect on Flight** fields to **Explain by**.

3. Set the selection at the top of the visual for **What influences Indicated Damage** to True.

   You notice that many different selections from those fields appear to correlate with damage and that the filter context is maintained:

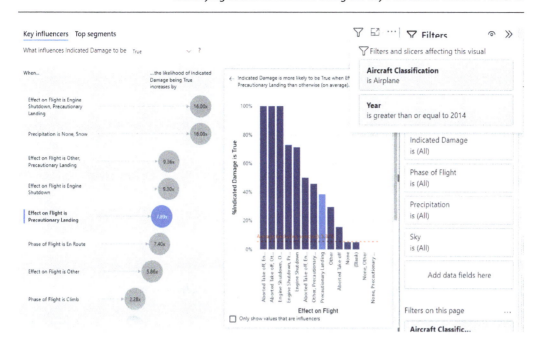

Figure 5.14 – Different field selections correlate to an outcome of damage

You can even add additional filters to the page, and the filter selections will result in a recalculated key influencers visual. You can take a deep dive into the data and relationships between different features.

As a result of feature discovery, you will be adding the following features to the ML queries:

Feature	Predict Damage	Predict Size	Predict Height
Number Struck	Yes	Yes	Yes
Aircraft Mass Code	Yes	Yes	Yes
Month Num	Yes	Already there	Yes
Number of Engines	Yes	Yes	Yes
Number of Engines Struck	Yes	Yes	Yes
Percentage of Engines Struck	Yes	Yes	Yes
Number of Engines Ingested	Yes	Yes	Yes
Percentage of Engines Ingested	Yes	Yes	Yes
Number of Engines Damaged	No	Yes	Yes
Percentage of Engines Damaged	No	Yes	Yes
Phase of Flight	Yes	Yes	Yes
Precipitation	Yes	Yes	Yes

| Sky | Yes | Yes | Yes |
| Effect on Flight | Yes | Yes | Yes |

Figure 5.15 – Features to be added to the ML queries in Power Query

Having discovered many new features for your ML queries, you can now add them to Power Query!

Adding new features to the ML queries in Power Query

Back in Power Query, you will now add the new features that were discussed in this chapter to the ML queries. Looking through the list, **Month Num** is the only one that will need some custom M code to convert **Incident Date** to a month. You've already done this in the previous chapter, so you can reuse the `Date.Month([Incident Date])` M code for a custom column.

Starting with Predict Damage highlighted in the group ML queries, follow these steps:

1. Double-click on **Remove Other Columns** under **Applied Steps**.

2. Add each of the features in the table shown in *Figure 5.16* (including **Incident Date** to be converted into **Month Num**).

   Your screen should look like this:

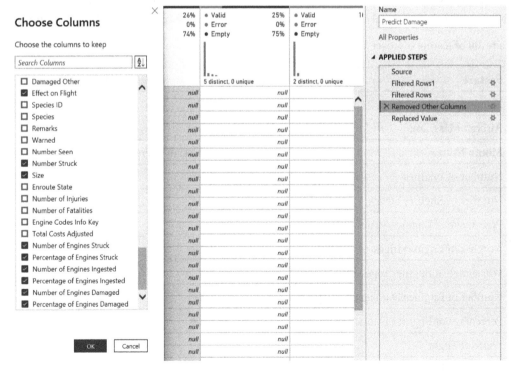

Figure 5.16 – Select the columns to be added to the ML query

3. Click **OK**.

4. **Phase of Flight**, **Sky**, **Precipitation**, and **Effect on Flight** all have some empty values. Replace the **null** (empty) values with the text value `empty`.

5. After adding a new column for **Month Num**, you can remove the **Incident Date** column.

Repeat these steps for the **Predict Size** and **Predict Height** ML queries and the new features in *Figure 5.16*. Your ML queries are now becoming much more robust with data that you have reason to believe may provide predictive value when used with Power BI ML.

Summary

In this chapter, you discovered new features and added them to pages of your Power BI report. You also used the Power BI key influencers visual to explore the FAA Wildlife Strike data to find interesting correlations. You then added the new features to your **Predict Damage**, **Predict Size**, and **Predict Height** ML queries. Finally, you ensured that the ML queries were cleaned up and ready for Power BI ML.

In the next chapter, you will continue to explore the FAA Wildlife Strike data using different types of capabilities in Power BI such as R and Python visuals. Newly discovered features will then be added to your ML queries as you finish them up and prepare to graduate to the Power BI cloud service.

6
Discovering New Features Using R and Python Visuals

In *Chapter 5* of this book, you discovered new columns and features for your queries using Power BI Desktop that will be migrated to the Power BI cloud service to train and test ML models. During your exploration and discovery of the data you also expanded the Power BI report that you will deliver to end users for interactive data exploration.

Before migrating your solution to the Power BI cloud service, you will take one last pass over the FAA Wildlife Strike data and seek out additional features to be added to the ML queries that will be used to build the Power BI ML models. In order to add some diverse capabilities to the analytic report, you'll leverage R/Python visuals within Power BI. At the end of this chapter, you will be ready to publish your solution to the Power BI cloud service.

Technical requirements

For this chapter, you'll need the following resources:

- Power BI Desktop April 2023 or later (no licenses required)
- FAA Wildlife Strike data files from either the FAA website or the Packt GitHub repo
- R installed on your local computer: `https://learn.microsoft.com/en-us/power-bi/create-reports/desktop-r-visuals`
- Python installed on your local computer: `https://learn.microsoft.com/en-us/power-bi/connect-data/desktop-python-visuals`

Exploring data with R visuals

Power BI has the capability to run R scripts and display R visuals. R is a powerful language that is often used by data scientists for statistics and ML. You will need to install R on your local machine to use it with Power BI Desktop per the instructions at `https://learn.microsoft.com/en-us/power-bi/create-reports/desktop-r-visuals`.

There are numerous R visualizations that can be useful for data analysis and finding new features for ML models. The FAA Wildlife Strike data contains several True/False flags related to the portions of the aircraft struck, the location of damage, the ingestion of animals into the engines, and more. These values should fit nicely on an R correlation plot, which will graphically show flags that tend to correlate either positively or negatively. Let's give it a shot!

You will follow three steps to find new features:

1. Prep are the data for the R correlation plot.
2. Build the R correlation plot visualization and add it to your report.
3. Identify new features for your Power BI ML queries.

Note that if you don't want to build all of these Power BI report pages as part of your journey through this book, the completed PBIT template for *Chapter 6* (including the R and Python components) is available at this link: `https://github.com/PacktPublishing/Unleashing-Your-Data-with-Power-BI-Machine-Learning-and-OpenAI/tree/main/Chapter-06`.

Preparing the data for the R correlation plot

Converting the True/False columns to an integer column where 1 represents True and 0 represents False is necessary to prepare the data for the R correlation plot. Let's identify the columns that will be used on the **Strike Reports** query of the **Curated Reporting Queries** group:

Ingested Other	Indicated Damage	Struck Random	Damaged Random
Struck Windshield	Damaged Windshield	Struck Nose	Damaged Nose
Struck Engine 1	Damaged Engine 1	Ingested Engine 1	Struck Engine 2
Damaged Engine 2	Ingested Engine 2	Struck Engine 3	Damaged Engine 3
Ingested Engine 3	Struck Engine 4	Damaged Engine 4	Ingested Engine 4
Struck Propeller	Damaged Propeller	Struck Wing or Rotor	Damaged Wing or Rotor
Struck Fuselage	Damaged Fuselage	Struck Landing Gear	Damaged Landing Gear
Struck Tail	Damaged Tail	Struck Lights	Damaged Lights
Struck Other	Damaged Other		

Figure 6.1 – True/False columns related to wildlife strikes

If you were to change the data type of a column, and the column was being used in Power BI, you could potentially break a report or a DAX expression. Generally, it is a best practice to avoid changing data types unless absolutely necessary. Report users will also generally better understand the options of True or False rather than 1 or 0 in a report. Go ahead and create a new version of each column that is of an integer data type. Further down the road, you can decide which version to include in each dataset or ML query depending on the use case. Perform the following steps for the columns in *Figure 6.1*:

1. In the **Curated Reporting Queries** group, duplicate all of these columns.
2. Rename the new column to have Int at the end such that **Indicated Damage – Copy** becomes **Indicated Damage Int**.
3. Change the data types of the new columns to Whole Number.
4. Click **Close & Apply** in Power Query to update the Power BI dataset.

These flags are primarily related to damage and location of impact, but could also be useful for predicting the height and size of the animals. For example, the landing gear will probably not be struck above a certain height because it is only down for takeoffs and landings. If multiple parts of a plane are struck, it may correlate with a flock of birds versus a lone animal.

Now you can return to the Power BI report and build the R correlation plot visual!

Building the R correlation plot visualization and adding it to your report

The integer versions of the True/False columns in the FAA Wildlife Strike data should now be available in your Power BI dataset. Also, per the technical requirements covered earlier in this chapter, you should have R installed on the local machine on which you're running Power BI Desktop:

1. Select the R script visual in Power BI Desktop, and add it to the canvas of a new page.
2. Set the filters on the page to match **Predict Damage** with **Aircraft Type** filtered to Airplane and **Year** filtered to be greater than or equal to 2014. Add the integer **Indicated Damage Int** column to **Values**.

Figure 6.2 – R script visual in Power BI

3. While the R visual is highlighted, a scripting window will be shown at the bottom of the page. Add some R code to activate the R correlation plot:

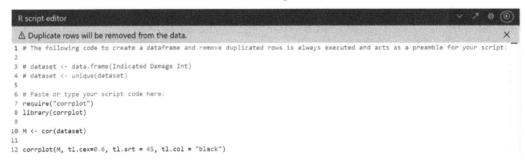

Figure 6.3 – Add the R code for an R correlation plot

Here is the code that was added to the visual:

```
require("corrplot")
library(corrplot)

M <- cor(dataset)

corrplot(M, tl.cex=0.6, tl.srt = 45, tl.col = "black")
```

4. Now add the new integer columns that you created to **Values**, along with the original field that was added:

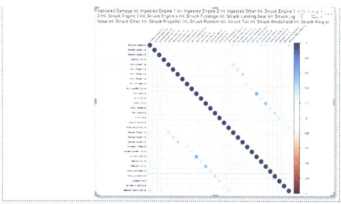

Figure 6.4 – R correlation plot with True/False integer columns

The plot is expanded in Figure 6.5.

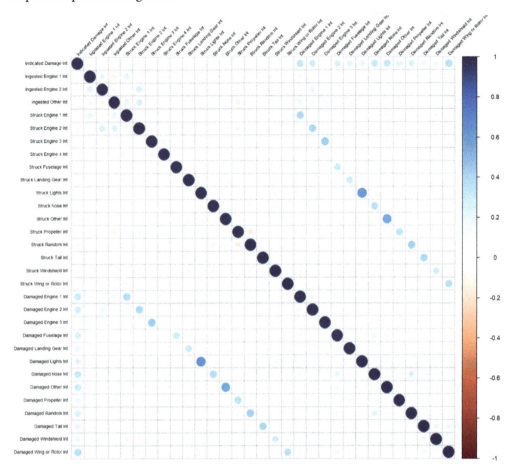

Figure 6.5 – R correlation plot with True/False integer columns

Text for the columns in *Figure 6.5* are too small to read, but represent all of the TRUE/FALSE indicators converted to integer values. The PBIT file for *Chapter 6* in the GitHub repository allows you to view these values.

```
R script editor
⚠ Duplicate rows will be removed from the data.
1 # The following code to create a dataframe and remove duplicated rows is always executed and acts as a preamble for your script:
2
3 # dataset <- data.frame(Indicated Damage Int)
4 # dataset <- unique(dataset)
5
6 # Paste or type your script code here:
7 require("corrplot")
8 library(corrplot)
9
10 M <- cor(dataset)
11
12 corrplot(M, tl.cex=0.6, tl.srt = 45, tl.col = "black")
```

Figure 6.6 – Code for R correlation plot with True/False integer columns.

Now you can dive into the data using an R correlation plot!

Identifying new features for your Power BI ML queries

The R correlation plot displays circles that increase in size and color intensity to indicate positive and negative correlation levels. Blue indicates a positive correlation (where the values go up and down together), white indicates no correlation (values go up and down randomly related to each other), and red indicates a negative correlation (one value tends to go up when the other goes down).

Looking at the initial rendering of the R correlation plot in *Figure 6.5*, there are not a great deal of blue or red circles besides the self-matches and a few light blue circles for different related damage flags. Adding a few filters to the page allows you to explore correlations within subsets of the data. The R correlation plot will re-calculate every time you select new filters. For example, *Figure 6.7* has the following filters selected on the dataset:

- **Year** is greater than or equal to 2014
- **Aircraft Type** is Airplane
- **Size** is Large
- **Aircraft Mass Code** is 3, 4 or 5
- **Effect on Flight** is not blank, none, or other
- **Number Struck** is 1 or 2-10

You can see this in the following screenshot:

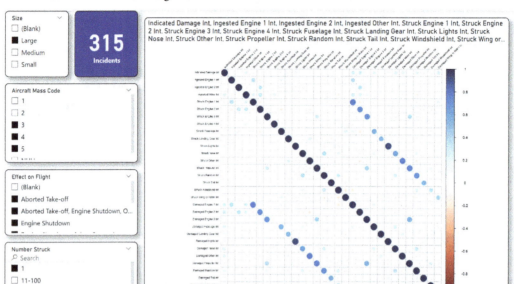

Figure 6.7 – When filters are selected, the R correlation plot is re-processed.

The text in the columns in *Figure 6.7* is too small to read, but represent all of the True/False indicators converted to integer values. The PBIT file for *Chapter 6* in the GitHub repository allows you to view these values.

After filtering down to a subset of data, correlations begin to emerge on the R correlation plot. Expand the visualization and focus on the **Indicated Damage Int** field correlations. The strongest correlations are for flags that also indicate some sort of damage. There are, however, some weaker positive correlations for other flags:

Figure 6.8 – A few weak positive correlations shown for Indicated Damage

After exploring additional filter combinations with the R correlation plot, the following features will be added to the ML queries:

Feature	Predict Damage	Predict Size	Predict Height
Ingested Other	Yes	Yes	Yes
Struck Windshield	Yes	Yes	Yes
Struck Engine 1	Yes	Yes	Yes
Damaged Engine 2	No	Yes	Yes
Ingested Engine 3	Yes	Yes	Yes
Struck Propeller	Yes	Yes	Yes
Struck Fuselage	Yes	Yes	Yes
Struck Tail	Yes	Yes	Yes
Struck Other	Yes	Yes	Yes
Damaged Windshield	No	Yes	Yes
Damaged Engine 1	No	Yes	Yes
Ingested Engine 2	Yes	Yes	Yes
Struck Engine 4	Yes	Yes	Yes
Damaged Propeller	No	Yes	Yes
Damaged Fuselage	No	Yes	Yes
Damaged Tail	No	Yes	Yes
Damaged Other	No	Yes	Yes
Struck Random	Yes	Yes	Yes
Struck Nose	Yes	Yes	Yes
Ingested Engine 1	Yes	Yes	Yes
Struck Engine 3	Yes	Yes	Yes
Damaged Engine 4	No	Yes	Yes
Struck Wing or Rotor	Yes	Yes	Yes
Struck Landing Gear	Yes	Yes	Yes
Struck Lights	Yes	Yes	Yes
Damaged Random	No	Yes	Yes
Damaged Nose	No	Yes	Yes
Struck Engine 2	Yes	Yes	Yes
Damaged Engine 3	No	Yes	Yes
Ingested Engine 4	Yes	Yes	Yes
Damaged Wing or Rotor	No	Yes	Yes

Feature	Predict Damage	Predict Size	Predict Height
Damaged Landing Gear	No	Yes	Yes
Damaged Lights	No	Yes	Yes

Figure 6.9 – Features will be added to the ML queries

You've discovered a great number of features for your ML queries, but you're not done yet! You can also use Python visuals to explore data in Power BI, which is your next task.

Exploring data with Python visuals

In addition to R, Power BI also supports Python queries and visuals. Python is a very popular language that is also frequently used by data scientists. Per the requirements at the beginning of this chapter, you'll need to install Python on your local machine for Power BI Desktop: `https://learn.microsoft.com/en-us/power-bi/connect-data/desktop-python-visuals`.

In the FAA Wildlife Strike data, **Height** and **Speed** are both fields that can be recorded for reports. Height is a measure in feet from the ground at which an incident happened, while speed is a measure of the speed the aircraft was traveling when it was struck by wildlife. You will take a look at both of these metrics using Python histograms so that you can compare the distribution of those values when selecting different filters.

You will follow these steps:

1. Preparing the data for the Python histogram.
2. Building the Python histogram visualization and add it to your report.
3. Identifying new features for your Power BI ML queries.

Let's proceed.

Preparing the data for the Python histogram

Both **Height** and **Speed** are integer columns that also contain empty values. Empty values with numeric columns of data can be tricky because you don't know whether it is zero or unknown. For the report page, you filter out the empty values for each visualization. Otherwise, the integer columns are ready to go for your Python histogram data visualizations.

Building the Python histogram visualization and add it to your report

Next, we need to build the visualization:

1. Select the Python script visual in Power BI Desktop, and add it to the canvas of a new page.

2. Set the filters on the page to match **Predict Damage** with **Aircraft Type** filtered to `Airplane` and **Year** filtered to be `greater than or equal to 2014`. Add the integer **Speed** column to **Values**:

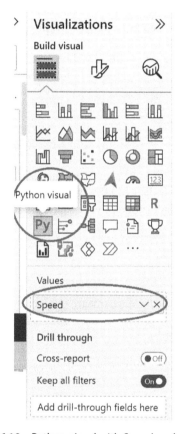

Figure 6.10 – Python visual with Speed under Values

3. While the Python visual is highlighted, a scripting window will be visible at the bottom of the page. Add some Python code to activate the Python histogram with a title of `Speed for Incidents with Damage`:

```
Python script editor                                                    ∨ ↗ ⚙ ⊙

⚠ Duplicate rows will be removed from the data.                                    ✕

1 # The following code to create a dataframe and remove duplicated rows is always executed and acts as a preamble for your script:
2
3 # dataset = pandas.DataFrame(Number of Engines Struck)
4 # dataset = dataset.drop_duplicates()
5
6 # Paste or type your script code here:
7 import matplotlib.pyplot as plt
8 dataset.plot(kind='hist',y='Speed')
9 plt.xlabel("Speed")
.0 plt.ylabel("Incidents")
.1 plt.title("Speed for Incidents with Damage")
.2 plt.show()
```

Figure 6.11– Python code that renders a histogram in Power BI

Here's the code entered into the script editor as shown in *Figure 6.11*:

```
import matplotlib.pyplot as plt
dataset.plot(kind='hist',y='Speed')
plt.xlabel("Speed")
plt.ylabel("Incidents")
plt.title("Speed for Incidents with Damage")
plt.show()
```

4.   For the filters on this visual, set **Indicated Damage** to True and **Speed** to is not (Blank). Now you can render the Python histogram visualization:

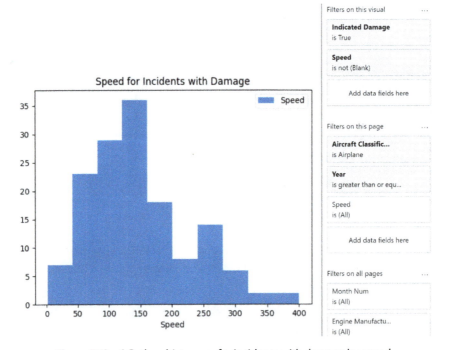

Figure 6.12 – A Python histogram for incidents with damage by speed

Now you can use the Python histogram visual to analyze the distribution of data!

Identifying new features for Power BI ML queries

Let's look at the visual:

1. Copy and paste the visual, and rename the title to `Speed for Incidents without Damage`. Here's the Python code, which can be entered in the same way as in *Figure 6.10*:

    ```
    import matplotlib.pyplot as plt
    dataset.plot(kind='hist',y='Speed')
    plt.xlabel("Speed")
    plt.ylabel("Incidents")
    plt.title("Speed for Incidents without Damage")
    plt.show()
    ```

2. Change the **Indicated Damage** filter on the second Python histogram visual to `False`, and you can compare the two visuals:

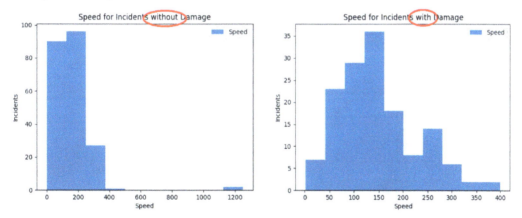

Figure 6.13 – Compare the speed of incidents with or without damage

Note that there are incidents without damage that are in the 1200 knots bucket, which skews the histogram further to the left.

3. Filter the page for **Speed** at `less than 700` to create comparable histograms. Also add some filters to the page (anything you'd like to explore) such as **Size, Effect on Flight**, and **Month Name**.

4. Next, copy and paste both charts and replace Speed with Height. Filter the whole page such that Height is not blank. Here's the Python code for the histogram of the heights when damage was reported:

```
import matplotlib.pyplot as plt
dataset.plot(kind='hist',y='Height',color='black')
plt.xlabel("Height")
plt.ylabel("Incidents")
plt.title("Height for Incidents with Damage")
plt.show()
```

5. And here is the Python script for a histogram without damage:

```
import matplotlib.pyplot as plt
dataset.plot(kind='hist',y='Height',color='black')
plt.xlabel("Height")
plt.ylabel("Incidents")
plt.title("Height for Incidents without Damage")
plt.show()
```

You can now interactively view the distribution of **Height** and **Speed** with many different filter settings:

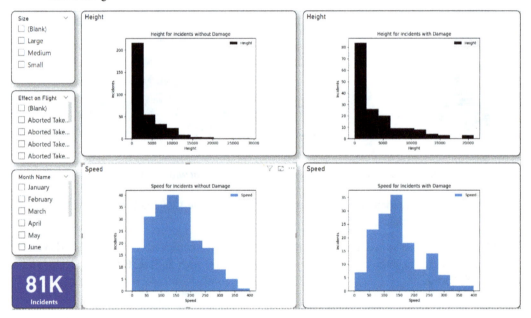

Figure 6.14 – Interactive Python histograms for Height and Speed

Height and speed both appear to change when damage has been reported. As a result of your exploration using Python histograms, you will be adding both **Height** and **Speed** to the ML queries. Using R and Python visuals, you have verified numerous new features that can be used to train and test your ML models in Power BI.

Adding new features to the ML queries

So far in this chapter, you have identified numerous new features to be added to the **Predict Damage**, **Predict Size**, and **Predict Height** ML queries for your Power BI ML models. As you did in section three of *Chapter 5, Adding New Features to the ML Queries in Power Query*, you can add these features to the ML queries in Power Query:

1. Double-click on **Remove Other Columns** under **Applied Steps**.
2. Add each of the features in *Figure 6.9* (also include **Speed** and **Height**).

Your screen should look like this while adding the features:

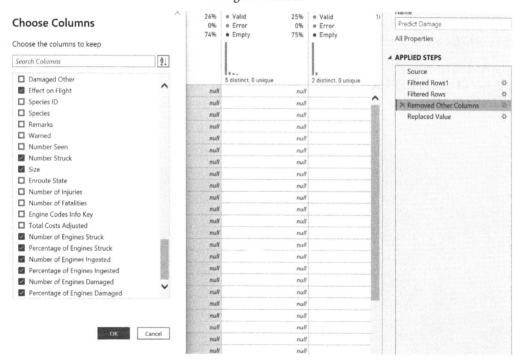

Figure 6.15 – Select the columns to be added to the ML query

After adding the new features, you may note that **Height** and **Speed** both contain some empty values. Since these are not categorical fields, there is no simple option for adding a text value such as empty. For example, with **Speed**, the impact of a collision at 5 knots versus 500 knots should be expected to be very different when hitting a large animal. Empty values could represent many different scenarios such as missing data or unknown speed. You will evaluate a few different options for handling these missing values when you build and test the ML models in Power BI.

Future iterations of your solution may very well contain additional features that you discover. For now, you have numerous features that you have identified and added to queries that are architected for ML, and you are ready to journey forward into the Power BI cloud services!

Summary

In this chapter, you added R and Python visuals to your Power BI reports to discover new features in the FAA Wildlife Strike data. Using an R correlation plot, you were able to interactively slice and dice several incident flag values for positive and negative correlations. With Python histograms you took a look at the impact of speed and height on the outcomes for your planned Power BI ML models. Finally, you added new features to your **Predict Damage**, **Predict Size**, and **Predict Height** ML queries that will be used for ML in Power BI.

In the next chapter, you will begin migrating content to the Power BI cloud service. After migrating the Power BI dataset and report, you will then migrate the Power Query scripts to dataflows for use with Power BI ML.

7

Deploying Data Ingestion and Transformation Components to the Power BI Cloud Service

In *Chapter 6*, you finalized the base design for your ML queries, which will be migrated to the Power BI cloud service to train and test ML models. You focused on using R and Python visuals within Power BI Desktop to visualize and evaluate potential features for these ML queries.

This chapter will be an adventure into the Power BI cloud service. You will migrate your work in Power Query to dataflows and publish your Power BI dataset and report to a Power BI workspace. The process of moving these queries is a repetitive but necessary step for your end-to-end project, the workshop that runs in parallel with this book. An experienced Power BI developer can probably move through this chapter quickly by cutting and pasting the M queries from GitHub. By the end of this chapter, your content will be fully migrated to the Power BI cloud service and ready for Power BI ML.

Technical requirements

For this chapter, you'll need the following resources:

- Power BI Desktop April 2023 or later (no licenses required)
- FAA Wildlife Strike data files from either the FAA website or the Packt GitHub site
- Power BI Pro license
- One of the following Power BI licensing options for access to Power BI dataflows:
  - Power BI Premium
  - Power BI Premium Per User

- One of the following options for getting data into the Power BI cloud service:

  - Microsoft OneDrive (with connectivity to the Power BI cloud service)

  - Microsoft Access and Power BI Gateway

  - Azure Data Lake (with connectivity to the Power BI cloud service)

Creating a Power BI workspace

Before we start importing content into the Power BI cloud service, you will need a **workspace** for the project. A workspace is a way to organize, secure, and govern content in the Power BI cloud service. For this project, you need a workspace that supports the use of both dataflows and ML, which at the time of writing requires either **Power BI Premium** with a **Pro** license or a **Premium Per User** license. If you do not have either of these licenses, you can still follow along with this book for learning purposes and explore the code samples in the Packt GitHub repository.

Workspaces can be extended to include integration with security capabilities, information protection, deployment pipelines for life cycle management, and more. This book will only cover how to create a basic workspace since extensive documentation about workspaces is available online. A tutorial for creating workspaces can be found at `https://learn.microsoft.com/en-us/power-bi/collaborate-share/service-create-the-new-workspaces`.

Follow these steps to create a new workspace in Power BI:

1. Log into the Power BI cloud service by going to `https://app.powerbi.com/`.
2. Ensure that you have either a Pro or Premium Per User license: `https://powerbi.microsoft.com/en-us/pricing/`.
3. You will also need to ensure that your Power BI administrators have given you access to create workspaces.
4. From the left-hand side vertical pane, select **Workspaces | + New Workspace**.
5. Choose a name for your workspace, describe it, and then select either **Premium Per User** or **Premium Per Capacity** for the **license mode** option.

Now, you are ready to go with a Power BI workspace, which supports reports, datasets, dataflows, and ML for your FAA Wildlife Strike data project!

Publishing your Power BI Desktop dataset and report to the Power BI cloud service

Next, you must import your dataset and report from Power BI Desktop into the Power BI cloud service. Once published to the cloud service, you will be able to share the analytical report with others who are stakeholders in the project. You will also be able to view the reports on the Power BI mobile app if you want to dive into the data while on the go.

The work that you have done up to this point used Power BI Desktop on your local machine. You have two options for migrating this content to the Power BI cloud service:

- Publish from Power BI Desktop: `https://learn.microsoft.com/en-us/power-bi/create-reports/desktop-upload-desktop-files`

- Import the `.pbix` file from the Power BI service

Both options are equally simple. For this tutorial, you will import the `.pbix` file from the Power BI service.

From your newly created Power BI workspace, select **Upload | OneDrive for Business**, and select the `.pbix` file that you have created. If you do not use OneDrive, you can also upload from other file locations too. Once you've uploaded the `.pbix` file, you'll see that the dataset has been separated from the report and that they are now two separate artifacts. Upon clicking on the report, you can validate that all the pages can now be browsed in the Power BI cloud service:

Figure 7.1 – The FAA Wildlife Strike report can now be browsed in the Power BI cloud service

Eventually, you may revisit this report and allow it to be refreshed with new data. Since you are working with a snapshot in time of FAA Wildlife Strike data for your ML efforts, you do not want to change the data in this report. The data in this report needs to reflect the data that you use to train your ML models during the initial training and testing phases of the project. That way, you can revisit this report to explore or validate the exact data used for ML.

Creating Power BI dataflows with connections to source data

The Power BI Desktop Power Query work from previous chapters is connected to data sources from your local machine. Power BI dataflows is a very similar tool to Power Query, but connectivity happens from the Power BI cloud service. When creating your dataflows, you will need to consider connectivity to the data sources. Earlier in this book, you determined that the sources of data for the FAA Wildlife Strike database were as follows:

- `wildlife.accdb`: All of the historical FAA Wildlife Strike reports. This file is an Access database that's been downloaded in ZIP file format from the FAA website.

- `read_me.xls`: Descriptive information about the data in the `Database.accdb` database file. This file is an Excel file that was downloaded within the same ZIP file as the Access database. The file has been changed to a `.xlsx` extension in the Packt GitHub repository and is available in the folder at `https://github.com/PacktPublishing/Unleashing-Your-Data-with-Power-BI-Machine-Learning-and-OpenAI/tree/main/Chapter-01`.

- `Date`: For this project, the Date table will be created using custom M code in Power Query and dataflows. The code is named `12 Date Table .M` and is available on the Packt GitHub site in the folder at `https://github.com/PacktPublishing/Unleashing-Your-Data-with-Power-BI-Machine-Learning-and-OpenAI/tree/main/Chapter-07`.

When using Power Query in Power BI Desktop, you created groups of queries to organize your project. Raw Data, Curated Reporting Queries, Curated Dataset Tables, and ML Queries were logical groupings based on the intended use of the queries within. With Power BI dataflows, you can break these down into smaller groups of queries so that you can monitor them, troubleshoot issues, and keep the logic in bitesize chunks. Your dataflows will have an architecture that looks as follows:

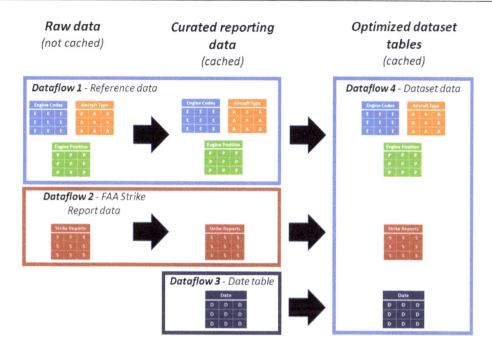

Figure 7.2 – The logic from Power Query will be migrated to four Power BI dataflows

You will start by creating **Dataflow 1**, which will bring the reference data into the Power BI cloud service.

Dataflow 1 – reference data from the read_me.xls file

You must start your adventure with Power BI dataflows using the data contained within the `read_me.xlsx` file, which contains descriptive information about the reported data from the FAA Wildlife Strike database. First, you will need to decide how to connect to the `read_me.xlsx` file. You have many options, including, but not limited to, the following:

- Store the file in OneDrive and connect from Power BI
- Store the file in SharePoint Online and connect from Power BI
- Connect to the file using a Power BI Gateway to your local machine or another storage location
- Store the file in an Azure Data Lake and connect from Power BI

You can find extensive documentation about all of these approaches with simple online searches. For the example in this book, we will be using OneDrive since it is simple and requires minimal configuration. Follow these steps to get started:

1. From your newly created Power BI workspace, from the ribbon, select **New** | **Dataflow**.

2. Select **Define new tables** | **Add new tables**.

3. Choose **Excel Workbook**.

4. Select **Browse OneDrive** and choose the `read_me.xlsx` file. This file was copied from the following folder location on the Packt GitHub site: `https://github.com/PacktPublishing/Unleashing-Your-Data-with-Power-BI-Machine-Learning-and-OpenAI/tree/main/Chapter-01`.

5. Click **Select**.

6. Click **Next** to proceed to table selection.

7. Select `Aircraft Type`, `Engine Codes`, and `Engine Position`.

8. Select **Transform Data**.

Your browser should look as follows:

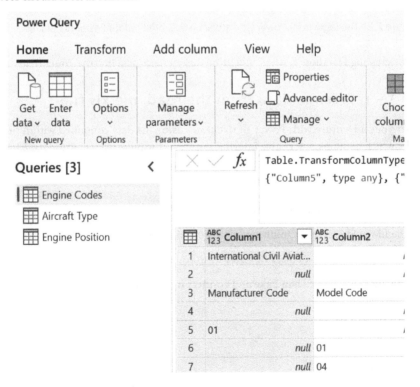

Figure 7.3 – Dataflows displaying three tables from the read_me.xls file

Now, you can begin migrating the logic from Power Query to dataflows. Rather than replicate the steps from previous chapters in this book, **M scripts** that can be copied from the Packt GitHub site can be found at `https://github.com/PacktPublishing/Unleashing-Your-Data-with-Power-BI-Machine-Learning-and-OpenAI/tree/main/Chapter-07`. M scripts are the code created by the Power Query SaaS interface, which can be pasted into the **Advanced editor** area or Power Query or dataflows.

You can cut and paste these scripts into dataflows to save time. The following is an example for the first query, **Engine Codes**:

1. Copy the **01 Raw Data - Engine Codes.M** M code from the GitHub repository folder at `https://github.com/PacktPublishing/Unleashing-Your-Data-with-Power-BI-Machine-Learning-and-OpenAI/tree/main/Chapter-07`.

2. Right-click on the **Engine Codes** query in your new dataflow and select **Advanced editor**.

3. Paste the M code into the **Advanced editor** area. Make sure you replace YOUR_ONEDRIVE_URL in the M code to reflect your OneDrive URL. The **Advanced editor** area should look as follows:

Advanced editor

```
1  let
2      Source = Excel.Workbook(Web.Contents("https://your_onedrive_url/read_me.xlsx"), null, true),
3      #"Navigation 1" = Source{[Item = "Engine Codes", Kind = "Sheet"]}[Data],
4      #"Changed column type 1" = Table.TransformColumnTypes(#"Navigation 1", {{"Column1", type text}, {"Column2", type text}, {"Column3", type text}, {"Column4", type text}, {"Column5",
          type text}, {"Column6", type text}}),
5      #"Removed top rows" = Table.Skip(#"Changed column type 1", 2),
6      #"Promoted headers" = Table.PromoteHeaders(#"Removed top rows", [PromoteAllScalars = true]),
7      #"Removed top rows 1" = Table.Skip(#"Promoted headers", 1),
8      #"Removed columns" = Table.RemoveColumns(#"Removed top rows 1", {"Column5", "Column6"}),
9      #"Transform columns" = Table.TransformColumnTypes(#"Removed columns", {{"Manufacturer Code", type text}, {"Engine Model", type text}}),
10     #"Replace errors" = Table.ReplaceErrorValues(#"Transform columns", {{"Manufacturer Code", null}, {"Engine Model", null}}),
11     #"Filled down" = Table.FillDown(#"Replace errors", {"Manufacturer Code"}),
12     #"Filled down 1" = Table.FillDown(#"Filled down", {"Engine Manufacturer"})
13  in
14     #"Filled down 1"
```

Figure 7.4 – Code pasted into your dataflow query

For clarity, *Figure 7.4* has also been enlarged and presented as two images. *Figure 7.5* shows the left side of the code:

Advanced editor

```
1  let
2      Source = Excel.Workbook(Web.Contents("https://
3      #"Navigation 1" = Source{[Item = "Engine Codes", Kind = "Sheet"]}[Data],
4      #"Changed column type 1" = Table.TransformColumnTypes(#"Navigation 1", {{"Column1", type text}
          type text}, {"Column6", type text}}),
5      #"Removed top rows" = Table.Skip(#"Changed column type 1", 2),
6      #"Promoted headers" = Table.PromoteHeaders(#"Removed top rows", [PromoteAllScalars = true]),
7      #"Removed top rows 1" = Table.Skip(#"Promoted headers", 1),
8      #"Removed columns" = Table.RemoveColumns(#"Removed top rows 1", {"Column5", "Column6"}),
9      #"Transform columns" = Table.TransformColumnTypes(#"Removed columns", {{"Manufacturer Code",
10     #"Replace errors" = Table.ReplaceErrorValues(#"Transform columns", {{"Manufacturer Code", nul
11     #"Filled down" = Table.FillDown(#"Replace errors", {"Manufacturer Code"}),
12     #"Filled down 1" = Table.FillDown(#"Filled down", {"Engine Manufacturer"})
13  in
14     #"Filled down 1"
```

Figure 7.5 – Code pasted into your dataflow query

Figure 7.6 shows the right side of the code.

×

```
                                        /read_me.xlsx"), null, true),

lumn1", type text}, {"Column2", type text}, {"Column3", type text}, {"Column4", type text}, {"Column5",

calars = true]),

"column6"}),
ufacturer Code", type text}, {"Engine Model", type text}}),
cturer Code", null}, {"Engine Model", null}}),
```

Figure 7.6 – Code pasted into your dataflow query

4. Click **OK**; your query should look as follows:

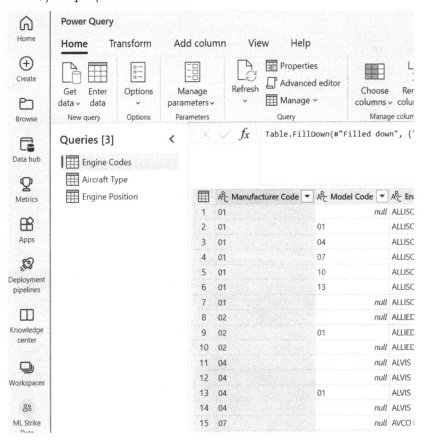

Figure 7.7 – The Engine Codes query with applied steps

Notice that these additional steps make some changes to the data formatting. These additional steps of cleanup are unique to the Engine Codes query due to some formatting issues with the Excel file. In a perfect architecture, the Raw Data queries would not have any transformations or formatting changes. Since you are working with real data in the real world, this compromise was necessary in this particular instance.

The queries for **Aircraft Type** and **Engine Position** should not need any transformations or formatting changes, but make sure that all of their columns have text for **Data Type**. In the same GitHub folder, you can also get M code for the **02 Raw Data - Aircraft Type.M** and **03 Raw Data – Engine Position.M** queries.

You can now add the queries for **Engine Codes Added Data**, **Aircraft Type Added Data**, and **Engine Position Added Data**. These tables were added to Power Query back in *Chapter 2* via a manual entry process. The tables account for mismatched key values and missing data. Either refer back to *Chapter 2* and enter these three queries using **Enter data** in dataflows or cut and paste the queries from the `Chapter-07` folder of the GitHub repository:

- `04 Raw Data - Engine Codes Added Data.M`

- `05 Raw Data - Aircraft Type Added Data.M`

- `06 Raw Data - Engine Position Added Data.M`

5. Right-click in the **Queries** column of the dataflow and select **New Group**. Name the group `Raw Data`, and add all six of the queries you created. Your dataflow should now look like this in your browser:

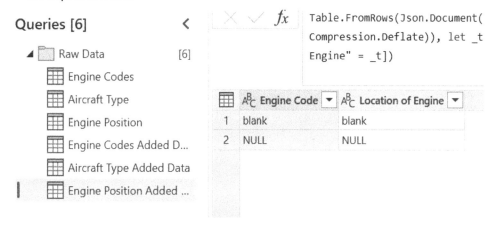

Figure 7.8 – Queries in the Raw Data group of a dataflow

6. Next, create a new group in the dataflow named **Curated Reporting Queries**. You need to add three new queries to this group for **Aircraft Type Info**, **Engine Codes Info**, and **Engine Position Info**. To do this in the dataflow, select **Get data | Blank query**. Paste the corresponding M code into the **Connect to data** source window for the new blank query. The M code can be found in the Packt GitHub folder at `https://github.com/PacktPublishing/ Unleashing-Your-Data-with-Power-BI-Machine-Learning-and-OpenAI/ tree/main/Chapter-07`. The following example shows the M code for **Aircraft Type Info**:

```
1  let
2      Source = #"Aircraft Type",
3      #"Promoted headers" = Table.PromoteHeaders(Source, [PromoteAllScalars = true]),
4      #"Changed column type" = Table.TransformColumnTypes(#"Promoted headers", {{"Aircraft Code", type text}, {"Aircraft Classification", type
         text}}),
5      #"Filtered rows" = Table.SelectRows(#"Changed column type", each ([Aircraft Code] <> null)),
6      #"Appended query" = Table.Combine({#"Filtered rows", #"Aircraft Type Added Data"})
7  in
8      #"Appended query"
```

Figure 7.9 – M code for Aircraft Type Info

7. After selecting **Next**, validate that the dataflows query works and looks as follows:

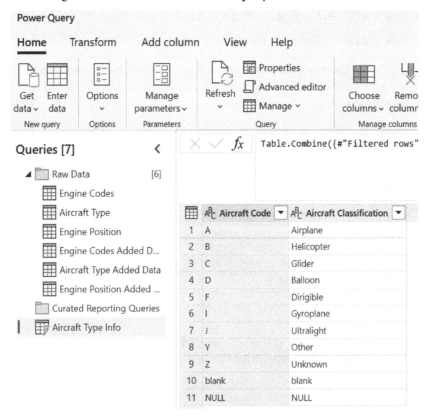

Figure 7.10 – New query for Aircraft Type Info in the Curated Reporting Queries group

Repeat the same process for the **Engine Codes Info** and **Engine Position Info** queries and ensure that all three queries are in the new **Curated Reporting Queries** group. The M code for all three queries are named as follows on the Packt GitHub site:

- `07 Curated Data - Aircraft Type Info.M`
- `08 Curated Data - Engine Codes Info.M`
- `09 Curated Data - Engine Position Info.M`

Once completed, **Save & close** your dataflow and name it **Reference Data**. Your first dataflow is complete!

Dataflow 2 – Wildlife Strike data from the database.accdb file

Now, you can move on to the second dataflow, which will bring in the report-level data for the FAA Wildlife Strike database. The `database.accdb` file contains incident-level data from the FAA Wildlife Strike database. The file is in a Microsoft Access database format. Official documentation for connecting to an Access database can be found at `https://learn.microsoft.com/en-us/power-query/connectors/accessdatabase`. You have a few options, including, but not limited to, the following:

- Connect to the Access file using a Power BI Gateway.
- Use an ELT/ETL tool such as Azure Data Factory to extract the data from the Access file and drop it in a Data Lake or database: `https://learn.microsoft.com/en-us/azure/data-factory/connector-microsoft-access?tabs=data-factory`.
- Export the data to a flat file from the Access database and use the extracted file as your source.

For this book, the data will be exported from Access to a flat text file. If you do not have Microsoft Access, you can also download the extract from the Packt GitHub site at `https://github.com/PacktPublishing/Unleashing-Your-Data-with-Power-BI-Machine-Learning-and-OpenAI/tree/main/Chapter-07`.

First, you must extract the data from Access to a text file:

1. Open the `wildlife.accdb` file using Microsoft Access.
2. Right-click on the **STRIKE_REPORTS** table and select **Export** | **Text File**.
3. Choose a destination for storing the text file, such as OneDrive.

Here's a screenshot of the export process:

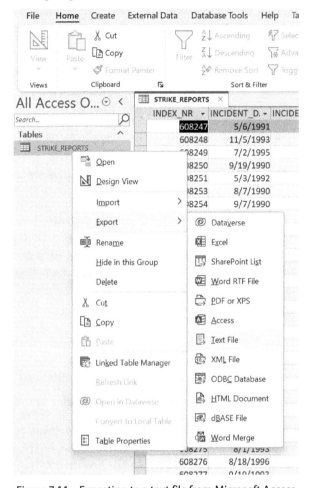

Figure 7.11 – Exporting to a text file from Microsoft Access

Now, you can create a dataflow named Strike Reports by following similar steps that you followed for your dataflow for Reference Data:

1. From your newly created Power BI workspace, from the ribbon, select **New | Dataflow**.
2. Select **Define new tables | Add new tables**.
3. Choose **Text/CSV**.
4. Select **Browse OneDrive** and choose the STRIKE_REPORTS.txt file.
5. Click **Select**.
6. Click **Next** to move to the next screen.

7. Select **Transform Data**. to bring the table into the editing view.

8. Depending on the source, dataflows might automatically change some of the data types. For the Raw Data layer, keep the text file unformatted by removing the **Changed column type** step:

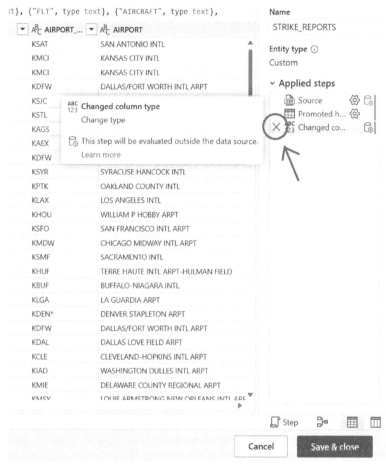

Figure 7.12 – Automatic column type changes are not needed in the Raw Data layer

9. Next, create two new groups in the dataflow for **Raw Data** and **Curated Reporting Queries**. Name the new query that you created **Strike Reports** and move it to the **Raw Data** group.

The curated version of **Strike Reports** includes a join to the **Engine Codes Info** query so that a primary key value can be added to **Strike Reports** that references **Engine Codes Info**. To reference **Engine Codes Info** from your new dataflow, follow these steps:

1. Click **Get data | Dataflows**.

2. Click **Next**.

3. Expand **Workspaces**.

4. Expand your Power BI workspace.

5. Expand the **Reference Data** dataflow.

6. Check **Engine Codes Info** and click **Create**.

7. Move the **Engine Codes Info** query to **Curated Reporting Queries**, and then right-click it and unselect **Load**. Your browser screen should look like this:

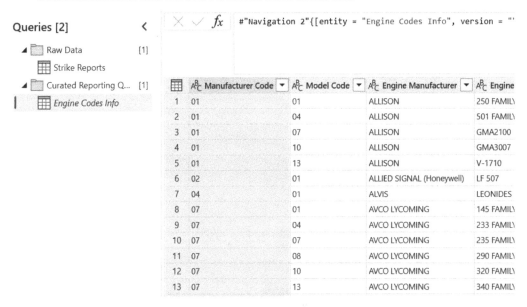

Figure 7.13 – Engine Codes Info can be referenced in the dataflow

Now, you can add the M code for the curated version of Strike Reports. The M code is available on the Packt GitHub site and has also been included here:

1. Select **Get data** | **Blank query**.

2. Paste in the 11 Curated Data - Strike Reports Info.M M code from the folder at https://github.com/PacktPublishing/Unleashing-Your-Data-with-Power-BI-Machine-Learning-and-OpenAI/tree/main/Chapter-07 and click **Next**.

3. Rename the query **Strike Reports Curated**.

4. Move it to the **Curated Reporting Queries** group.

Once you've validated that all of the data appears as it does in Power BI Desktop, you can **Save & close** the dataflow, name the dataflow **Strike Reports**, and then refresh it! You're now ready to move on to your third dataflow, which will be a Date table.

Dataflow 3 – the Date table

Creating a separate dataflow for your Date table may seem unnecessary from the perspective of this individual project, but it will allow you to reuse the Date table with other future projects. Follow these steps to create a **Date table** dataflow that begins on January 1, 1990 (the first year of FAA Wildlife Strike data) and runs through 2024:

1. From your newly created Power BI workspace, from the ribbon, select **New** | **Dataflow**.
2. Select **Define new tables** | **Add new tables**.
3. Select **Blank query**.
4. Paste in the **12 Date Table.M** M code, which can be found on the Packt GitHub site at `https://github.com/PacktPublishing/Unleashing-Your-Data-with-Power-BI-Machine-Learning-and-OpenAI/tree/main/Chapter-07`.
5. Click **Next**.
6. Rename the query **Date**.
7. Click **Save & close**.
8. Name your new dataflow **Date Table**.
9. Refresh the dataflow.

Now, you are ready to pull everything you've created together for your fourth dataflow, which will contain the data for populating a Power BI dataset!

Dataflow 4 – data to populate a Power BI dataset

Your fourth dataflow will combine all of the queries that you've created and organize them in a single place so that they can be used with a Power BI dataset. You won't be making any transformations to the source tables, but having a separate dataflow gives you the flexibility to add new transformations if needed without impacting queries that will also be used to populate ML queries in the next chapter. Creating this dataflow should be straightforward:

1. From your newly created Power BI workspace, from the ribbon, select **New** | **Dataflow**.
2. Select **Define new tables** | **Link tables from other dataflows**.
3. Sign in and click **Next**.
4. Expand your workspace.
5. Expand the **Date Table** dataflow and check **Date**.
6. Expand the **Strike Reports** dataflow and check **Strike Reports Curated**.

7. Expand the **Reference Data** dataflow and check **Aircraft Type Info**, **Engine Codes Info**, and **Engine Position Info**.

8. Click **Transform Data**.

9. Rename the queries **Date**, **Strike Reports**, **Aircraft Type**, **Engine Codes**, and **Engine Position**.

10. Select **Save & close**.

11. Name the dataflow **FAA Wildlife Strike Dataset Tables**.

12. Save and refresh the dataflow.

With that, you've migrated your primary ingestion and transformation queries from Power BI Desktop to dataflows in the Power BI service. Later in this project, you can circle back to redirect your Power BI dataset to the new FAA Wildlife Strike dataset tables. For now, you have what you need to start building out your ML queries in Power BI dataflows. These will be used to train and test your Power BI ML models.

Adding a dataflow for ML queries

Now that you've ingested, cleaned up, and transformed the data from the FAA Wildlife Strike database, you can build out your specialized queries for Power BI ML models. Before you get started, note that Power BI ML is a version of Azure AutoML that has been built into Power BI as a SaaS offering. Data science teams using advanced tools will often apply transformations to data, such as imputing missing values, normalizing numeric ranges, and weighting features within a model. The advanced transformations of features won't be covered in this book since AutoML has featurization capabilities to optimize data for ML. The queries you will be creating could probably be improved upon with advanced featurization techniques, but for this project, we will keep things simple and let the AutoML featurization capabilities in Power BI ML handle some of the advanced feature transformations.

Adding the Predict Damage ML query to a dataflow

You will now create a fifth dataflow that contains the logic for the ML queries. The expanded architecture will look like this:

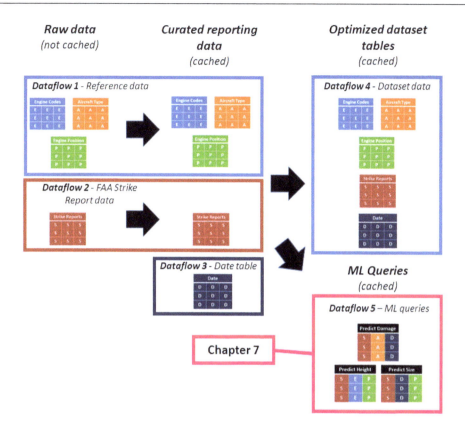

Figure 7.14 – ML Queries added to a Power BI dataflow

You will start by migrating the Predict Damage ML query you created in Power Query to a new dataflow:

1. From your newly created Power BI workspace, from the ribbon, select **New** | **Dataflow**.
2. Select **Define new tables** | **Link tables from other dataflows** | **Add linked tables**.
3. Sign in and click **Next**.
4. Expand your workspace.
5. Expand the **Strike Reports** dataflow and check **Strike Reports Curated**.
6. Click **Transform Data**.
7. Create a group named **Sources** and move **Strike Reports Curated** into that group.
8. Right-click **Strike Reports Curated** and unselect **Enable load**.

Next, you must add a new query for **Predict Damage** that has been built using the **Strike Reports Curated** query:

1. Select **Get data | Blank query**.

2. Paste in the **13 Predict Damage.M** M code. This can be found on the Packt GitHub site at `https://github.com/PacktPublishing/Unleashing-Your-Data-with-Power-BI-Machine-Learning-and-OpenAI/tree/main/Chapter-07`.

3. Click **Next**.

4. Rename the query **Predict Damage**.

5. Create a new group named **ML Queries** and move **Predict Damage** to that group.

    Your dataflow should now look as follows:

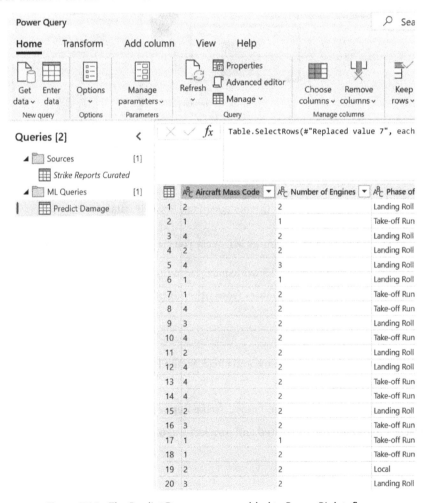

Figure 7.15 – The Predict Damage query added to Power BI dataflows

Before you move on to the next query, save and process your dataflow to ensure that you do not lose your work.

6. Click **Save & close**.

7. Name your new dataflow **ML Queries**.

8. Refresh the dataflow.

Now, you are ready to add another ML query to your dataflow!

Adding the Predict Size ML query to a dataflow

The **Predict Size** ML query that you created in Power Query for Power BI can also be added to the **ML Queries** dataflow you created. Open the **Edit tables** view for the dataflow and proceed as follows:

1. Select **Get data | Blank query**.

2. Paste in the **14 Predict Size.M** M code. This can be found on the Packt GitHub site for the **Predict Size** query: `https://github.com/PacktPublishing/Unleashing-Your-Data-with-Power-BI-Machine-Learning-and-OpenAI/tree/main/Chapter-07`.

3. Click **Next**.

4. Rename the query **Predict Size**.

5. Move **Predict Size** to the **ML Queries** group.

Once you've validated that the data previews correctly, you can **Save & close** the dataflow to ensure that you don't lose your work. Now, you are ready to add your third ML query for predicting height!

Adding the Predict Height ML query to a dataflow

Finally, you must add a query for predicting height to the ML Queries dataflow. The query can be added similarly to the other two queries:

1. Select **Get data | Blank query**.

2. Paste in the **15 Predict Height.M** M code. This can be found on the Packt GitHub site for the **Predict Height** query: `https://github.com/PacktPublishing/Unleashing-Your-Data-with-Power-BI-Machine-Learning-and-OpenAI/tree/main/Chapter-07`.

3. Click **Next**.

4. Rename the query **Predict Height**.

5. Move **Predict Height** to the **ML Queries** group.

Once your query has been added, your dataflow should look as follows in your browser:

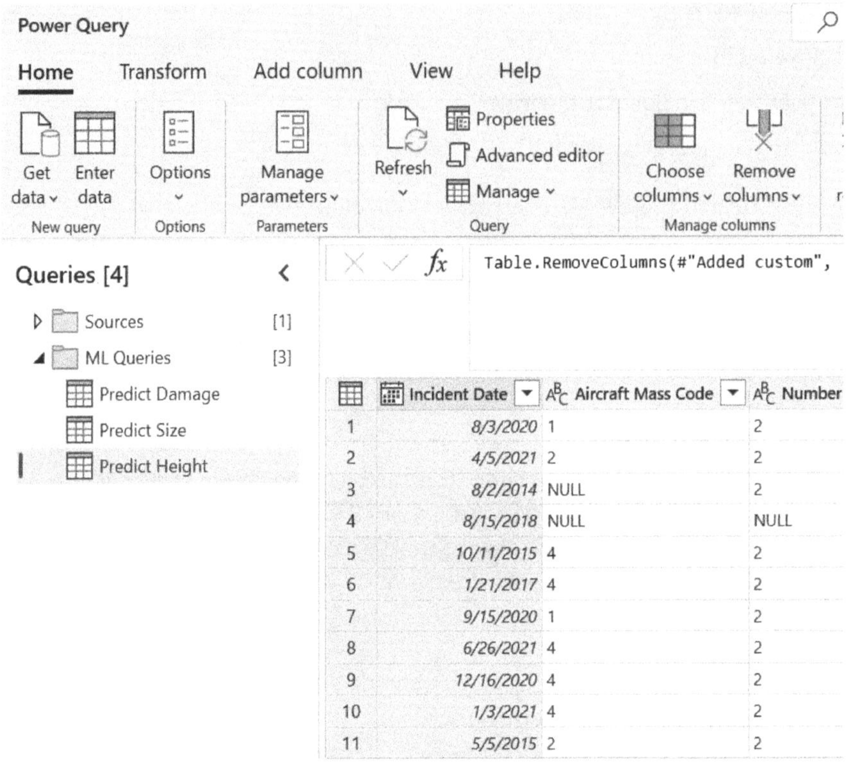

Figure 7.16 – All three ML queries have been added to a dataflow

Now, you can **Save & close** your dataflow, and then refresh it in the Power BI cloud service. With that, you are ready to move on to ML in Power BI!

Summary

In this chapter, you migrated queries from Power BI Desktop Power Query to dataflows in the Power BI cloud service. These queries ingest, prep, and create tables designed for your Power BI dataset. Then, you migrated your ML queries from Power Query for Power BI Desktop to dataflows in the Power BI cloud service. In doing so, you created a new dataflow that is populated by the dataflows you created in the previous chapter. The new ML Queries dataflow was saved and refreshed in your Power BI workspace.

In *Chapter 8*, you will begin working with Power BI ML in the cloud. You will use the three ML queries you created here to build and test the Binary Prediction, Categorical, and Regression ML models in Power BI.

Part 3: Machine Learning in Power BI

In this part, you will build an ML model in Power BI, evaluate the model, and then configure it to work with new and updated data.

This process will be covered in the following chapters:

- *Chapter 8, Building Machine Learning Models with Power BI*
- *Chapter 9, Evaluating Trained and Tested ML Models*
- *Chapter 10, Iterating Power BI Machine Learning Models*
- *Chapter 11, Applying Power BI Machine Learning Models*

8

Building Machine Learning Models with Power BI

In *Chapter 7* of this book, you built three queries in Power BI dataflows that will be used for ML in Power BI. FAA Wildlife Strike data was the source of that data, which you will use to build your Power BI ML models. Those queries are sets of features associated with reports of incidents in which an aircraft struck wildlife.

In this chapter, you will build and train ML models using the queries created in *Chapter 7*. In *Chapter 1*, you determined that you would create a binary prediction model for predicting whether damage occurred, a general classification model to predict the size of the wildlife, and a regression model to predict the height from the ground associated with wildlife strikes that caused damage. At the end of this chapter, you will be ready to assess the results of the ML models you have built. We'll do that in the following chapter.

Technical requirements

You'll need the following for this chapter:

- FAA Wildlife Strike data files from either the FAA website or the Packt GitHub site

- Power BI Pro license

- One of the following Power BI licensing options for access to Power BI dataflows:

  - Power BI Premium

  - Power BI Premium Per User

- One of the following options for getting data into the Power BI cloud service:

  - Microsoft OneDrive (with connectivity to the Power BI cloud service)

  - Microsoft Access and Power BI Gateway

  - Azure Data Lake (with connectivity to the Power BI cloud service)

Building and training a binary prediction ML model in Power BI

You're finally ready to build and train your first ML model in Power BI! We will start with a binary prediction model to predict whether damage happened when wildlife struck an airplane. As discussed in *Chapter 1*, a binary prediction model will make a yes/no prediction for a given row of data containing columns that are the predictive features. The query that you built in *Chapter 7* is in your **ML Queries** dataflow and is named **Predict Damage**.

You'll build your prediction model as follows:

1. Create a new dataflow in your Power BI workspace by selecting **New | Dataflow**.
2. Select **Link tables from other dataflows**.
3. Ensure you are signed in to your organizational account and select **Next**.
4. Expand your Power BI workspace folder, expand the **ML Queries** dataflow, select **Predict Damage**, and click **Transform data**.
5. Save and close the new dataflow.
6. Name the new dataflow `Predict Damage ML`.
7. Refresh the new dataflow.

    Now you can begin building your binary prediction ML model in Power BI.

8. Click on the new dataflow, **Predict Damage ML**, from your workspace.
9. Click on the ribbon header for **Machine learning models**.
10. Select **Get started**, as shown in the following screenshot:

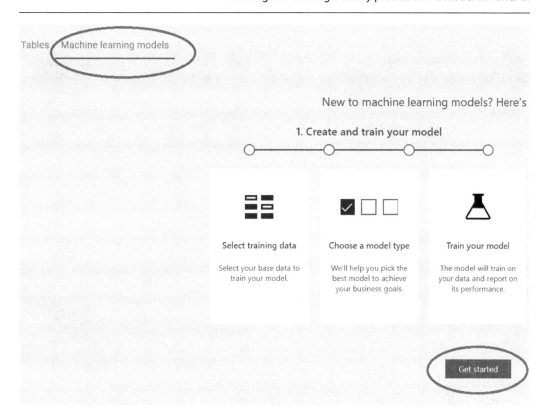

Figure 8.1 – Start an ML model from within a Power BI dataflow

Now, select the column of data that the ML model will predict. For your binary prediction model, you must select a column with two possible outcomes. The column named Indicated Damage within the Predict Damage table contains a 1 value when damage was reported for a wildlife strike and a 0 value when damage was not reported. Each row represents a unique wildlife strike event.

11. Select the Predict Damage table.

12. Select the **Outcome column** value named Indicated Damage.

13. Click **Next**. Your screen should look as follows:

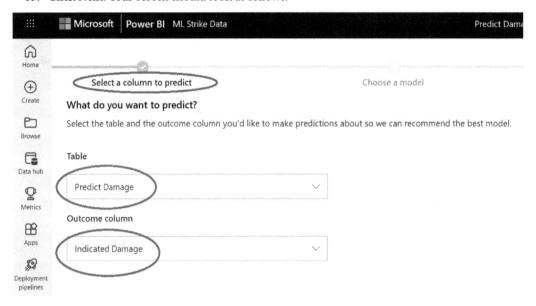

Figure 8.2 – The table and outcome column for a binary prediction model are selected

Power BI automatically recognizes that a **Binary Prediction** model was the best choice. Next, you will select the target outcome from the Indicated Damage column. The 1 value indicates that damage was reported, and that is the prediction that is most interesting for the ML model. Damage is the less frequent outcome and will also be associated with possible safety issues and costs.

14. Select **1** from the **Choose a target outcome** field.

15. For **Match label**, enter 1 to indicate that the prediction accurately matches the outcome.

16. For **Mismatch label**, enter Not 1 to indicate that the prediction missed the mark.

17. Your screen should look like the following screenshot before you click **Next**:

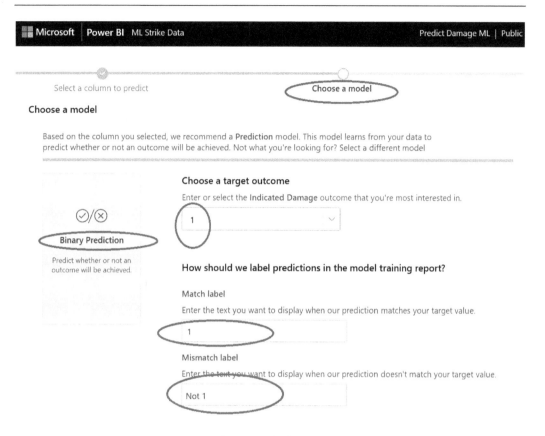

Figure 8.3 – Power BI detected a fit for a Binary Prediction model

Selecting features that will be used to train the binary prediction ML model is the next step. As you can see in *Figure 8.4*, Power BI has detected columns that are correlated to the outcome. At the time this screenshot was taken, the recommended columns were **Speed**, **Struck Windshield**, **Struck Nose**, **Ingested Engine 2**, **Struck Propeller**, **Struck Wing or Rotor**, **Struck Fuselage**, **Struck Landing Gear**, **Struck Tail**, and **Size**. You check the boxes for all of the columns in the data that do not directly indicate some form of damage beyond those that are recommended. The recommendations are based on a sampling of data, so there may be some hidden gems within features that were not flagged. Unless there are too many unique values, there's no harm in adding all the features to your first pass at the Power BI AutoML tool. You will whittle down the features as you iterate the ML model and attempt to improve future results. Here's a screenshot of the selection page before you check all of the features:

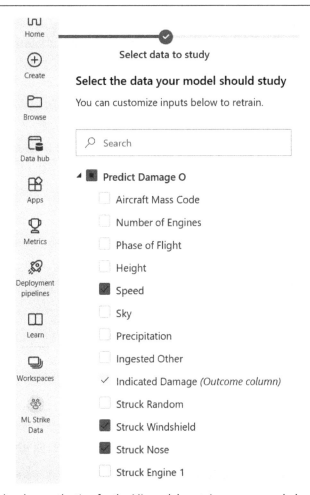

Figure 8.4 – Default column selection for the ML model contains recommended columns by Power BI

Now you can select settings for the ML model that will be trained.

18. Give the ML model a name such as `Predict Damage ML Model`.

19. Add a description in the **Description** field.

20. Select the **Training time** value. In theory, longer training times should provide better results due to running more iterations. In reality, you will usually reach a point of diminishing returns with small datasets. You selected 29 minutes. Note that you can also re-run the training process at different durations to compare results.

21. Note that at the bottom of the screen, Power BI says it will automatically use **20%** of the data for testing and **80%** for training. Here's a screenshot before you select **Save & train**:

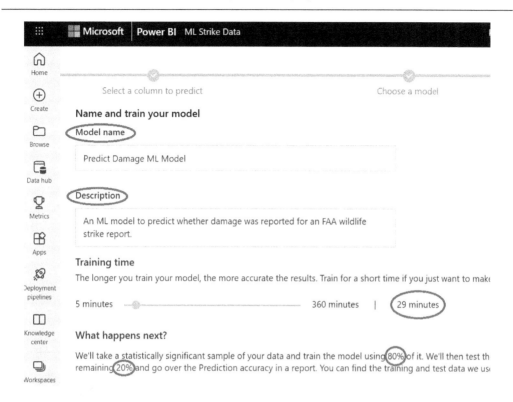

Figure 8.5 – Settings for naming and training the ML model

Once you select **Save & train**, Power BI will begin training and testing different ML algorithms to find the best fit for your data. Now you can kick back, let Power BI do the work, and move on to your next ML model! After the ML model has been trained, you will take a deep dive into the testing results in the next chapter.

Building and training a general classification ML model in Power BI

Moving on to your second ML model, you will predict the size of wildlife that struck an aircraft based on data collected about the strike. This ML model could be useful in predicting possible species that struck an aircraft. Use the query from the **ML Queries** dataflow named **Predict Size**:

1. Create a new dataflow in your Power BI workspace by selecting **New** | **Dataflow**.

2. Select **Link tables from other dataflows**.

3. Ensure you are signed in to your organizational account and select **Next**.

4. Expand your Power BI workspace folder, expand the **ML Queries** dataflow, select **Predict Size**, and click **Transform data**.

5. Save and close the new dataflow.

6. Name the new dataflow `Predict Size ML`.

7. Refresh the new dataflow.

   Now you can begin building your general classification ML model in Power BI.

8. Click on the new **Predict Size ML** dataflow from your workspace.

9. Click on the ribbon header for **Machine learning models**.

10. Select **Get Started**.

    For a general classification ML model, you now select a column with more than two possible values to be predicted. The column named **Size** within the **Predict Size** table contains three values: **Large**, **Medium**, and **Small**. Each row still represents a unique wildlife strike event, just as in the previous binary classification ML model.

11. Select the **Predict Size** table.

12. Select the Outcome column named **Size**.

13. Click **Next**.

14. Power BI automatically recognizes that a **General Classification** model was the best choice. Your screen should look like the following screenshot before you click **Next**:

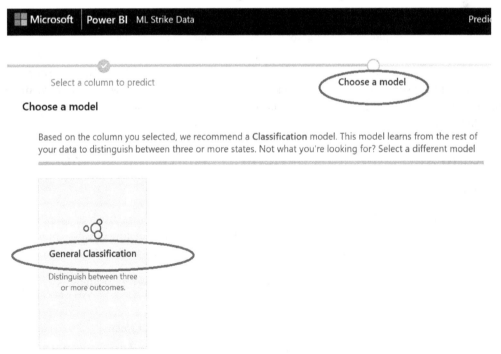

Figure 8.6 – Power BI detected a fit for a General Classification model

As with the previous binary prediction ML model, Power BI will recommend features for your first attempt to build the model. The recommended columns for your general classification ML model at the time this book was written were **Airport ID**, **Aircraft Mass Code**, **Number of Engines**, **Phase of Flight**, **Height**, **Speed**, **Sky**, **Precipitation**, **ingested Other**, **Indicated Damage**, **Struck Random**, **Damaged Random**, **Struck Windshield**, **Damaged Windshield**, **Struck Nose**, **Damaged Nose**, **Struck Engine 1**, **Damaged Engine 2**, **Struck Engine 3**, **Struck Propeller**, **Struck Wing or Rotor**, **Damaged Wing or Rotor**, **Struck Fuselage**, **Damaged Fuselage**, **Struck Landing Gear**, **Struck Tail**, **Damaged Tail**, **Struck Lights**, **Damaged Lights**, **Struck Other**, **Effect on Flight**, **Number of Engines Ingested**, **Percentage of Engines Ingested**, **Number of Engines Damaged**, and **Month Number**. Take note of these features, and then also check the box for the other features for your first pass at the Power BI ML tool.

Now you can select settings for the ML model that will be trained.

15. Give the ML model a name, such as `Predict Size ML Model`.

16. Add a description in the **Description** field.

17. Select a value in **Training time**.

18. Once you select **Save & train**, Power BI will begin training and testing different ML algorithms to find the best fit for your data.

Once you have given your ML model some time for building, you can circle back to it in the next chapter to review the testing data.

Building and training a regression ML model in Power BI

Finally, you will build an ML model to predict the height of impact associated with wildlife strikes. A regression ML model can predict numeric values based on features used to train the model. This ML model could be useful in predicting expected costs when a wildlife strike causes damage. Use the query from the **ML Queries** dataflow named **Predict Height**:

1. Create a new dataflow in your Power BI workspace by selecting **New | Dataflow**.

2. Select **Link tables from other dataflows**.

3. Ensure you are signed in to your organizational account and select **Next**.

4. Expand your Power BI workspace folder, expand the dataflow **ML Queries**, select **Predict Height**, and click **Transform data**.

5. Save and close the new dataflow.

6. Name the new dataflow `Predict Height ML`.

7. Refresh the new dataflow.

Now you can begin building your regression ML model in Power BI.

8. Click on the new **Predict Height ML** dataflow from your workspace.

9. Click on the ribbon header for **Machine learning models**.

10. Select **Get Started**.

A regression ML model will predict a numeric value based on features. In this use case, you will be building an ML model that predicts the height related to a wildlife strike. The column named **Height** within the **Predict Height** table contains integer values representing feet above the ground. Each row still represents a unique wildlife strike event.

11. Select the **Predict Height** table.

12. Select the **Outcome column** named **Height**.

13. Click **Next**.

14. If a regression use case is not auto-detected, Power BI gives you all three choices of ML model types to choose from. As shown in *Figure 8.7*, click on **Regression** before clicking **Next**:

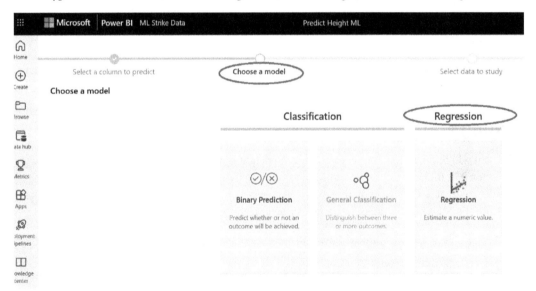

Figure 8.7 – The regression model will predict numeric values

Power BI again recommends features, and you can select all of them for the first run of the ML model.

Now you can select settings for the ML model that will be trained.

15. Give the ML model a name, such as `Predict Height ML Model`.

16. Add a description in the **Description** field.

17. Select a value in **Training time**.

18. Once you select **Save & train**, Power BI will begin training and testing different ML algorithms to find the best model for your data.

You've now reached a point in the project where the first attempts at all three ML models have been built. While it may have seemed easy, there is still much work to do in the coming chapters!

Summary

In this chapter, you used Power BI to build dataflows and train a binary prediction ML model, a general classification model, and a regression model. All three relied on the work you had done through *Chapter 7* to identify features in the FAA Wildlife Strike data, prep queries for ML, and then publish everything to the Power BI cloud service.

In *Chapter 9*, you will review the testing results of the ML models and evaluate the accuracy of the tested predictions. ML models needing improvement can be modified and re-trained as needed until acceptable results are attained.

9

Evaluating Trained
and Tested ML Models

In *Chapter 8* of this book, you built three ML models in Power BI. The models were trained and tested using FAA Wildlife Strike data and attempted to predict the following:

- Whether wildlife striking an aircraft caused damage

- The size of the wildlife that struck the aircraft

- The height at which the wildlife strike occurred

This chapter will review the results of the testing that Power BI does after training the ML models. After reviewing the testing results, you will make changes to the training data with the intent of improving predictive capabilities of the ML models. At the end of this chapter, all three ML models will be ready to deploy and configure for use with Power BI.

Technical requirements

There are a few key terms that you may want to research before reading this chapter if you are new to ML. The definitions given here are taken verbatim from the documentation at this link: `https://learn.microsoft.com/en-us/azure/machine-learning/how-to-understand-automated-ml?view=azureml-api-2#classification-metrics`:

- **The area under the curve (AUC)**: The AUC can be interpreted as the proportion of correctly classified samples. More precisely, the AUC is the probability that the classifier will rank a randomly chosen positive sample higher than a randomly chosen negative sample.

- **Recall**: Recall is the ability of a model to detect all positive samples.

- **Precision**: Precision is the ability of a model to avoid labeling negative samples as positive.

As with the previous chapters, you'll need the following:

- FAA Wildlife Strike data files from either the FAA website or the Packt GitHub site

- A Power BI Pro license

- One of the following Power BI licensing options for access to Power BI dataflows:

  - Power BI Premium

  - Power BI Premium Per User

- One of the following options for getting data into the Power BI cloud service:

  - Microsoft OneDrive (with connectivity to the Power BI cloud service)

  - Microsoft Access + Power BI Gateway

  - Azure Data Lake (with connectivity to the Power BI cloud service)

Evaluating test results for the Predict Damage ML model in Power BI

After the three ML models have completed training, you can take a look at the testing results for each of those models using a pre-built report in Power BI. The training report will provide metrics to help you determine whether the models have some feedback about the value of the predictions. You start with **Predict Damage ML Model**, which is a binary prediction ML model. While in your workspace, follow these steps:

1. Click on the **Predict Damage ML Model** dataflow.

2. On the ribbon, select **Machine learning models**.

3. Under the **ACTIONS** column, click the clipboard to access **View training report**, per the following screenshot:

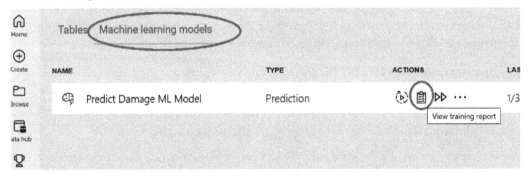

Figure 9.1 – Navigation for the Predict Damage ML Model training report

4. The report should open to look like the following figure:

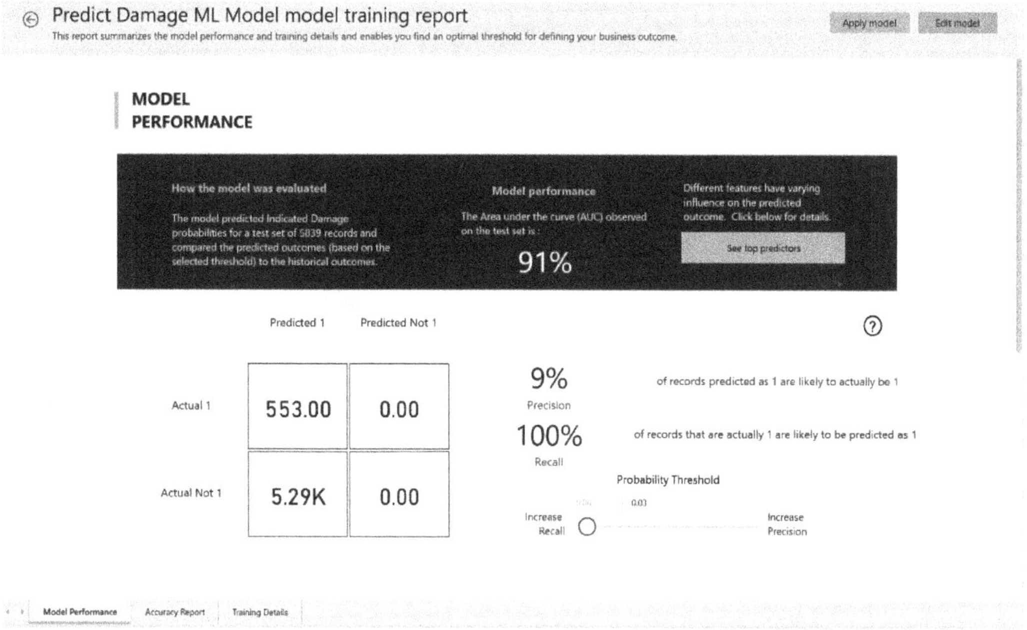

Figure 9.2 – The training report for Predict Damage ML Model

Note that your metrics on this page may differ due to random sampling of the testing data and any changes to the scope of source data used for training and testing. Also, Power BI ML will randomly split the data into testing and training subsets, which may be different every time it runs.

Model performance for Predict Damage ML Model

The **Predict Damage ML Model** testing has yielded some interesting results. In the example provided above, you can see that the model performance, or AUC, is listed at 91%. The closer that the AUC is to 100%, the better an ML model is at overall correct predictions. Your first inclination might be to claim success, but there are some additional details to consider.

For a binary prediction ML model, the prediction is for either a value of 1 (yes) or 0 (no). When predicting whether damage happened due to a wildlife strike, there are four possible outcomes for each row of data and comparing it to the real result:

Prediction	What really happened	Outcome
Damage happened	Damage really happened	True positive
Damage happened	Damage didn't happen	False positive
Damage didn't happen	Damage really happened	False negative
Damage didn't happen	Damage didn't happen	True negative

Figure 9.3 – Four possible outcomes of testing the ML model versus reality

As seen in *Figure 9.2*, there is a sliding bar filter in the bottom-right portion of the report called **Probability Threshold**. The probability threshold is a value assigned to each prediction between zero and one to indicate the certainty of the prediction. A probability score of 99 could be interpreted as *"The ML model is 99% certain that this incident caused damage."* Can you rely on the certainty of the ML model, and does that number reflect reality? The testing results can help you find out!

You move **Probability Threshold** to 0.50 and view the results. Notice that other values on the page change:

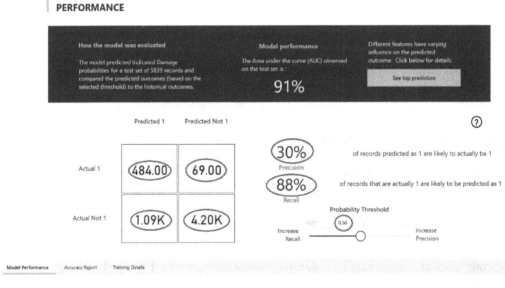

Figure 9.4 – Model performance report with Probability Threshold set to 0.50

Starting with the grid having four boxes, you note that 484 incidents were correctly predicted to have had damage. However, 69 incidents that had real damage were missed by the ML model. 484/(484 + 69) is about an **88%** success rate for correctly flagging incidents with damage. This is the **Recall** value on the report. Also, 1.09K incidents were incorrectly predicted to have caused damage when they did not. **Precision** indicates that with **Probability Threshold** set to 0.50, only **30%** of the incidents that are flagged as causing damage will actually have caused damage.

With **Probability Threshold** set to 0.80, the metrics change:

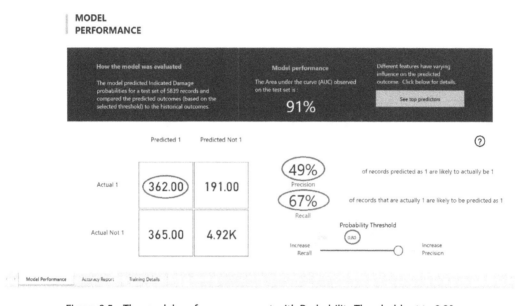

Figure 9.5 – The model performance report with Probability Threshold set to 0.80

With **Probability Threshold** set to 0.80, **Precision** increases to **49%**. 49% sounds better, but there's a catch! Yes, more incidents that were predicted to cause damage did in fact cause damage, but only 362 incidents were flagged out of 551 damaging incidents! Setting **Probability Threshold** at 0.80 might eliminate false positives but 33% (1 – **Recall** of 0.67) of actual real damage events would be missed.

In summary, **Probability Threshold** functions as a cut-off value that can impact the four possible outcomes of this binary prediction ML model, as illustrated in the following charts.

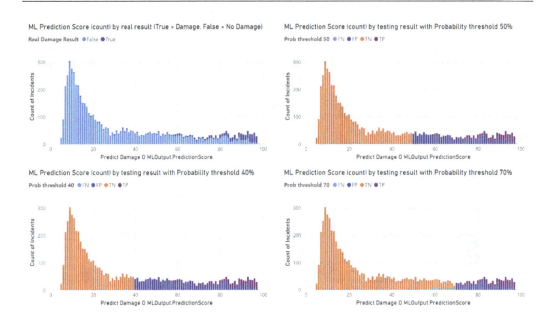

Figure 9.6 – Impact of Probability Threshold on results versus real tested results

Let's break down *Figure 9.6*:

- The top-left chart shows the real results of each incident with **ML Prediction Score** on the *x* axis
- The top-right chart shows the impact of setting **Probability Threshold** to 0.50 on **False Negative (FN)**, **False Positive (FP)**, **True Negative (TN)**, and **True Positive (TP)**
- The bottom-left chart shows the impact of setting **Probability Threshold** to 0.40
- The bottom-right chart shows the impact of setting **Probability Threshold** to 0.70

Figure 9.7 sums up the impact of changing **Probability Threshold** for this ML model in practical terms:

Testing outcome	Increase Probability Threshold	Decrease Probability Threshold
True Positive	Fewer	More
True Negative	More	Fewer
False Positive	Fewer	More
False Negative	More	Fewer

Figure 9.7 – Impact of Probability Threshold on testing outcomes

You'll need to go back to your stakeholders to ask for feedback about the importance of the different possible outcomes in *Figures 9.6* and *9.7*. Verbalizing this impact to non-technical stakeholders can be a challenge. The optimal **Probability Threshold** will depend upon the requirements of your stakeholders. You'll need to ask something like the following:

Do you want to flag incidents more frequently to capture as many real incidents with damage as possible, at the expense of having more incorrectly flagged incidents that did not cause damage? Or do you want fewer flagged incidents, with fewer incorrectly flagged incidents, but at the expense of not flagging and missing some incidents with damage?

The screen has been split in half to improve visibility. *Figure 9.8* shows the left half of the screen:

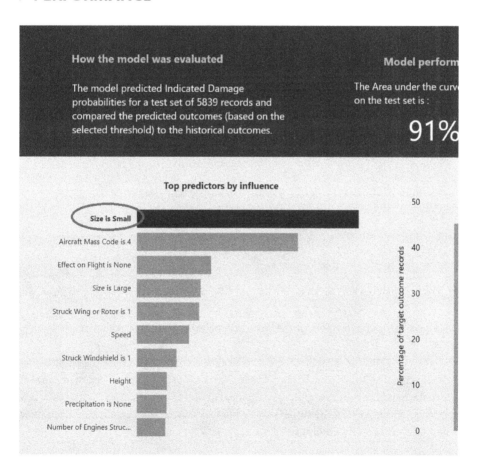

Figure 9.8 – Top predictors for the Predict Damage ML binary prediction model

In the upper-right portion of the report page (see *Figure 9.9*), you click a yellow box labeled **See top predictors**. A list of the top predictive features is shown, and you click on **Size is Small**:

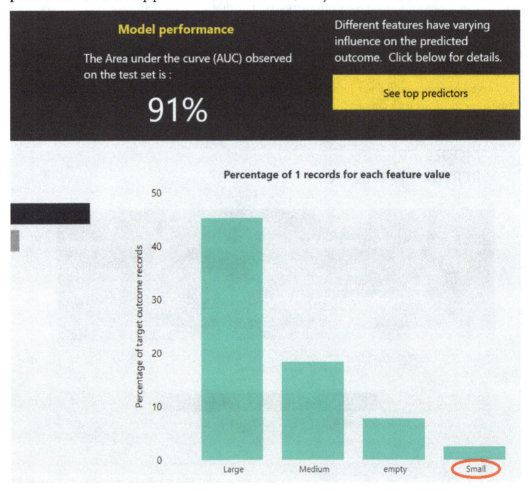

Figure 9.9 – Top predictors for the Predict Damage ML binary prediction model

You see that when you click on a predictor (feature) value, a chart pops up on the right to visualize that feature. You can also hover over bars on these charts for greater detail. For **Size is Small**, the chart shows that when **Size is Large**, damage happened about 45% of the time. When **Size is Small**, damage happened about 2.5% of the time. That's a big difference! You can click on each of the top predictors and take notes on the findings.

At the bottom of the **MODEL PERFORMANCE** page, you find a **Cost-Benefit Analysis** chart with filters, as shown in *Figure 9.9*:

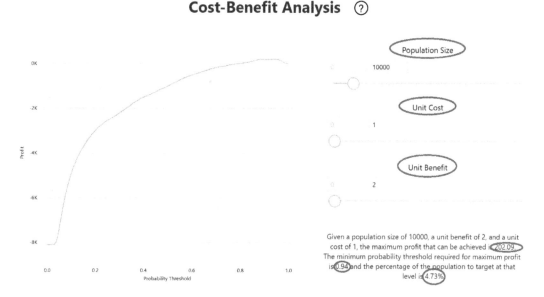

Figure 9.10 – Cost-Benefit Analysis for Predict Damage ML

The best way to summarize this chart, in practical terms, is that it allows you to determine the impact of different **Probability Threshold** settings. If the total count of predictions (**Population Size**) is set to 10,000, the cost of a prediction (**Unit Cost**) is set to 1, and the relative benefit of a correct prediction is set to 2, then the maximum profit per the testing would be 202.09 if the threshold were set to 0.94, and only 4.73% of the population would be targeted. With this particular use case, the setting of **Probability Threshold** will probably require a conversation with your stakeholders. While an interesting discussion point, there are other factors to consider for the implications of wildlife striking aircraft, such as passenger safety, impact on wildlife, end user use of the predictions, and more.

Accuracy report for Predict Damage ML

Next, you move to the next page of the training report, named **ACCURACY REPORT**, as you can see in the following screenshot.

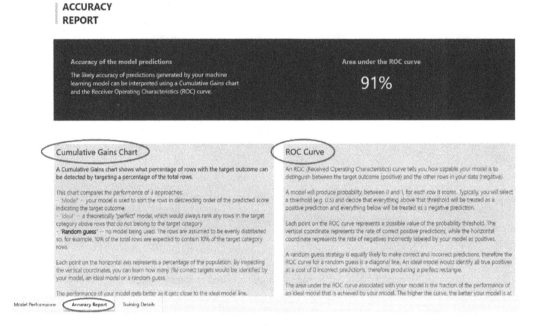

Figure 9.11 – Accuracy report for the Predict Damage ML binary prediction model

The top of the accuracy report provides detailed explanations for **Cumulative Gains Chart** and **ROC Curve** breakdowns. Scroll down the page to view those charts. **Cumulative Gains Chart** is on the left and shows how the ML model performs compared to a perfect model and random guessing. As you hover over the line and move to the right, you can see the performance as **Probability Threshold** decreases:

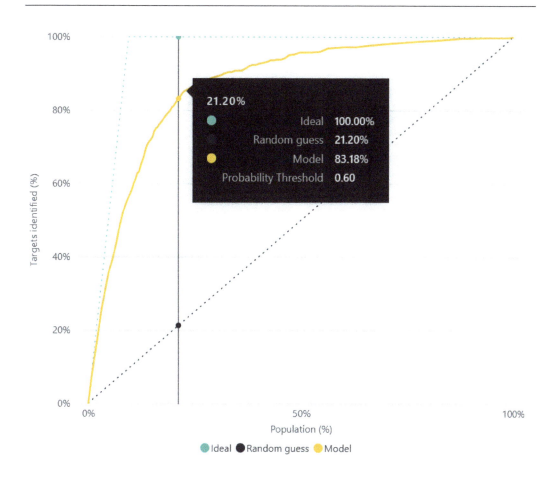

Figure 9.12 – Cumulative Gains Chart (left) displays testing results
against a perfect model and random guesses

ROC Curve on the right side of the page shows how well the model predicts positives as positives (true positive) and negatives as negatives (true negative). A curve elevated upward and to the left indicates good performance:

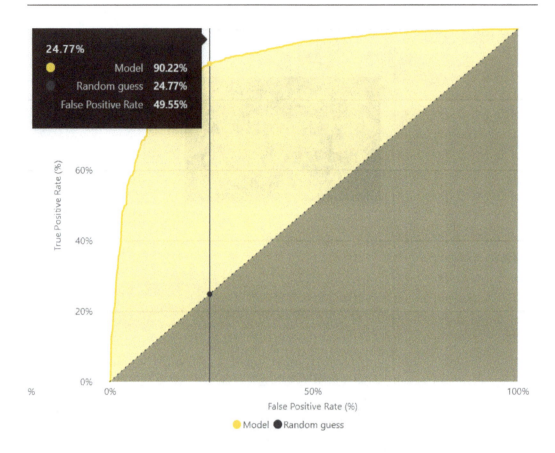

Figure 9.13 – ROC Curve (right) visualizes the ML model's ability to distinguish the target outcome

Training Details for Predict Damage ML

Finally, you move to the last page of the report, named **TRAINING DETAILS**. The top of this page displays details about the testing such as the number of rows sampled, the number of rows used for testing, the type of model that was selected as having the best results, and the number of iterations run to determine the best-fit model. The page can be seen in *Figure 9.13*:

TRAINING DETAILS

How the model was trained

Power BI used the automated ML capability in Azure Machine Learning to train your model. Automated ML was used to find the best way to prepare your data, determine the algorithms used and select the algorithm parameters likely to yield the best accuracy. These steps were used in the machine learning pipeline which generated your machine learning model.

Sampled rows	2359	**Final model used**	Pre-fitted Soft Voting Classifier
Training rows	766	**Iterations run**	32

Model quality over iterations

Figure 9.14 – TRAINING DETAILS for the Predict Damage ML binary prediction ML model

You'll also notice the **Model quality over iterations** chart, showing ML model quality comparisons during the iterative training and testing. Scrolling down the page, you can view details about the ML model such as the features in the model, the data types and imputation of those features, and the parameters that were used to create the model. Here's a screenshot:

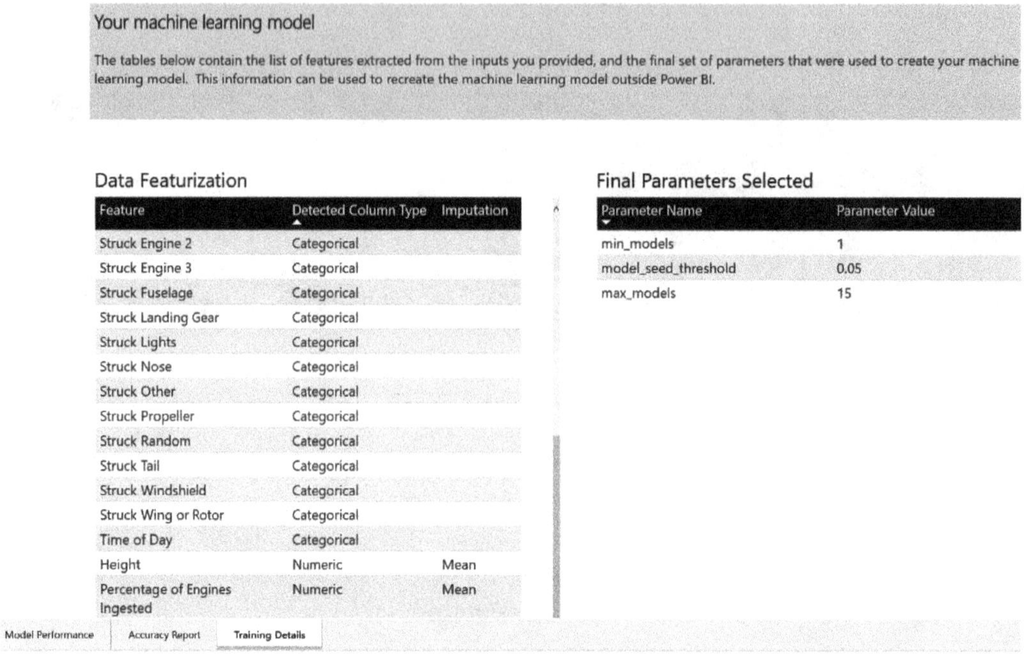

Your machine learning model

The tables below contain the list of features extracted from the inputs you provided, and the final set of parameters that were used to create your machine learning model. This information can be used to recreate the machine learning model outside Power BI.

Data Featurization

Feature	Detected Column Type	Imputation
Struck Engine 2	Categorical	
Struck Engine 3	Categorical	
Struck Fuselage	Categorical	
Struck Landing Gear	Categorical	
Struck Lights	Categorical	
Struck Nose	Categorical	
Struck Other	Categorical	
Struck Propeller	Categorical	
Struck Random	Categorical	
Struck Tail	Categorical	
Struck Windshield	Categorical	
Struck Wing or Rotor	Categorical	
Time of Day	Categorical	
Height	Numeric	Mean
Percentage of Engines Ingested	Numeric	Mean

Final Parameters Selected

Parameter Name	Parameter Value
min_models	1
model_seed_threshold	0.05
max_models	15

Model Performance   Accuracy Report   **Training Details**

Figure 9.15 – Details about the ML model including features and parameters

Scrolling down to the bottom third of the **TRAINING DETAILS** page, you will see a donut chart of the different ML algorithms used as part of an ensemble model. Hovering over an algorithm, you can see details about how it has been used. With Power BI, you use a SaaS ML tool, so there isn't a need to dive deeper into these details. If a data science team wants to extend your findings by building custom ML models in a tool such as Azure ML, this information might be of value to them as they plan their follow-up project:

Ensemble machine learning models

Ensemble models use multiple learning algorithms to obtain better predictive performance than may be obtained from a single learning algorithm. Ensemble models are useful for improving accuracy in certain cases.

Automated ML in Power BI generates ensemble models, if they are found to be optimal. If an ensemble model is used, then the constituent model details will be presented below.

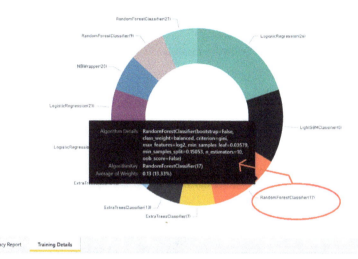

Figure 9.16 – Ensemble machine learning model algorithms for the Predict Damage ML model

Looking back at the process to create the **Predict Damage ML** model, you included a long list of features that you considered possible candidates for having predictive capabilities. In *Chapter 10*, you will revisit this ML model to retrain it with a more succinct and carefully chosen list of features before deploying the ML model. Now, you are ready to move on to the next ML model for this chapter.

Evaluating test results for Predict Size ML Model in Power BI

Your next ML model to review is a classification model for predicting the size of wildlife that struck an aircraft. These predictions don't necessarily indicate the size of the actual animal. For example, a large flock of smaller birds might also be considered a large impact. Predicting these values could help understand the likelihood of incidents that are perceived to be more severe.

Model performance for Predict Size ML

Moving on to the test results for your ML model to predict the size of an animal or animals that struck an aircraft, you follow similar steps as in the previous section to open the report. From your Power BI workspace, do the following:

1. Click on the **Predict Size ML Model** dataflow.

2. On the ribbon, select **Machine learning models**.

3. Under the **ACTIONS** column, click the clipboard to access **View training report**.

4. The report should look like the following figure, and on the bar chart, you can click on the **Small** class:

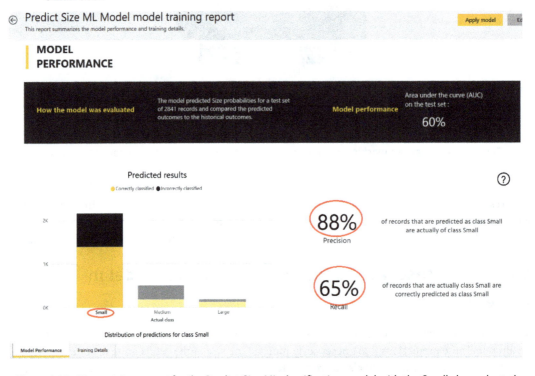

Figure 9.17 – The training report for the Predict Size ML classification model with the Small class selected

First, you notice that this report looks slightly different since it is for a different type of ML model, a classification model. The AUC, at the top right of the report page, is 60%. As a general rule of thumb, an AUC under 70% is not very good. An AUC of 50% generally represents random guessing, and 60% is only slightly above that value. You'll need to dive deeper into the testing results to find opportunities for improvement.

The **Small** class (you clicked on in *Figure 9.16*) had a **Precision** rating of **88%**, which means that when a prediction of **Small** was made, it turned out to be true 88% of the time. **Recall** for **Small** was only **65%**, which means that only 65% of actual small incidents were captured.

Now, click on the **Medium** class:

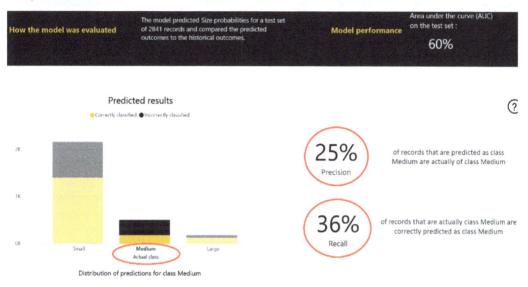

Figure 9.18 – Training report for the Predict Size ML classification model with the Medium class selected

The results for predicting **Medium** are not very good. With a **Precision** rating of **25%**, most of the predictions for **Medium** turned out to be wrong. Adding to the disappointment, only **36%** of actual medium strike incidents were captured by the **Medium** prediction.

Let's move on to the **Large** class:

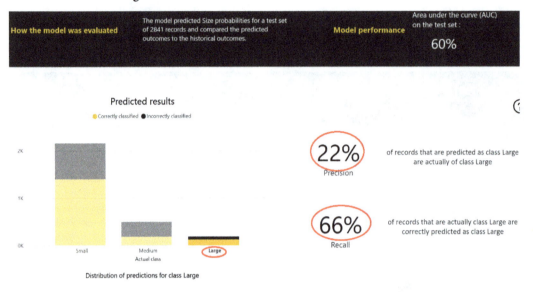

Figure 9.19 – The training report for the Predict Size ML classification model with the Large class selected

The **Large** class had a **Precision** rating of **22%**, indicating that a prediction of **Large** is only correct about 1 out of 5 times. **66%** of actual large-sized incidents were captured in those predictions. In summary, a prediction of **Large** is usually inaccurate but about two-thirds of actual large events are captured in that prediction.

Scrolling to the bottom of the **MODEL PERFORMANCE** page, you can click on the different classes that were predicted to see the top predictors. Within the **Large** class, you click on the bar for **Indicated Damage** to pop up a chart on the right, which shows details about that feature:

Top Predictors

An important aspect to analyze is the impact of different features in your data on your predictions. Certain features might have a high impact on predictions, whereas others might have very low. The **Top predictors** visual shows the relative impact of each feature on outcomes. Clicking on a predictor will show the breakdown in the test data.

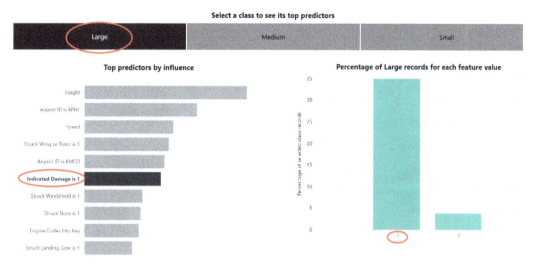

Figure 9.20 – Top Predictors for the Large class with Indicated Damage details

When the class is **Large**, the features on the left side chart of *Figure 9.18* were determined to influence that class. You've clicked on the **Indicated Damage** feature and can see that when that value is **1**, the class will be **Large** 35% of the time. When set to **0**, a classification of **Large** occurs less than 5% of the time. You can click through the different classes (**Large**, **Medium**, and **Small**) to view the features that were top influencers and take notes for your next iteration of the ML model.

Training details for Predict Size ML

Moving on to the **TRAINING DETAILS** page for **Predict Size ML**, you'll see a similar page to that for **Predict Damage ML**:

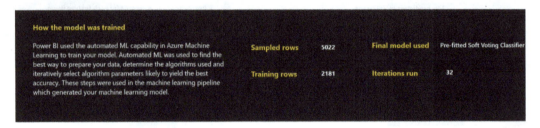

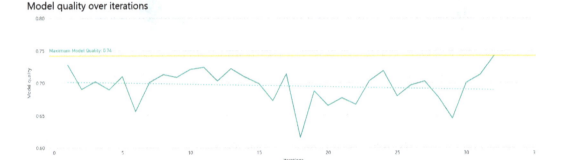

Figure 9.21 – TRAINING DETAILS includes details about training the ML model

Interestingly, the quality of the ML model declined with an increase in the number of iterations. With machine learning, more data is not always better, and greater complexity does not always yield better results. As a novice with these tools, sometimes, trial and error is the best way to familiarize yourself with these concepts.

Scrolling to the middle of the **TRAINING DETAILS** page, you can view details about the features used in the ML model and the final parameters. Again, this is a similar page to the **Predict Damage ML** report:

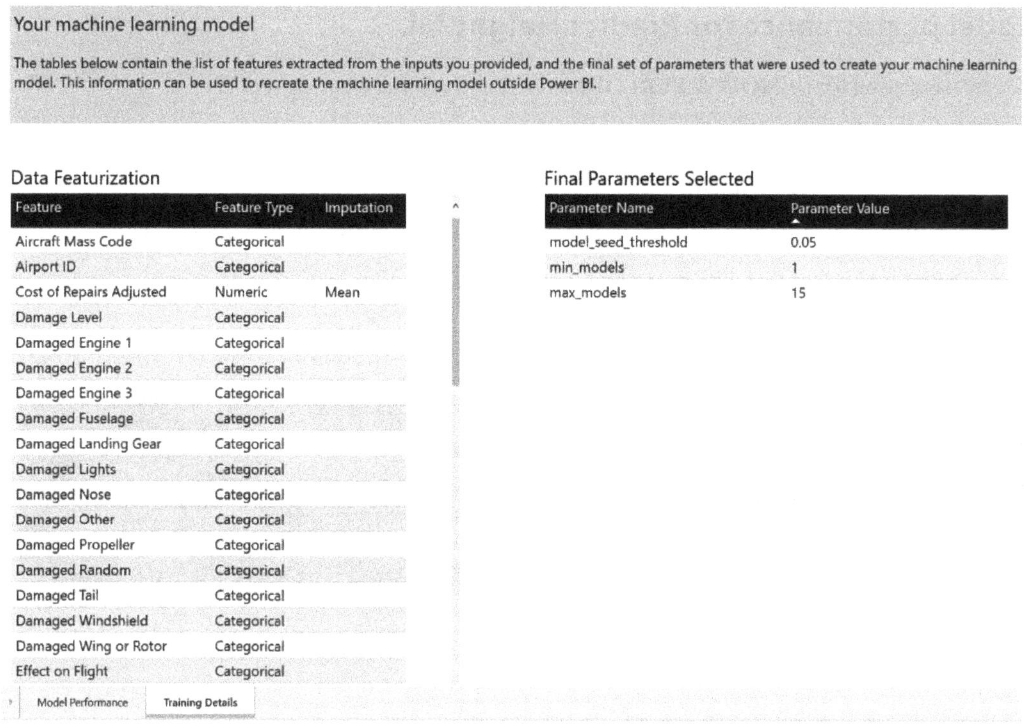

Your machine learning model

The tables below contain the list of features extracted from the inputs you provided, and the final set of parameters that were used to create your machine learning model. This information can be used to recreate the machine learning model outside Power BI.

Data Featurization

Feature	Feature Type	Imputation
Aircraft Mass Code	Categorical	
Airport ID	Categorical	
Cost of Repairs Adjusted	Numeric	Mean
Damage Level	Categorical	
Damaged Engine 1	Categorical	
Damaged Engine 2	Categorical	
Damaged Engine 3	Categorical	
Damaged Fuselage	Categorical	
Damaged Landing Gear	Categorical	
Damaged Lights	Categorical	
Damaged Nose	Categorical	
Damaged Other	Categorical	
Damaged Propeller	Categorical	
Damaged Random	Categorical	
Damaged Tail	Categorical	
Damaged Windshield	Categorical	
Damaged Wing or Rotor	Categorical	
Effect on Flight	Categorical	

Final Parameters Selected

Parameter Name	Parameter Value
model_seed_threshold	0.05
min_models	1
max_models	15

Model Performance   Training Details

Figure 9.22 – Features and parameters for the Predict Size ML model

You can also scroll down to the bottom third of the page and view the **Ensemble machine learning** information. As stated for **Predict Damage ML**, this information is interesting but mostly useful for data scientists who might want to extend the findings of this project into a tool such as Azure ML. You'll revisit this ML model in the next chapter, but for now, you can move on to the **Predict Height ML** model.

Evaluating test results for the Predict Height ML model in Power BI

Finally, you review the test results for the **Predict Height ML** model. This was a regression model attempting to predict the height at which wildlife strikes happened to aircraft. This model does not predict a yes/no answer or a categorical value, but rather a numeric value representing the height in feet from the ground.

Model performance for Predict Height ML

Start by navigating to the **MODEL PERFORMANCE** page of the training report:

1. Click on the **Predict Height ML Model** dataflow.

2. On the ribbon, select **Machine learning models**.

3. Under the **ACTIONS** column, click the clipboard to access **View training report**.

4. The report should look like the following figure:

**MODEL
PERFORMANCE**

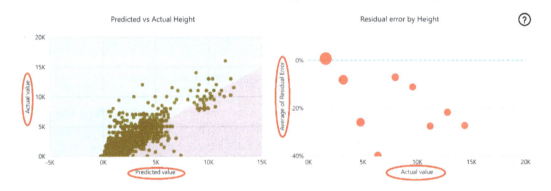

Figure 9.23 – Performance for the Predict Height ML regression model

First, you notice at the top of the page that **Model Performance** is **80%**. With a regression model, the numeric differences between predicted and real results are represented by this value. The features provide predictability, but you'd like to get that number even higher for better results.

The chart on the left side of the page, **Predicted vs Actual Height** plots **Actual value** versus **Predicted value** for the height at which an impact occurred. Variation is expected due to different aircraft models, weather, species, and many other factors. Perfect predictability would display the dots on the line separating the red and blue portions of the chart. You can see that the regression line generally follows through results.

On the right side of the page in *Figure 9.22*, the chart for **Residual error by Height** shows the average error for different values that were tested. A value of -5% would mean that the prediction is usually 5% too low for a range of values. You notice that the first bubble on the *x* axis appears close to 0%. When you hover over it, you see the values, and you can click it to filter the chart on the left:

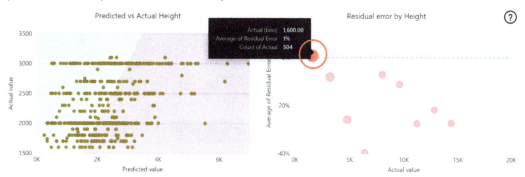

Figure 9.24 – The lowest range in height had an extremely high number of residual errors

Looking at the **Predicted vs Actual Height** chart, you can see that a low height above the ground had a residual error of **1%**.

If you click on the third bubble from the left, a height of 6,500-7,800 feet, the average residual error is now **-40%**:

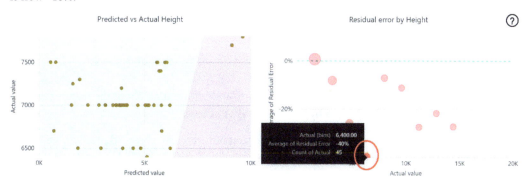

Figure 9.25 – The bins covering heights of 3,200-4,500 feet have a lower average number of residual errors

On the **Predicted vs Actual Height** chart for the third bin, notice that many actual values are reported at a height of 6,500, 7,000, and 7,500 when you click on the bubble to filter the chart on the left. Looking into reasons for this conformity might help you understand the nuances in the source data. Are pilots estimating the height of a wildlife strike incident? Are these common stable altitudes for aircraft flight plans when they are not increasing or decreasing height? Is the conformity just a coincidence? The root cause of this pattern can only be discovered with additional investigation.

Training details for Predict Height ML

Moving on to the final page of the training report for **Predict Height ML,** named **TRAINING DETAILS**, you see a similar report structure to the previous two ML model training reports. The top of the page displays the number of rows sampled, the number of rows used for training, the final model used, and the number of iterations that were run:

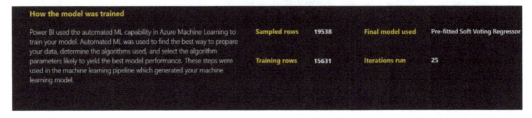

Power BI used the automated ML capability in Azure Machine Learning to train your model. Automated ML was used to find the best way to prepare your data, determine the algorithms used, and select the algorithm parameters likely to yield the best model performance. These steps were used in the machine learning pipeline which generated your machine learning model.

How the model was trained			
Sampled rows	19538	Final model used	Pre-fitted Soft Voting Regressor
Training rows	15631	Iterations run	25

Model quality over iterations

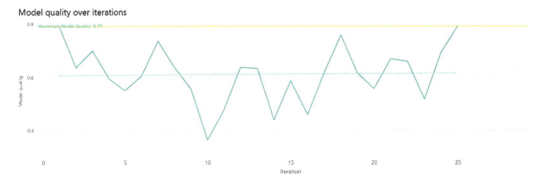

Figure 9.26 – TRAINING DETAILS for the Predict Height ML regression model

Scrolling down the page, you will again see similar charts and information about the features used, the parameters, and the algorithms used by automated ML in Power BI.

Having completed your review of the testing and training report for all three ML models, you are ready to move on to the next chapter of this book.

Summary

This chapter took a deep dive into the training and testing reports for your **Predict Damage ML, Predict Size ML**, and **Predict Height ML** models. In doing so, you reviewed the reports for all three types of ML models in Power BI: binary prediction, classification, and regression. You evaluated how well each of these models made predictions by reviewing the testing data in Power BI. You also explored lists of features that were highly predictive.

In the next chapter, you will modify the filter criteria and features selected for your ML models, with the goal of improving the predictive capabilities. Iterative training and testing are the best way to improve your ML models, and this process will help you prepare for your own Power BI ML projects beyond the scope of this book.

10
Iterating Power BI ML models

In *Chapter 8*, you trained Power BI ML models using all of the features that you had selected for each of the three ML models – that is, **Predict Damage ML**, **Predict Size ML**, and **Predict Height ML** – using data from the FAA Wildlife Strike database. In *Chapter 9*, you evaluated the test results of the automated training and testing process that is part of Power BI. The test results helped you understand the strengths and weaknesses of the predictive models, along with details about features that contributed to correct predictions.

This chapter will revisit the findings from *Chapter 9* and use them to decide if you need to modify and retrain the ML models to achieve better results via iterative development. The list of features that are used to train these ML models can be whittled down, the filter criteria can be adjusted, and the result of the new round of training and testing can be compared to those from *Chapter 9*.

Technical requirements

The requirements for this chapter are the same as the preceding chapters:

- FAA Wildlife Strike data files from either the FAA website or the Packt GitHub site
- A Power BI Pro license
- One of the following Power BI licensing options for access to Power BI dataflows:
  - Power BI Premium
  - Power BI Premium Per User
- One of the following options for getting data into the Power BI cloud service:
  - Microsoft OneDrive (with connectivity to the Power BI cloud service)
  - Microsoft Access and Power BI Gateway
  - Azure Data Lake (with connectivity to the Power BI cloud service)

Considerations for ML model iterations

Numerous books have been written about ML and reasons that ML models perform well or poorly, including books from Packt Publishing. The purpose of this book is to help you learn Power BI so that you can explore the FAA Wildlife Strike data, analyze that data, and then create SaaS ML models. At this point in this book, you are at a crossroads. Do you continue to iterate these ML models in the SaaS tool? Have you demonstrated enough value to hand an ML model project over to a data science team who will improve upon the model using Azure ML or advanced tools? Or do you go back to your stakeholders, report your findings, and ask for guidance on the next steps? The following diagram shows a few options for the next steps you could consider:

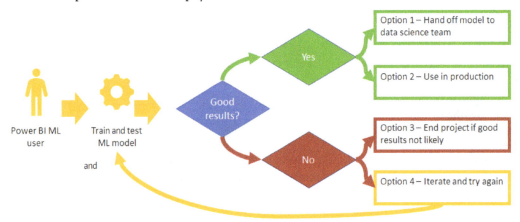

Figure 10.1 – Possible next steps for your Power BI ML models

Rather than diving into the technicalities of ML theory, you will focus on a few possible causes of inaccuracy that can be easily addressed with modifications that can be made for each of your SaaS Power BI ML models. Based on your assessment of each model, you will decide on the next steps based on the options shown in *Figure 10.1*. Let's look at a few topics you should consider.

Inaccurate data

"Garbage in, garbage out" is a popular saying in the data world. Training an ML model with bad data, or scoring bad data through an ML model, can cause inaccurate results. This issue can be addressed through your work as a data professional, but what if the source data collection mechanisms are bad? If the source data is inaccurate, there is only so much you can do to address the problem without making changes to the source data collection process.

Features with low predictive value

In the first round of training and testing your ML models, you ran every feature you identified or created from the FAA Wildlife Strike database through the Power BI SaaS ML tool. Without getting too technical, keeping things small and simple is a good goal for ML (especially using a SaaS tool such as Power BI). Many of the features you included in the ML models may have little value for making predictions. You took notes of the features that were identified as having predictive value, but trial and error with new iterations of training and testing may be needed. You may eventually reach a point of diminishing returns. Will that be the best you can do, or should you hand off the ML model to a data science team with advanced tools and skill sets?

Data volumes

Discussing the impact of data volumes on ML models could fill an entire book. As a general rule, simple ML models with good data will require less training data than complex ML models or models trained using imperfect data. Again, venturing into the topic of optimal data volumes for ML goes beyond the scope of this book, which is to create simple SaaS ML models in Power BI. With the Power BI SaaS ML tool, keeping your training datasets in the tens of thousands of rows or less is a good rule of thumb.

Data characteristics

ML models can be impacted by various data characteristics, such as the following:

- **High cardinality of features**: Too many unique values in a categorical column can reduce the predictive value of the column. For example, including the airport codes for every airport in the FAA Wildlife Strike database would result in a high cardinality column.

- **Skewed data**: Results are captured in a numerical range or for a few categories, but other options are lacking. An example would be if the FAA Wildlife Strike data is missing strikes at high altitudes, or if most of the data is captured from a single airport. If the accurate data is naturally skewed, there are advanced techniques beyond the scope of this book that can address skew for ML models.

- Other characteristics such as **bias**, **overfitting**, **underfitting**, and many more potential issues can be assessed. Again, these topics are discussed at length in books that focus on ML theory.

Before proceeding, you need to be clear about your goals and objectives. You aren't trying to create perfect ML models using the Power BI ML tool. Instead, you are proving the predictive value of the FAA Wildlife Strike data for your use cases of predicting damage, predicting wildlife size, and predicting the height of impact. The decisions you make for each of these ML models will be presented back to your stakeholders to demonstrate the results of your project, along with recommendations for future iterations of the ML models and the overall project.

Assessing the Predict Damage binary prediction ML model

The **Predict Damage ML** model that you built and reviewed in the previous two chapters is designed to predict the likelihood that damage was reported due to wildlife striking an aircraft. A few key metrics from the training report for that binary prediction model can be seen in the following table:

Metric name	Metric value	Comments
Area Under the Curve (AUC)	91%	The AUC indicates the performance of an ML model, with 100% being perfect. 50% would be random guessing, while less than 50% indicates predictions worse than random guessing.
Row Count for Training	23,356	The number of rows used to train the ML model.
Row Count for Testing	5839	The number of rows used to test against the trained ML model.
Cost-Benefit Analysis Best Probability Threshold	0.94	The probability threshold with the greatest return on investment when considering precision and recall.

Figure 10.2 – Metrics for the initial Predict Damage ML model

The testing results for the **Predict Damage ML** model were discussed at length in *Chapter 10*. Generally speaking, a 91% AUC is not a bad start for your first effort at an ML model. Can you make the model even better at predicting damage? If so, what changes could you make? You can review different metrics from the perspective of the **Probability Threshold** setting:

Probability Threshold setting	Precision – How many flagged incidents had damage?	Recall – How many incidents of real damage were flagged to have damage?	Comments
0.94	67%	38%	Maximum cost-benefit analysis threshold
0.70	44%	75%	Less than half of flagged incidents had real damage, but 75% were captured

Probability Threshold setting	Precision – How many flagged incidents had damage?	Recall – How many incidents of real damage were flagged to have damage?	Comments
0.50	30%	88%	88% of all damage incidents were captured, but flagged incidents were false alarms 70% of the time
0.03	9%	100%	All damage incidents were captured, but 91% of the flagged incidents were false alarms

Figure 10.3 – The Probability Threshold setting's impact on the Predict Damage ML model

By browsing through these features using Power BI and searching through the different considerations mentioned earlier in this chapter, you can weigh the pros and cons of your options. For example, of the 29,195 rows in the dataset used for training and testing, the **Phase of Flight** feature **Parked** is used on only six rows. None of those six rows had damage. Logically, this makes sense since damaging a large parked aircraft would require the strength of a grizzly bear or elephant. How do you handle an underrepresented category such as this? Is it time to call upon the data science team? Your options have been summarized in the following table:

Options	Considerations
Hand off to the data science team	<ul><li>A large number of features could probably be whittled down for better results with a simpler ML model</li><li>91% AUC could be difficult to improve with a SaaS ML tool</li><li>ML experts could review the model for bias and skew</li></ul>
Use in production	<ul><li>Is the ML model good enough to provide value for stakeholders?</li><li>What are the consequences of incorrect predictions?</li><li>Can you truly explain what contributes to the predictions? Do you need to be able to do this?</li></ul>
End the project	Unless the predictions provide little value, ending the project for this ML model now doesn't make much sense
Iterate the ML model	<ul><li>Can you improve upon the ML model?</li><li>How much better can you make it?</li></ul>

Figure 10.4 – Options and considerations for the Predict Damage ML model

The most likely real-world decision would be to circle back with stakeholders and review your results. The best option would likely be handing off to a data science team who can review and assess your findings, improve upon the ML model, and quantify the business value for the stakeholders. You could also iterate upon the existing ML model, but with a 91% AUC, your effort might be better directed toward other efforts within the larger FAA Wildlife Strike data project.

Assessing the Predict Size ML classification model

The **Predict Size ML** model was an attempt at building an ML classification model to predict if the size of a wildlife strike was Small, Medium, or Large. The following table shows some key metrics about the initial version of the ML model:

Metric Name	Metric Value	Comments
AUC	60%	The AUC indicates the performance of an ML model, with 100% being perfect. 60% is better than random guessing, but not very good!
Row Count for Training	11,368	Number of rows used to train the ML model
Row Count for Testing	2,841	Number of rows used to test against the trained ML model

Figure 10.5 – Key metrics for the Predict Size ML classification model

The AUC for this model was only 60%, which is not very good. What can you do to make it better? First, take a look at the precision and recall metrics by class:

Class	Precision – How many flagged incidents matched the class?	Recall – How many real members of this class were captured?	Comments
Small	88%	65%	Good precision, but 35% of Small incidents were still misclassified
Medium	25%	36%	Not very good precision and recall metrics
Large	22%	66%	Not very good precision, but 2/3 of all large incidents were captured

Figure 10.6 – Precision and recall metrics by class for the Predict Size ML classification model

While the **Predict Size ML** model is doing a good job of predicting the Small class, the predictions for Medium and Large are disappointing. Having taken notes on the features with strong predictive capabilities, you can change some of the filter criteria when performing a second iteration of the ML model:

Filter criteria	First ML model	New ML model iteration	Comments
Date	>= 1/1/2010	>= 1/1/2010	Same
Aircraft Class Code	A	A	Same
Airport ID	Top 10 Airports	Top 15 Airports	Larger sample size
Height		Not null and Not 0	Eliminates rows with missing data for a predictive column
Speed		Not null and Not 0	Eliminates missing data and removes a speed of 0
Size	Not null and Not blank	Not null and Not blank	Same – removes rows with missing data

Figure 10.7 – Changes to the filter criteria for Predict Size ML

Based on the notes you took while reviewing the training report, as well as your findings from using Power BI for data exploration, you can whittle down the list of features for your next iteration of training the **Predict Size ML** model:

Features in the Curated FAA Wildlife Strike query	Included in the first iteration of the Predict Size ML model?	Included in the second iteration of the Predict Size ML model?	Notes
Incident Date			Too many unique values rolled into Month
Time of Day		Yes	
Airport ID	Yes	Yes	Filtered to the top 15 to avoid cardinality issues
Airport Name			Describes Airport ID
Latitude			Too many unique values
Longitude			Too many unique values
Runway			Too many unique values
State			Location information covered by Airport ID

Features in the Curated FAA Wildlife Strike query	Included in the first iteration of the Predict Size ML model?	Included in the second iteration of the Predict Size ML model?	Notes
FAA Region			Location information covered by Airport ID
Operator ID		Yes	
FLT			Too many unique values
Aircraft		Yes	
Aircraft Class Code			Filtered to A for both iterations
Aircraft Mass Code	Yes	Yes	
Number of Engines	Yes	Yes	Filtered to 2 for the second iteration
Phase of Flight	Yes	Yes	
Height	Yes	Yes	
Speed	Yes	Yes	
Distance			
Sky	Yes		
Precipitation	Yes		
Cost of Repairs Adjusted		Yes	
Ingested Other		Yes	
Indicated Damage	Yes	Yes	
Damage Level		Yes	
Struck Random	Yes	Yes	
Damaged Random	Yes	Yes	
Struck Windshield	Yes	Yes	
Damaged Windshield	Yes		
Struck Nose	Yes	Yes	
Damaged Nose	Yes	Yes	
Struck Engine 1	Yes		
Damaged Engine 1	Yes	Yes	
Ingested Engine 1	Yes		
Struck Engine 2	Yes		
Damaged Engine 2	Yes	Yes	

Features in the Curated FAA Wildlife Strike query	Included in the first iteration of the Predict Size ML model?	Included in the second iteration of the Predict Size ML model?	Notes
Ingested Engine 2	Yes		
Struck Engine 3	Yes		
Damaged Engine 3	Yes		
Ingested Engine 3	Yes		
Struck Engine 4	Yes		
Damaged Engine 4	Yes		
Ingested Engine 4	Yes		
Struck Propeller	Yes	Yes	
Damaged Propeller	Yes	Yes	
Struck Wing or Rotor	Yes	Yes	
Damaged Wing or Rotor	Yes	Yes	
Struck Fuselage	Yes		
Damaged Fuselage	Yes		
Struck Landing Gear	Yes	Yes	
Damaged Landing Gear	Yes	Yes	
Struck Tail	Yes	Yes	
Damaged Tail	Yes	Yes	
Struck Lights	Yes	Yes	
Damaged Lights	Yes	Yes	
Struck Other	Yes		
Damaged Other	Yes		
Effect on Flight	Yes	Yes	
Number Seen		Yes	
Number Struck		Yes	
Number of Engines Struck	Yes		
Percentage of Engines Struck	Yes		
Number of Engines Ingested	Yes		

Features in the Curated FAA Wildlife Strike query	Included in the first iteration of the Predict Size ML model?	Included in the second iteration of the Predict Size ML model?	Notes
Percentage of Engines Ingested	Yes		
Number of Engines Damaged	Yes		
Percentage of Engines Damaged	Yes		
Month Number	Yes	Yes	
Total Features	50	36	
Total Rows	7,203	4,928	

Figure 10.8 – Features selected for the first and second iterations of the Predict Size ML model

You have two options for performing a second iteration of the **Predict Size ML** model. First, you can make changes to the filter criteria in your **ML Queries** dataflow, and then edit and retrain the ML model, as per *Figure 10.9*:

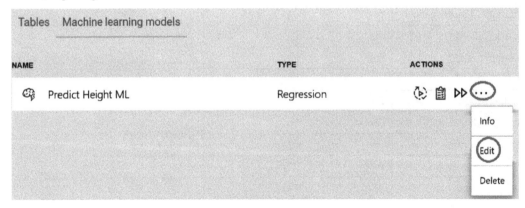

Figure 10.9 – You can iterate the existing ML model if a copy of the older version is not needed

The second option would be to create a second version of the query for training and testing, and also create a new ML model. It's up to you if you'd prefer to keep things simple with a single query and ML model, or if you'd rather build multiple versions for comparison. If you are keeping accurate notes and documentation, a single copy of each is probably the most efficient option.

After retraining the ML model (or building a new one for the second iteration), check the training report. You will see that the AUC only went up to 61%!

**MODEL
PERFORMANCE**

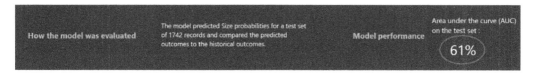

10.10 – AUC only went up slightly for the second iteration of the Predict Size ML model

Despite trimming down the number of features and removing some rows with missing data, your results are still only slightly better than random guesses. Notice that the Small class has a precision of 81% (how many were flagged as Small that were Small) and a recall of 70% (total percentage of small values that were captured by the Small prediction).

At first, you will be hesitant to report your findings to your stakeholders since the results are not great. Before being disappointed, think about the following points:

- With an AUC of 61%, your ML model is still better than random guesses and the Small class had decent results.

- The Small, Medium, and Large classes might be chosen subjectively by the people filling out the report. Different people, in different places, referencing different sizes of planes, might judge these criteria using different contexts. If so, one person's Medium might be another person's Large.

- Maybe a highly accurate classification ML model isn't possible with the data you are using.

After several attempts to modify the **Predict Size ML** model using Power BI, you will be unable to significantly improve the results. As a next step, you have a few viable options:

- Engage a data science team who can help you identify opportunities for improvement by selecting different features and using different filter criteria. Perhaps you are missing something that a data science professional with advanced tools can discover.

- Circle back to your stakeholders, present the results, and ask them to define success. Is 81% precision and 70% recall for the Small class of value to them? If not, how do they define successful predictions?

- Another option would be to convert this ML model into a binary prediction ML model. Since the Small class is getting decent results, you could flag Small as 1 and Medium or Large as a 0. If this was acceptable to the stakeholders, maybe Medium and Large can be lumped together for better results.

Next, we'll assess another model.

Assessing the Predict Height ML regression model

The **Predict Height ML** model is a regression model that's designed to predict the height at which an aircraft was impacted by wildlife. The regression ML model predicts a numeric value representing height in feet from the ground, at which an impact happened based on the features in the report. Features such as **Speed**, **Distance**, and **Phase of Flight** were listed as top predictors.

80% of the variation in the testing results is explained by the model. Is 80% good? It depends on the use case and the requirements! If the variation (R squared) is 100%, then the ML model will give perfect predictions. 80% could indicate that the predictions are good but that independent and random variables might be 100% impossible. Or, maybe a higher value is possible and the data is either missing important features or measures are inaccurate.

In this use case, common sense dictates that explaining 100% of the variation would be impossible. You can go outside and watch a duck take off from water, ascend into the sky, and then descend. An aircraft could potentially strike it at any of those heights along the way!

You decide to iterate on the ML model to see if you can get better predictive results. Based on the features that were identified as top predictors, performing additional analysis using Power BI with the source data, and some trial and error, you can get slightly better results. The following changes were made to the filter criteria for the ML model:

Filter criteria	First ML model	New ML model iteration	Comments
Date	>= 1/1/2010	>= 1/1/2010	Same.
Aircraft Class Code	A	A	Same.
Airport ID	Top 15 Airports	Top 15 Airports	Same.
Height	Not null	Not null and Not 0	Added Not 0 since there are too many possibilities while still on the ground. This limits the pool to flying animals.
Number of Engines		= 2	New filter to limit the data to the most common commercial planes.
Aircraft Mass Code		Not null	New filter criteria to eliminate entries with missing data.
Speed		Not null	Eliminates missing data.

Filter criteria	First ML model	New ML model iteration	Comments
Distance		Not null	Eliminates missing data.
Species		Top 35 animal species; removed "unknown" entries	Allows Species to be a feature.

Figure 10.11 – Changes to filter criteria for the new Predict Height ML model iteration

As per the final row in *Figure 10.7*, adding **Species** as a new feature to the data could be valuable for improving predictive results. Different flying animal species prefer cruising altitudes that can also vary by location and time of year.

To add **Species**, you can add another query to the **ML Queries** dataflow. The relevant M code can be found at `https://github.com/PacktPublishing/Unleashing-Your-Data-with-Power-BI-Machine-Learning-and-OpenAI/tree/main/Chapter-10` and is named `02 Top 40 Species for Height.M`. Paste it in as a new query named **Top 40 Species**.

This query will create a list of the top 40 animals from the filtered data, with species containing "unknown" removed. A new query can then be added for your second iteration of the ML model. Alternatively, you can modify the existing **Predict Height** query. If you replace the existing query, be sure to document all the changes in case you want to step things back to a previous version. If you create a new query for each iteration, be careful that data sprawl doesn't get out of control, with numerous versions of the same query confusing other users. You can join the **Top 40 Species** query to the **Predict Height** query, and then filter for rows that matched one of the Top 40 species. Or, you can copy the `03 Predict Height v2.M` query from GitHub and paste it into the **Predict Height** dataflow. The join is part of that M code.

Your queries in the **ML Queries** dataflow should now look like this:

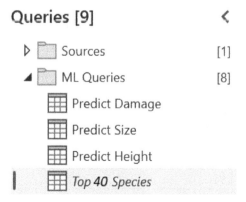

Figure 10.12 – Queries in the ML Queries dataflow

The changes to features that were used to predict height are summarized in the following table:

Features in the Curated FAA Wildlife Strike query	Included in the first iteration of the Predict Height ML model?	Included in the second iteration of the Predict Height ML model?	Notes
Time of Day	Yes		
Airport ID	Yes	Yes	Filtered to Top 15 to avoid cardinality issues
Aircraft Class Code			Filtered to A for both
Aircraft Mass Code	Yes		
Number of Engines	Yes		Filtered to 2 for the second iteration
Phase of Flight	Yes	Yes	
Height			Removed 0 for the second iteration
Speed	Yes	Yes	
Distance	Yes	Yes	
Sky	Yes		
Precipitation	Yes		
Cost of Repairs Adjusted	Yes	Yes	
Ingested Other	Yes		
Indicated Damage	Yes	Yes	
Damage Level	Yes	Yes	
Struck Random	Yes		
Damaged Random	Yes	Yes	
Struck Windshield	Yes	Yes	
Damaged Windshield	Yes		
Struck Nose	Yes		
Damaged Nose	Yes	Yes	
Struck Engine 1	Yes		
Damaged Engine 1	Yes		
Ingested Engine 1	Yes		

Features in the Curated FAA Wildlife Strike query	Included in the first iteration of the Predict Height ML model?	Included in the second iteration of the Predict Height ML model?	Notes
Struck Engine 2	Yes		
Damaged Engine 2	Yes		
Ingested Engine 2	Yes		
Struck Propeller	Yes		
Damaged Propeller	Yes		
Struck Wing or Rotor	Yes	Yes	
Damaged Wing or Rotor	Yes	Yes	
Struck Fuselage	Yes		
Damaged Fuselage	Yes		
Struck Landing Gear	Yes	Yes	
Damaged Landing Gear	Yes		
Struck Tail	Yes		
Damaged Tail	Yes	Yes	
Struck Lights	Yes		
Damaged Lights	Yes		
Struck Other	Yes		
Damaged Other	Yes		
Effect on Flight	Yes	Yes	
Species ID		Yes	Filtered to Top 35 to avoid cardinality issues
Warned	Yes		
Number Seen	Yes		
Number Struck	Yes	Yes	
Size	Yes	Yes	
Number of Engines Struck	Yes		
Percentage of Engines Struck	Yes		
Number of Engines Ingested	Yes		
Percentage of Engines Ingested	Yes		
Number of Engines Damaged	Yes		

Features in the Curated FAA Wildlife Strike query	Included in the first iteration of the Predict Height ML model?	Included in the second iteration of the Predict Height ML model?	Notes
Percentage of Engines Damaged	Yes		
Engine Codes Info Key	Yes		
Month	Yes	Yes	
Total Features	**50**	**20**	
Total Rows	**35,169**	**9,751**	

Figure 10.13 – Features for the first and second iterations of the Predict Height ML model

As with the **Predict Size ML** model, you can either retrain the existing ML model or build a new one. Again, retraining the existing ML model will prevent artifact sprawl in your workspace (especially if you retrain several times). After retraining with the criteria from *Figure 10.11* and *Figure 10.13*, you will get a slightly better AUC for your results – that is, 83% versus 80% for the first attempt:

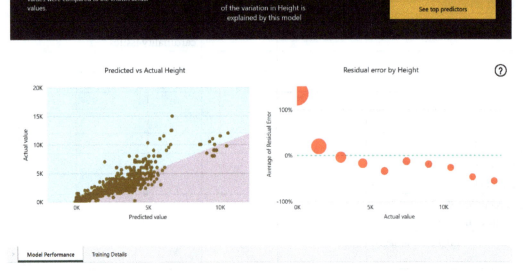

Figure 10.14 – Better AUC at 83% for the second iteration of Predict Height ML

An 83% AUC is good, but can you get it over 90% or even higher? While looking at the **Residual error by Height** chart, click on the largest bubble, which also has the highest residual error, at the top left of the chart:

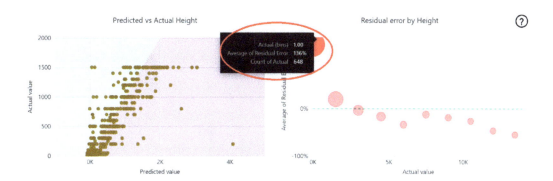

10.15 – High residual error and clustering of reports at 100- and 500-foot increments

As per *Figure 10.15*, there is a 136% residual error at heights between 0 and 2,000 feet. Also, as in *Chapter 9*, notice that reports are still appearing to cluster at 100-foot increments, and even more strongly at 500-foot increments. Have the heights been rounded to 100- or 500-foot increments on the report? Without knowing more about the data collection process, you cannot answer this question.

Upon realizing some improvements you can make when trimming down the features and optimizing the filter criteria for your training and testing data, you have a few good options moving forward:

- If you can engage a data science team, your testing has proven that predicting the height of impact is possible within a range of expectations. A data science team could probably use advanced tools and techniques to improve upon the existing model.

- You can report to your stakeholders that predicting height is a realistic goal, but be sure to describe the residual error at different height ranges.

Now, let's wrap this chapter up.

Summary

In this chapter, you reviewed each of the ML models that you have built. You decided to seek guidance on the next steps for the **Predict Damage ML** model from either a data science team or your stakeholders. For the **Predict Size ML** model, you found only slight predictive value and will need to seek guidance for your next course of action. The **Predict Height ML** model improved when you added new filter criteria and whittled down the feature selection, and the results are promising. At this point, you must either work with a data science team or circle back with your stakeholders for guidance on future plans for the model.

In *Chapter 11*, you will bring in newly added data from the FAA Wildlife Strike database and run it through your **Predict Damage ML** model to test the results. In doing so, you will learn how to score new data with your ML model whenever data refreshes in Power BI. You will also explore opportunities to find new value by adding Microsoft OpenAI capabilities to the solution.

11

Applying Power BI ML Models

In *Chapter 10*, we reviewed the results of training and testing all three of your ML models. Your options for future iterations and plans for your ML models were reviewed and discussed. The Predict Damage ML and Predict Height ML models had promising testing results, while the Predict Size ML model had room for improvement. For all three of your models, the best next steps were to review the results with your stakeholders, and, if possible, meet with your data science team to determine whether more advanced tooling and techniques could improve upon your initial work.

For this chapter, you will apply the ML models that you built to new data from the FAA Wildlife Strike database. The data used up to this point in the book ended on October 16, 2022. The new data for this chapter will be reports that have been added to the publicly available data between that date and March 11, 2023. The purpose of this chapter will be to review the process through which you can bring in new data and automate the process to score it and make predictions with your ML models. At the end, you will review the results of your newly scored data to see whether the results are similar to the ML testing done on the ML models by Power BI.

Technical requirements

As always, make sure you have access to the following:

- The FAA Wildlife Strike data files from either the FAA website or the Packt GitHub site

- A Power BI Pro license

- One of the following Power BI licensing options for access to Power BI dataflows:

  - Power BI Premium

  - Power BI Premium Per User

- One of the following options for getting data into the Power BI cloud service:

  - Microsoft OneDrive (with connectivity to the Power BI cloud service)

  - Microsoft Access + Power BI Gateway

  - Azure Data Lake (with connectivity to the Power BI cloud service)

- Power BI Desktop April 2023 or later (no licenses required)

Bringing the new FAA Wildlife strike data into Power BI

Meetings with project stakeholders and data science teams will determine the best next steps for your Power BI ML models. In the meantime, you can apply these ML models to new data and then compare the predictions to real results. Taking these steps will help you learn how to add your ML models to an automated refresh process in Power BI.

Downloading and configuring the new FAA Wildlife Strike data

As in *Chapter 1*, you should begin by downloading a new copy of the FAA Wildlife Strike data. The copy you've been using to date for this book contained data through October 16, 2022. Now, you'll pull in new data to score with the Power BI ML models that were trained and tested with historical data. The new file contains data through March 1, 2023. You can download a copy of the text file used for this part of the book at the Packt GitHub site here: `https://github.com/PacktPublishing/Unleashing-Your-Data-with-Power-BI-Machine-Learning-and-OpenAI/tree/main/Chapter-11/STRIKE_REPORTS_new.txt`.

In a real-world data project, the most common path of action would be to either update the source file with the newer version of the file or have an automated incremental refresh process data from the source on a schedule. Since we are just using this data to test against your ML models, and since this is a simple workshop, the instructions for this book will pull in the new data as a separate query in a dataflow. As a separate query, the original source data will still exist unchanged in case source-to-target comparisons for the ML models are needed.

Power BI can automate data pulls from many sources, but the source of the FAA Wildlife Strike data is an Access database in a zip file that cannot easily be pulled into Power BI automatically. If you'd like to automate the process of downloading the FAA Wildlife Strike data from the web for your own future use, you'll need to configure a nightly pull using a tool such as Azure Data Factory. Azure Data Factory and other data movement tools are outside the scope of this book, but plenty of online documentation should be able to guide you through the process of a nightly pull that serves up a file for storage in a destination such as Azure Data Lake or Azure SQL Database.

For the example provided in the book, an assumption will be made that the text file from the Packt GitHub site was downloaded and added to OneDrive. If you use another method, you should be able to easily adjust the source of the Power BI dataflow in the proceeding instructions.

Adding new FAA Wildlife Strike data to the Strike Reports dataflow

Once the new file of FAA Wildlife Strike data is in OneDrive, you can add it to the Power BI Cloud service using dataflows. First, open up the dataflow named **Strike Reports** and navigate to the **Edit Tables** screen. Follow these steps to add the new data to the **Raw Data** group:

1. Go to **Get Data** | **Text/CSV**.
2. **Browse OneDrive…** | select the STRIKE_REPORTS_new.txt file.
3. Click **Select** and then click **Next**.
4. Click **Create**.
5. Move the query to the **Raw Data** group.
6. If Changed column type was added to **Applied steps**, remove it.
7. Rename the query Strike Reports New.

    Now, you can add a version of the new strike reports query to the **Curated Queries** group, which will be prepped for use with ML queries.

8. Right-click on **Strike Reports New** and select **Reference**.
9. Move the new file to the **Curated Report Queries** group.
10. Rename the file Strike Reports Curated New.

Next, you replicate the logic of the **Strike Reports Curated** query and also filter the new query so that it only contains new data added to the FAA Wildlife Strike database after 10/16/2022. You can cut and paste M code to do this, or just copy and paste the code for 02 Curated Data - Strike Reports Curated New.M from the Packt GitHub site at this link: https://github.com/PacktPublishing/Unleashing-Your-Data-with-Power-BI-Machine-Learning-and-OpenAI/tree/main/Chapter-11.

Your **Strike Reports** dataflow should now look like this:

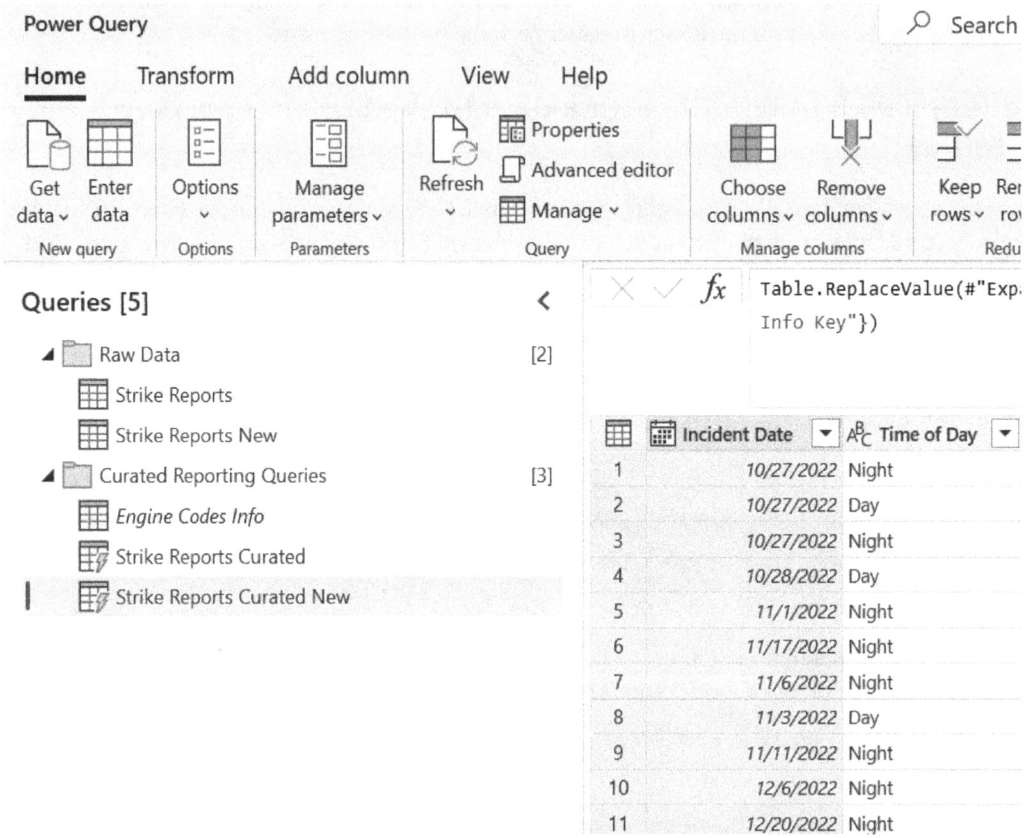

Figure 11.1 – The Strike Reports dataflow with queries for new data added

Once you've added the new queries, go ahead and process the dataflow. Now you are ready to move on to the **ML Queries** dataflow, which will be used to prep the data for Power BI ML. You will apply the same filter and transformation criteria to the new data before running it through the ML models to be scored.

Transforming the new data to prep it for scoring with Power BI ML queries

In order to prep the new FAA Wildlife Strike data to be scored by the three Power BI ML models, start by opening up the **Edit Tables** view for the **ML Queries** dataflow. Once it's open, follow these steps:

1. Select **Get data | Dataflows**, and click **Next**.
2. Select **Strike Reports Curated New**, and click **Create**.

3. Move the new query to the **Sources** group.

4. Right-click **Strike Reports Curated New** and uncheck **Enable load** so that you don't store a duplicate copy of the data.

Now you are ready to create new queries that will be transformed and filtered to meet the criteria of your Power BI ML models!

Your next step is to recreate the logic that was created for each of the three ML models, and then apply that logic to the new FAA Wildlife Strike data. The ML models are trained for specific filter and transformation criteria applied to rows of data through 10/16/2022. You will be applying that same filter and transformation steps to the data that was added to the database after 10/16/2022 so that it can be scored by the ML models.

Rather than walking through the process of cutting and pasting from the existing queries, you can use the M queries from the Packt GitHub repository at this link: `https://github.com/PacktPublishing/Unleashing-Your-Data-with-Power-BI-Machine-Learning-and-OpenAI/tree/main/Chapter-11`. Follow these steps:

1. Create a new group in the **ML Queries** dataflow called **ML Scoring Queries**.

2. Select **Get data | Blank query**.

3. Copy the M code from the Packt GitHub site from the query titled `03 ML Scoring Queries - Predict Damage ML Score.M`.

4. Paste that code into the blank query field and click **Next**.

5. Rename the query `Predict Damage ML Score` and move it to the **ML Scoring Queries** group.

6. Repeat *steps 2-5* for the query from the Packt GitHub site named `04 ML Scoring Queries - Predict Size ML Score.M` and name the query `Predict Size ML Score`.

7. Repeat *steps 2-5* for the query from the Packt GitHub site named `05 ML Scoring Queries - Predict Height ML Score.M` and name the query `Predict Height ML Score`.

8. Click on **Save & close** to save and close your dataflow.

Your **ML Queries** dataflow should now look like this:

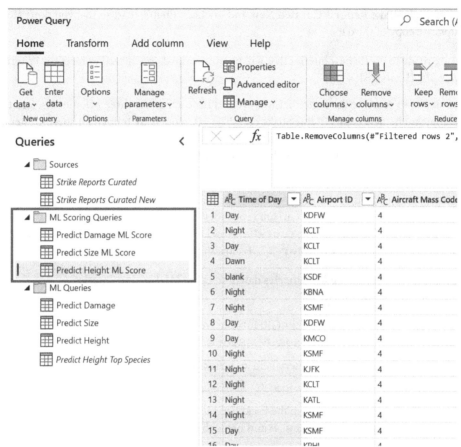

Figure 11.2 – The new group of queries added that will be used
to score the new data with Power BI ML models

Now you have the new FAA Wildlife Strike data ready to go for scoring with Power BI ML models! The new data, which was not used to train or test the original ML models, and which was added to the source database after the original data, has now been prepped for scoring so that you can evaluate the utility of your ML models when used with newly generated data.

Applying Power BI ML models to score new FAA Wildlife Strike data

After 11 chapters of work, you are finally ready to run new data through your Power BI ML models and evaluate the resulting predictions! You will run through the process of applying each ML model to the new data, and then browse the results of the scoring to compare predictions with the real results.

Applying the Predict Damage ML model in Power BI

You will now reference the **Predict Damage ML Score** data from the **ML Queries** dataflow against the **Predict Damage ML** model so that it can be scored. *Figure 11.3* is a quick summary of the data that you have used to train, test, and now apply the **Predict Damage ML Model**:

	Training	Testing	Apply (new)
Rows	10,165	4,326	653
Date Range	>= 1/1/2014 & <= 10/16/2022	>= 1/1/2014 & <= 10/16/2022	> 10/16/2022 & <= 3/1/2023

Figure 11.3 – Details about data used for training, testing, and applying new data to Predict Damage ML

Follow these steps to add the new data to the **Edit Tables** view of the **Predict Damage ML** dataflow:

1. Select **Get data | Dataflows**, and click **Next**.

2. Select **Predict Damage ML Score** from the **ML Queries** dataflow and click **Create**.

3. Click **Save & close**.

4. Refresh the **Predict Damage ML** dataflow.

Now you can apply **Predict Damage ML** model to score the new data. First, navigate to the ML model and click on the icon to apply the model:

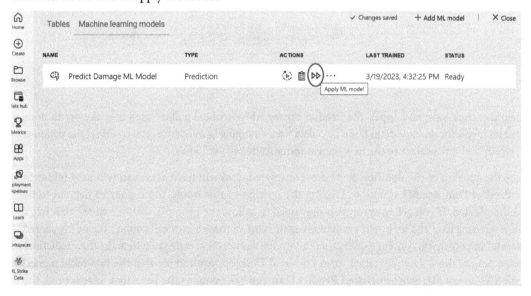

Figure 11.4 – Icon to apply the ML model

Next, select the query for the new data to be scored, and enter the threshold you'd like to use as the cutoff for predicting damage. As you recall from *Chapter 9*, the probability threshold with maximum profit was 0.74, but you can choose any value between **0** and **1**. The following example shows **0.5**:

Apply Predict Damage ML Model   ✕

Apply your model to get predictions

Input table

The model can be applied to these tables, as they have the same attributes as the ones the model was trained on.

Predict Damage ML Score ⌄

New output column name

This column will contain predictions

Predict Damage ML ModelOutput

Threshold

Scores ≥ threshold will be predicted as positive

0.5

[Save]   [Save and apply]   [Cancel]

Figure 11.5 – Choosing the input table and threshold for applying the ML model

When you click **Save and apply**, the **Predict Power BI ML** model will be used to make predictions about incidents for the new data! If the new data were changing at a cadence, you could set the dataflow to refresh and it would score the new data automatically on a schedule.

Once the scoring of the dataflow has been completed, you will have access to two new tables in the **Predict Damage ML** dataflow. During the writing of this book, some queries needed to be reauthenticated. If you get an error, you may need to follow the prompts within a query that has a yellow warning icon and save your credentials again. One of these tables will contain the newly scored data, and the other will contain explanations about the features that were used to make the prediction. Connecting to these dataflow tables from Power BI Desktop, you can see that the first table named **Predict Damage ML Score enriched Predict Damage ML** contains the rows that were scored, the outcome of the prediction based on the probability threshold, the score used to compare with the probability threshold, an explanation about the prediction, and an index column, which is a foreign key for the second table:

```
"Predict Damage O (2) enriched Predict Damage O ML_",{{"Predict Damage O MLOutput.PredictionExplanation", "Predict Damage
```

Predict Damage MLOutput.Outcome	1.2 Predict Damage MLOutput.PredictionScore	Predict Damage MLOut...	1²₃ Predict Damage MLOutput.ExplanationIndex
		"Number Struck","Categorical",17.	
FALSE	42	"Effect on Flight","Categorical",...	3
		"Aircraft Mass Code","Categorical"	
		"Base Probability","ExpectedValue	
		"Phase of Flight","Categorical",9.4;	
		"Struck Windshield","Categorical",	
TRUE	51	"Aircraft Mass Code","Categoric...	4
		"Base Probability","ExpectedValue	
		"Number of Engines","Categorical"	
		"Struck Windshield","Categorical",	
		"Phase of Flight","Categorical",4.7!	
FALSE	22	"Size","Categorical",54.6878509...	5

Figure 11.6 – Table of scored new data with predictions and explanations added

The second table is named **Predict Damage ML Score enriched Predict Damage ML explanations** and contains a separate row for each feature that was used to make the prediction. During the writing process of this book, an occasional bug would show up in the Power BI Service resulting in this table showing as blank within the dataflow. If you encounter this bug, connecting to this table using Power BI Desktop will allow you to see the data. The **Contribution** field is added up to calculate the prediction score value for the first table, which is compared to the probability threshold. Negative scores reduce the resulting score, and positive scores increase the score:

```
amage O ML explanations_",{{"Predict Damage O MLOutput.ExplanationIndex",
```

ᴬᴮC Type	1.2 Contribution	ᴬᴮC Value
Categorical	54.68785093	
ExpectedValueType	51.78815991	
Categorical	16.88266296	
Categorical	9.28471924	
Categorical	9.02325503	
Numeric	7.905516919	
Categorical	4.92984778	
Categorical	0.504534367	
Categorical	0.156815001	
Numeric	-0.037589651	

Figure 11.7 – Table of features explaining the predictions for each scored row

In the **Power BI Desktop Model** view, you can see that the tables have a one-to-many relationship:

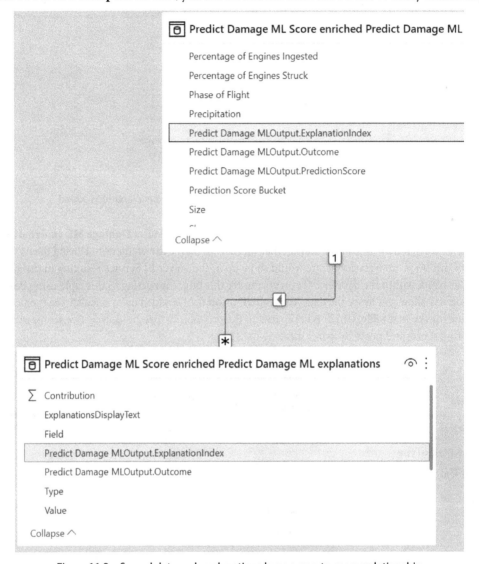

Figure 11.8 – Scored data and explanations have a one-to-many relationship

You can create an interactive report using Power BI to explore the results of the ML model scoring new data. First, you review the explanations of the different features for a single row of scored data. To clarify, the following screenshot is for a single event, indicated by an index of 7, which was given a prediction score of **18.00** and registers as predicting **No Damage** since the prediction score of 18 is less than the probability threshold of 50. You can see that the prediction score of 18 is the result of adding up all of the **Contribution** values in the table (bottom right) and waterfall chart (bottom left):

Figure 11.9 – Left half – Contribution of features used to predict damage for a single wildlife strike incident

This screenshot has been split into two figures to make sure you can read it.

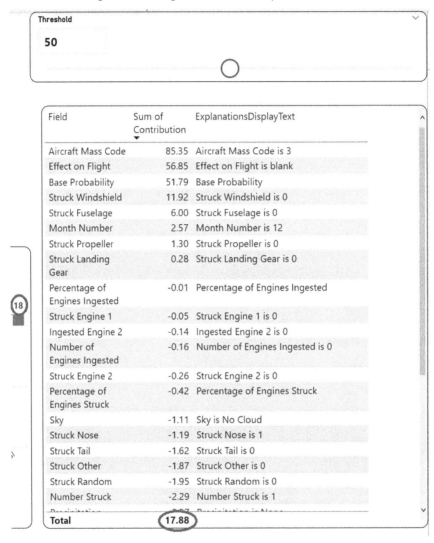

Field	Sum of Contribution	ExplanationsDisplayText
Aircraft Mass Code	85.35	Aircraft Mass Code is 3
Effect on Flight	56.85	Effect on Flight is blank
Base Probability	51.79	Base Probability
Struck Windshield	11.92	Struck Windshield is 0
Struck Fuselage	6.00	Struck Fuselage is 0
Month Number	2.57	Month Number is 12
Struck Propeller	1.30	Struck Propeller is 0
Struck Landing Gear	0.28	Struck Landing Gear is 0
Percentage of Engines Ingested	-0.01	Percentage of Engines Ingested
Struck Engine 1	-0.05	Struck Engine 1 is 0
Ingested Engine 2	-0.14	Ingested Engine 2 is 0
Number of Engines Ingested	-0.16	Number of Engines Ingested is 0
Struck Engine 2	-0.26	Struck Engine 2 is 0
Percentage of Engines Struck	-0.42	Percentage of Engines Struck
Sky	-1.11	Sky is No Cloud
Struck Nose	-1.19	Struck Nose is 1
Struck Tail	-1.62	Struck Tail is 0
Struck Other	-1.87	Struck Other is 0
Struck Random	-1.95	Struck Random is 0
Number Struck	-2.29	Number Struck is 1
Total	17.88	

Figure 11.10 – Right half – contribution of features used to predict damage for a single wildlife strike incident

In the waterfall chart split into *Figure 11.9* and *Figure 11.10*, you can zoom in to see that the features on the left contributed to keeping the Prediction Score low while the features on the right increased the result:

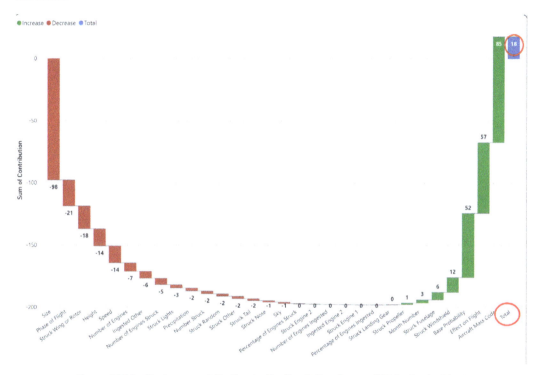

Figure 11.11 – Features contributing to the Prediction Score of 18 for the incident

Switching to another incident given an **Index** value of **2**, you'll see that the prediction was a false positive because it predicted damage when none was reported. The features that were weighted strongly within the prediction score of 85 can be sorted to the top of the table. This type of analysis can help you identify features or combinations of features that might contribute to inaccurate predictions or features that have little impact on the prediction. For example, looking at the explanations, you can see that having hit 2-10 large animals contributed to the high prediction score:

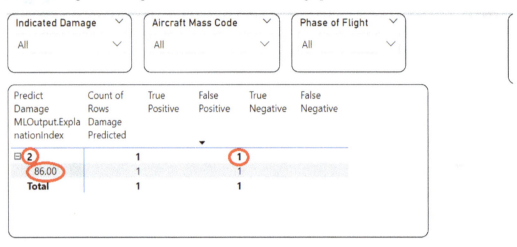

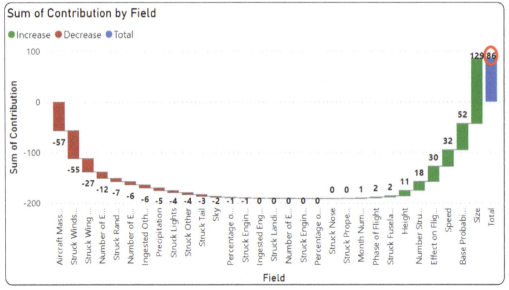

Figure 11.12 – Left half – the incident was predicted to have damage when it did not

Figure 11.12 and *Figure 11.13* each show half of the screen, to make it easier to read.

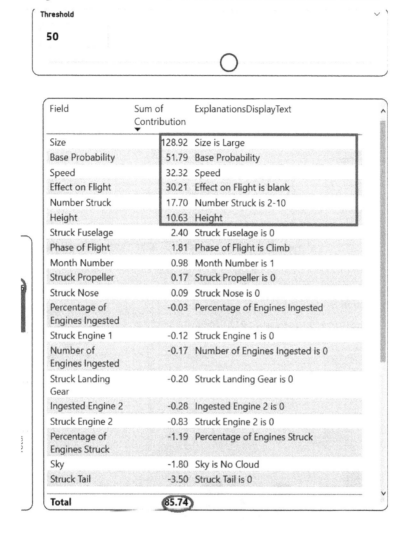

Field	Sum of Contribution	ExplanationsDisplayText
Size	128.92	Size is Large
Base Probability	51.79	Base Probability
Speed	32.32	Speed
Effect on Flight	30.21	Effect on Flight is blank
Number Struck	17.70	Number Struck is 2-10
Height	10.63	Height
Struck Fuselage	2.40	Struck Fuselage is 0
Phase of Flight	1.81	Phase of Flight is Climb
Month Number	0.98	Month Number is 1
Struck Propeller	0.17	Struck Propeller is 0
Struck Nose	0.09	Struck Nose is 0
Percentage of Engines Ingested	-0.03	Percentage of Engines Ingested
Struck Engine 1	-0.12	Struck Engine 1 is 0
Number of Engines Ingested	-0.17	Number of Engines Ingested is 0
Struck Landing Gear	-0.20	Struck Landing Gear is 0
Ingested Engine 2	-0.28	Ingested Engine 2 is 0
Struck Engine 2	-0.83	Struck Engine 2 is 0
Percentage of Engines Struck	-1.19	Percentage of Engines Struck
Sky	-1.80	Sky is No Cloud
Struck Tail	-3.50	Struck Tail is 0
Total	85.74	

Figure 11.13 – Right half – the incident was predicted to have damage when it did not

Using these tables in Power BI, you can also aggregate the results to understand differences at scale. For example, in the following report, you can see the **Precision %** and **Accuracy** metrics broken down by **Size**, with an adjustable probability threshold, distribution buckets for prediction scores, and aggregate values for the feature explanations:

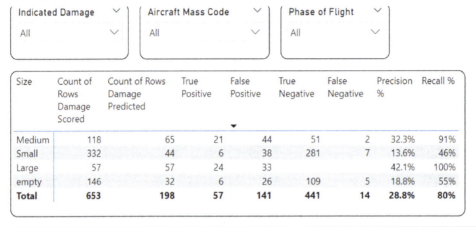

Size	Count of Rows Damage Scored	Count of Rows Damage Predicted	True Positive	False Positive	True Negative	False Negative	Precision %	Recall %
Medium	118	65	21	44	51	2	32.3%	91%
Small	332	44	6	38	281	7	13.6%	46%
Large	57	57	24	33			42.1%	100%
empty	146	32	6	26	109	5	18.8%	55%
Total	**653**	**198**	**57**	**141**	**441**	**14**	**28.8%**	**80%**

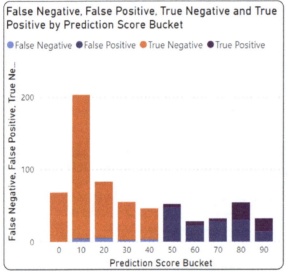

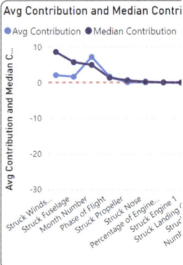

Figure 11.14 – Left half – aggregate scoring results for the new rows of data

The other half of the screen is shown in *Figure 11.15*.

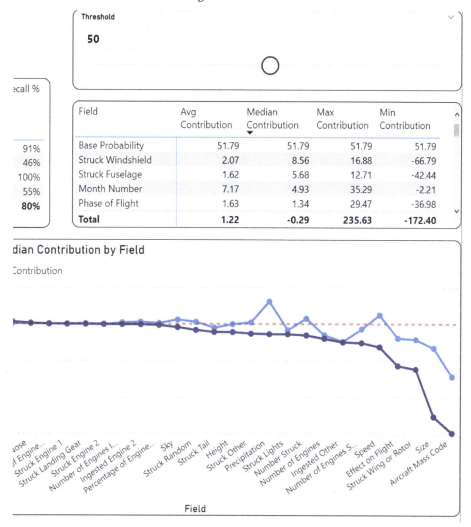

Figure 11.15 – Right half – aggregate scoring results for the new rows of data

Clicking on **Small** under **Size** to filter the whole page, you can see that from an average and median perspective, **Size** being **Small** strongly contributes to lower prediction scores:

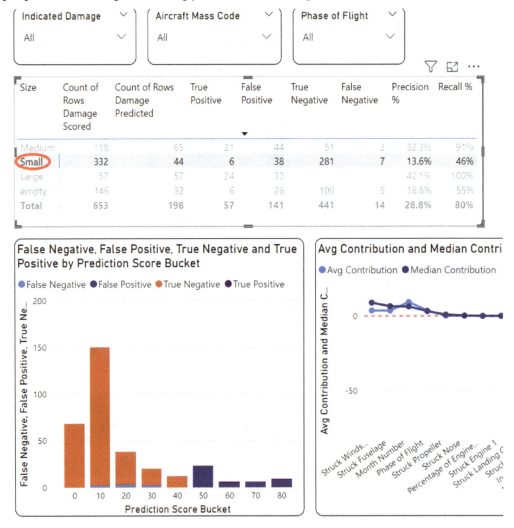

Size	Count of Rows Damage Scored	Count of Rows Damage Predicted	True Positive	False Positive	True Negative	False Negative	Precision %	Recall %
Medium	118	65	21	44	51	2	32.3%	91%
Small	332	44	6	38	281	7	13.6%	46%
Large	57	57	24	33			42.1%	100%
empty	146	32	6	26	109	5	18.8%	55%
Total	653	198	57	141	441	14	28.8%	80%

Figure 11.16 – Left half – report filtered with Size set to Small

Figure 11.17 shows the other half of the screen.

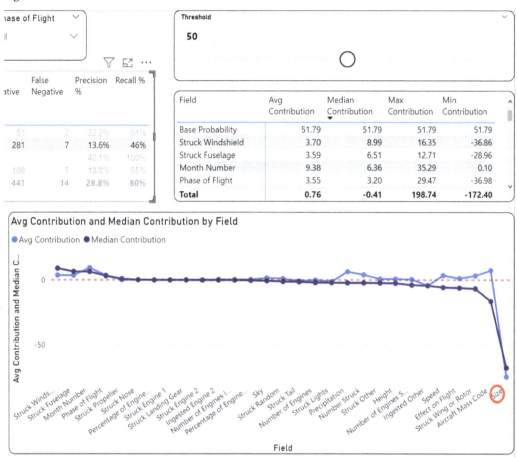

Figure 11.17 – Right half – Report filtered for Size of Small

You can compare some of the metrics to the values from the Model Performance Report that was reviewed in *Chapter 9*. Remember, *Recall* is the percentage of incidents with damage that are likely to be predicted as having damage, and *Precision* is the number of records predicted to have damage that actually have damage:

	Testing	New data scoring
Recall at Probability Threshold .5	88%	80%
Precision at Probability Threshold .5	30%	29%
Recall at Probability Threshold .74	67%	59%
Precision at Probability Threshold .74	49%	49%

Figure 11.18 – New data Recall and Precision compared to original testing results

The results for the new data appear to be somewhat consistent with the testing, but now you can dive into the data and judge for yourself! You are now ready to move on to the **Predict Size ML** model to test it on new data.

Applying the Predict Size ML model in Power BI

Applying the new data to the **Predict Size ML** model will be a repetitive task compared to what was just done for **Predict Damage ML**. As you recall from *Chapter 10*, the **Predict Size ML** model did not get very good results during testing, with a 61% AUC. The ML model probably needs either re-evaluation by a data science team or significant work to improve the AUC. Scoring new data against the model can still be a valuable exercise to help identify areas for improvement.

In order to minimize repetition, here's a summary of the steps to add new data and apply the ML model. Follow these steps to add the new data to the **Edit Tables** view of the **Predict Size ML** dataflow:

1. Select **Get data | Dataflows**, and click **Next**.
2. Select **Predict Size ML Score** from the **ML Queries** dataflow and click **Create**.
3. Click **Save & close**.
4. Refresh the **Predict Size ML** dataflow.
5. Navigate to the screen for **Predict Size ML Model**, and click **Apply ML model**.
6. Choose the **Predict Size ML Score** input table and click **Save & apply**.

Once the scoring is complete, you can pull tables of both the scored data and the related feature contributions into Power BI Desktop to review the results. You build a similar report for the **Size** predictions as you did for **Damage** predictions:

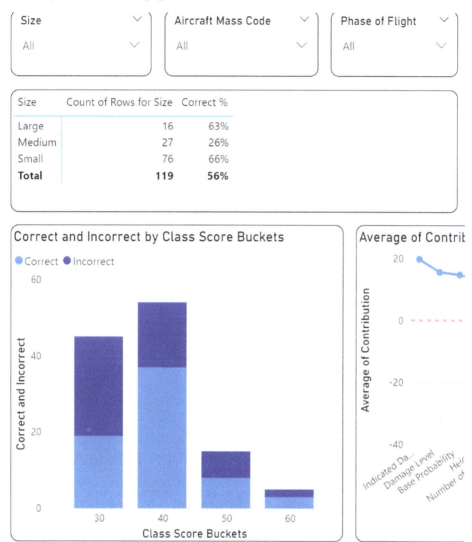

Size	Count of Rows for Size	Correct %
Large	16	63%
Medium	27	26%
Small	76	66%
Total	**119**	**56%**

Figure 11.19 – Left half – evaluation of the Predict Size ML scoring of new data

For ease of viewing, *Figure 11.19* shows the left half of the screen, while *Figure 11.20* shows the right side.

Field	Average of Contribution	Median of Contribution	Max of Contribution	Min of Contribution
Indicated Damage	19.64	29.83	150.85	-58.02
Damage Level	15.44	19.89	48.72	-33.93
Base Probability	14.61	14.35	15.06	14.05
Speed	5.75	10.47	77.04	-93.53
Height	12.81	10.41	143.24	-146.58
Effect on Flight	4.23	8.74	53.91	-121.97
Number of Engines	5.97	5.14	99.84	-20.26
Aircraft Mass Code	1.92	3.27	124.47	-26.61
Struck Wing or Rotor	1.48	2.83	68.84	-82.06
Struck Windshield	2.03	2.39	27.90	-89.44
Cost of Repairs Adjusted	-0.93	2.33	13.35	-85.20
Struck Nose	2.00	1.74	44.21	-110.18
Total	**1.71**	**1.04**	**150.85**	**-284.11**

Figure 11.20 – Right half – evaluation of the Predict Size ML scoring of new data

As with the original testing of this ML model, the results were barely better than random guessing. Only 119 rows of data met the criteria for the testing, which likely adds to the lackluster results. You can compare the results that were correctly classified to the original testing outcomes:

Size	Testing	New data scoring
Small	70%	66%
Medium	36%	26%
Large	61%	63%

Figure 11.21 – Comparing original test results versus newly scored data for Predict Size ML

While the new results are still not good, they do appear to be in the same range as the original test results. You can now move on to scoring new data for your final ML model, **Predict Height ML**!

Applying the Predict Height ML model in Power BI

As you did with the **Predict Size ML** model scoring of new data, you can follow similar steps starting in the **Edit Tables** view of the **Predict Height ML** dataflow to score the new data:

1. Select **Get data** | **Dataflows**, and click **Next**.
2. Select **Predict Height ML Score** from the **ML Queries** dataflow and click **Create**.
3. Click **Save & close**.
4. Refresh the **Predict Height ML** dataflow.
5. Navigate to the screen for **Predict Height ML** model, and click **Apply ML model**.
6. Choose the **Predict Height ML Score** input table and click **Save & apply**.

As with the previous two ML models, you can pull tables of both the scored data and the related feature contributions into Power BI Desktop to review the results. With a regression ML model, you aren't predicting yes/no or categorical values, but rather numeric values that can be compared to the actuals. With a regression, there isn't necessarily a right or wrong answer, but instead, you can compare how close the predicted numbers compare to reality. For example, you can predict that a plane struck a bird at 2,000 feet above the ground, but is that a good prediction if it actually happened at 2,052 feet? The answer to that question in the real world depends on the requirements of the stakeholders and end users!

The following figure illustrates the predicted height, actual height, and contribution information for features for the new data scored with the **Predict Height ML** model:

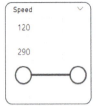

Incident Index	Height	Predicted Height	Residual	Residual % of Height
128	13000	11,263.14	-1,736.86	-13%
64	12500	6,274.13	-6,225.87	-50%
114	11000	9,683.38	-1,316.62	-12%
Total		**2,073.20**		**-6%**

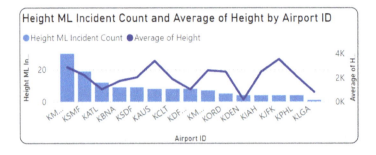

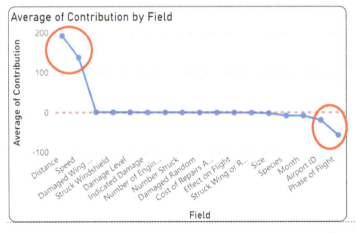

Figure 11.22 – Left half – comparing the predicted height to the actual height

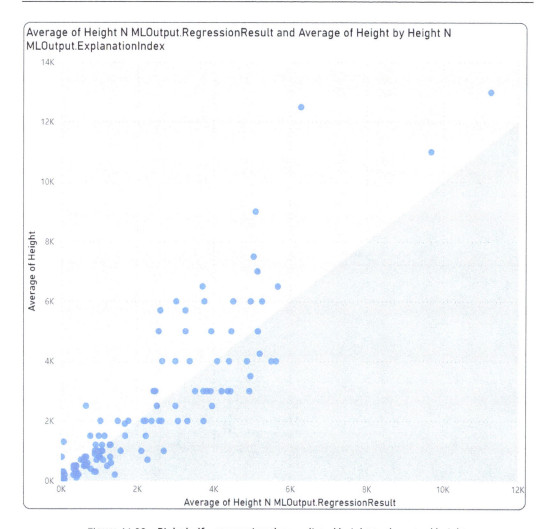

Figure 11.23 – Right half – comparing the predicted height to the actual height

As mentioned previously in the book, the actual **Height** values tend to land on round numbers in the hundreds or thousands. For example, 8 reports in the new data illustrated here were recorded to be at 4,000 feet. Is this due to rounding by the report filer? Is it due to standard heights for aircraft that are near an airport? Are there other reasons? Without additional information, it is impossible to know the reason. On the **Average of Contribution by Field** chart in the bottom left of the page, you notice that at both the aggregate level and filtered level, the **Distance**, **Speed**, **Airport ID**, and **Phase of Flight** features tend to have the greatest contribution.

Expanding the table in *Figure 11.24* that lists each individual incident, you can see the **Residual** value of the predicted height versus the actual height:

< Back to report

Incident Index	Height	Predicted Height	Residual	Residual % of Height
128	13000	11,263.14	-1,736.86	-13%
64	12500	6,274.13	-6,225.87	-50%
114	11000	9,683.38	-1,316.62	-12%
66	9000	5,093.35	-3,906.65	-43%
71	7500	5,039.52	-2,460.48	-33%
80	7000	5,141.27	-1,858.73	-27%
21	6500	3,710.49	-2,789.51	-43%
123	6500	5,675.46	-824.54	-13%
24	6000	3,024.83	-2,975.17	-50%
28	6000	3,757.06	-2,242.94	-37%
31	6000	5,263.42	-736.58	-12%
48	6000	4,964.49	-1,035.51	-17%
60	6000	4,511.99	-1,488.01	-25%
54	5700	3,267.31	-2,432.69	-43%
55	5700	2,607.87	-3,092.13	-54%
50	5000	2,562.04	-2,437.96	-49%
51	5000	3,934.82	-1,065.18	-21%
73	5000	5,152.84	152.84	3%
76	5000	4,464.88	-535.12	-11%
130	5000	3,269.93	-1,730.07	-35%
105	4250	5,198.89	948.89	22%
5	4000	2,656.44	-1,343.56	-34%
32	4000	3,378.20	-621.80	-16%
52	4000	5,628.21	1,628.21	41%
65	4000	5,504.60	1,504.60	38%
75	4000	3,005.51	-994.49	-25%
95	4000	4,088.59	88.59	2%
97	4000	4,867.52	867.52	22%

Figure 11.24 – The individual event's predicted height, actual height, and residual value

In *Figure 11.24*, notice that the range of accuracy for the predictions shifts considerably between incidents. There are probably many different factors contributing to the inaccuracies. Can the predictions be better? Or is there natural variability in the data due to the nature of the incidents and the process for recording data about the incidents? Conversations with the project stakeholders, people in charge of recording the data, and data science experts can help you learn more about this particular use case.

You've reached a point in your project where you have designed your ML models in Power BI, trained them, tested them, and then applied them to new data in a way that could work with an automated process in Power BI.

Summary

In this chapter, you brought new FAA Wildlife Strike data into Power BI and transformed the data to match the design of your original architecture. You then transformed the data to meet the filtering and transformation requirements of the data used to train and test your **Predict Damage ML**, **Predict Size ML**, and **Predict Height ML** models. Then, you made predictions for the new data by applying the trained Power BI ML models. Finally, you reviewed the results of the predictions and compared them to the actual results.

Chapter 12 will add a special twist to your project! For those of you out in the real world, changing scope and expectations is a frequent occurrence with data projects. When this book was being written, **OpenAI** and **Microsoft OpenAI** were fast becoming media sensations. Your stakeholders have asked you to find some use cases for OpenAI in your project. It's a scope change to your project, but it will be an exciting adventure! *Chapter 12* will review the OpenAI and Microsoft OpenAI offerings, as they can be applied to this project for added value.

Part 4: Integrating OpenAI with Power BI

In the final part of the book, you will see how you can make use of Open AI and Azure OpenAI to enhance your BI work. In the final chapter, you will look at some of the key ideas and lessons covered in the book, and think about how you can use them in your own work.

The following three chapters make up *Part 4*:

- *Chapter 12, Use Cases for OpenAI*
- *Chapter 13, Using OpenAI and Azure OpenAI in Power BI Dataflows*
- *Chapter 14, Project Review and Looking Forward*

12

Use Cases for OpenAI

In the previous chapter, you scored fresh data via the Power BI ML models and assessed the output in comparison to the automated testing performed by Power BI during the training phase. The FAA Wildlife Strike database provided fresh data that was generated in the real world beyond the scope of the training and testing datasets. This data could potentially serve as a framework for scheduling the scoring of new data utilizing a Power BI ML model in collaboration with dataflows. The recently evaluated data produced outcomes that were relatively consistent with the expected results derived from the testing data.

In this chapter, you are tasked by your stakeholders to incorporate OpenAI functionalities into the solution. OpenAI is garnering a lot of attention in the IT sector, and this project is being implemented during this trend. Although this entails a change in scope, the project's beneficiaries are fully supportive of and optimistic about this initiative. In this chapter, you will examine several use cases for OpenAI with your project, followed by a review of the prerequisites necessary to commence.

Technical requirements

The requirements are slightly different for this chapter:

- An account with the original open source OpenAI: `https://openai.com/`.

- Optional – Azure OpenAI in your Azure subscription: `https://azure.microsoft.com/en-us/products/cognitive-services/openai-service`. The book is written so that this is optional since it is not available to everyone at the time of publication.

- FAA Wildlife Strike data files from either the FAA website or the Packt GitHub site.

- A Power BI Pro license.

- One of the following Power BI licensing options for access to Power BI dataflows:

  - Power BI Premium

  - Power BI Premium Per User

- One of the following options for getting data into the Power BI cloud service:

  - Microsoft OneDrive (with connectivity to the Power BI cloud service)

  - Microsoft Access + Power BI Gateway

  - Azure Data Lake (with connectivity to the Power BI cloud service)

Brief overview and reference links for OpenAI and Azure OpenAI

In the latter part of 2022, the global media and information technology enthusiasts were captivated by the potential of **ChatGPT**. ChatGPT is a vast **large language model** (**LLM**) chatbot that facilitates natural language communication, code generation, and other functionalities, and was developed by OpenAI.

> **OpenAI**
>
> OpenAI is an AI research organization, and interested readers may find more information about it at this link: `https://openai.com/about`.

The renowned ChatGPT is constructed utilizing **generative pre-training** (**GPT**) models, and OpenAI also produces other types of AI models such as **DALL-E** for image generation. This book abstains from delving into OpenAI's intricate details, as there is already a plethora of information available on the internet.

The OpenAI platform is constructed upon Microsoft's Azure cloud infrastructure, which provides a powerful and reliable foundation for the platform's diverse range of services. In order to leverage the robust security, governance, and enterprise integration capabilities of the Azure platform, Microsoft offers Azure OpenAI to seamlessly access the models and features of OpenAI, while simultaneously benefiting from the capabilities of the Azure platform.

> **Azure OpenAI**
>
> To gain a deeper understanding of the many advantages of Microsoft Azure OpenAI, please visit the following link: `https://azure.microsoft.com/en-us/products/cognitive-services/openai-service`.

These next two chapters will home in on the analysis of FAA Wildlife Strike data using OpenAI technology. Building on the previous chapters, we will explore a range of simple use cases for OpenAI and Azure OpenAI, both of which are rapidly evolving within the information technology industry. Specifically, we will concentrate on basic summarization and description techniques utilizing GPT models. While code snippets for both OpenAI and Azure OpenAI will be provided, the accompanying screenshots will exclusively feature traditional OpenAI examples, as Azure OpenAI is currently unavailable for use in this publication.

As an active participant in the technical field, it is important to constantly evaluate and improve written content. In this chapter, readers may have already noticed a change in the writing style that can be attributed to the use of OpenAI ChatGPT. While the author remains the same, the assistance of ChatGPT has significantly enhanced the clarity and readability of the text. In fact, the very paragraph that you are currently reading has been optimized using ChatGPT based on the modifications shown in the accompanying screenshot. As we continue to incorporate advanced technology into our writing processes, it is essential to understand its potential benefits and limitations in order to fully leverage its capabilities.

 Rewrite the following text to sound like a technical book in the information technology industry: "Question for the reader: Does the content so far in this chapter feel like it was written by a different author? Well, the author is the same but OpenAI ChatGPT was used to improve upon the original text. For the paragraph that you are reading right now, the original content was modified in ChatGPT per the following screenshot:"

 As an active participant in the technical field, it is important to constantly evaluate and improve upon written content. In this chapter, readers may have noticed a change in the writing style that can be attributed to the use of OpenAI ChatGPT. While the author remains the same, the assistance of ChatGPT has significantly enhanced the clarity and readability of the text. In fact, the very paragraph that you are currently reading has been optimized using ChatGPT based on the modifications shown in the accompanying screenshot. As we continue to incorporate advanced technology into our writing processes, it is essential to understand the potential benefits and limitations in order to fully leverage its capabilities.

Figure 12.1 – Paragraph for this book rewritten using OpenAI ChatGPT

Let's embark on a journey with OpenAI as we explore techniques for analyzing FAA Wildlife Strike data within Power BI solutions!

Generating descriptions with OpenAI

Our first step will be to identify a suitable use case for leveraging the power of GPT models to generate descriptions of elements of FAA Wildlife Strike data. Our objective is to unlock the potential of external data by creating prompts for GPT models that can provide detailed information and insights about the data we are working with. Through this use case, we will explore the value that GPT models can bring to the table when it comes to data analysis and interpretation.

For example, a description of the FAA Wildlife Strike database by ChatGPT might look like this:

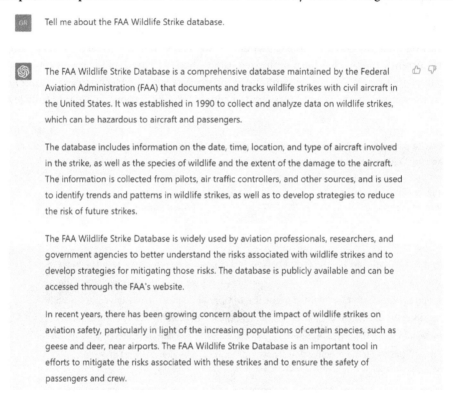

Figure 12.2 – OpenAI ChatGPT description of FAA Wildlife Strike database

Within your solution using the FAA Wildlife Strike database, you have data that could be tied to external data using the GPT models. A few examples include additional information about the following:

- Airports
- FAA regions
- Flight operators

- Aircraft
- Aircraft engines
- Animal species
- Time of year

When the scoring process for a large number of separate rows in a dataset is automated, we can use a GPT model to generate descriptive text for each individual row. It is worth noting that ChatGPT's approach varies from this, as it operates as a chatbot that calls upon different GPT models and integrates past conversations into future answers. Despite the differences in how GPT models will be used in the solution, ChatGPT can still serve as a valuable tool for testing various use cases.

When using GPT models, the natural language prompts that are used to ask questions and give instructions will impact the context of the generated text. Prompt engineering is a topic that has surged in popularity for OpenAI and LLMs. The following prompts will provide different answers when using "dogs" as a topic for a GPT query:

- `Tell me about dogs`
- `From the perspective of an evolutionary biologist, tell me about dogs`
- `Tell me the history of dogs`
- `At a third-grade level, tell me about dogs`

When planning for your use of OpenAI on large volumes of data, you should test and evaluate your prompt engineering strategy. For this book, the use cases will be kept simple as the goal is to teach tool integration with Power BI. Prompt engineering expertise will probably be the topic of many books and blogs this year.

You can test different requests for a description of an FAA region in the data:

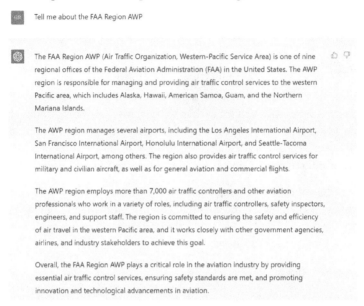

Figure 12.3 – Testing the utility of describing an FAA region using OpenAI ChatGPT

You can also combine different data elements for a more detailed description. The following example combines data fields with a question to ask (Tell me about the Species in State in Month):

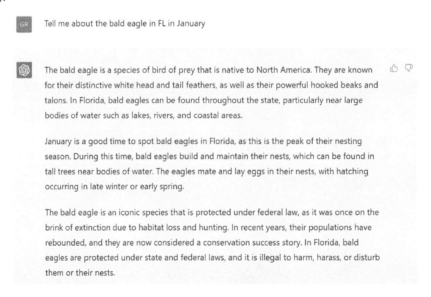

Figure 12.4 – Using ChatGPT to test a combination of data about species, state, and month

There are many different options to consider. In order to both combine a few fields of data, and provide useful context about the data, you decide to plan a use case for describing the aircraft and operator. An example can be tested in OpenAI ChatGPT with a formula such as the following: `Tell me about the airplane model Aircraft operated by Operator in three sentences` Here is an example using data from a single row of the FAA Wildlife Strike database:

Tell me about the airplane model B-737-700 operated by SOUTHWEST AIRLINES in three sentences

The B-737-700 is a narrow-body, short to medium-range airplane model that can carry up to 140 passengers. Southwest Airlines operates one of the largest fleets of B-737-700s in the world, with over 500 aircraft in operation. Known for its fuel efficiency, range, and advanced avionics, the B-737-700 is a highly capable aircraft that has contributed significantly to the success of Southwest Airlines.

Figure 12.5 – Information about an airplane in the fleet of an operator as described by OpenAI ChatGPT

From a prompt engineering perspective, asking this question for multiple reports in the FAA Wildlife Strike database would require running the following natural language query on each row of data (column names are depicted inside brackets):

```
Tell me about the airplane model [Aircraft] operated by [Operator] in
three sentences:
```

In the next chapter, you will use this prompt for reports in the FAA Wildlife Strike database in which the **Aircraft** and **Operator** fields are populated. After selecting a use case for augmenting your solution with additional information via OpenAI, it is recommended that you obtain approval from stakeholders to verify the practicality of the use case. Once approved, you can proceed with exploring new use cases that involve utilizing OpenAI to generate summaries of data derived from FAA Wildlife Strike data within your solution.

Summarizing data with OpenAI

You can also use OpenAI GPT models to summarize data. Numerous databases feature free text fields that comprise entries from a diverse array of sources, including survey results, physician notes, feedback forms, and comments regarding incident reports for the FAA Wildlife Strike database that we have used in this book. These text entry fields represent a wide range of content, from structured data to unstructured data, making it challenging to extract meaning from them without the assistance of sophisticated natural language processing tools.

The **Remarks** field of the FAA Wildlife Strike database contains text that was presumably entered by people involved in filling out incident forms about aircraft striking wildlife. A few examples of the remarks for recent entries are shown in Power BI in the following screenshot:

	Remarks
22	eReport ID: RBIRD10-23Description: At approximately 100 kts on the take off roll on runway 08L, we saw a large
23	eReport ID: RBIRD11-23Description: During the takeoff roll, around 130 knots, bird strike on upper fuselage , jus⟩
24	unknown aircraft reported FOD or a strike. Runway closed and one bird recovered from 35L north of EL. No pire⟩
25	Conditional inspection performed at destination. No damage foundModel737-8H4, Engine ManufacturerCFM IN
26	Model: A321-271N. Engine Manufacturer: IAE. Engine Model: PW1133G-JM.
27	No damage found. Model: A321-231. Engine Manufacturer: IAE. Engine Model: V2533-A5. 1 PHOTO.
28	eReport ID: RBIRD6-23Description: I flew an LPV approach to the GPS RNAV Runway 35 at Lubbock International
29	eReport ID: RBIRD1-23Description: During arrival into GYY I thought I caught a glimpse of something going by t⟩
30	eReport ID: RBIRD12-23Description: On landing rollout, at approximately 60 knots, a bird strike was encountered⟩
31	Description: After rotation at approximately 400 feet agl, bird strike to captains side front windshield. No abnorm⟩
32	No effect on flight. Continued to landing and could only see a mark on the windshield. Maintenance is addressin⟩
33	Model737-8H4, Engine ManufacturerCFM INTLClassificationStandardEngine ModelCFM56-7B27E
34	eReport ID: RBIRD16-23Description: On departure at approximately 100 to 150 ft we saw a large bird coming to
35	MULTIPLE SPECIES. 1 noticeable strike on captain wing; 2 birds found on perimeter road of 22L approach path. 1
36	RPA5710 (N212JQ) reported bird strike on final after landing RWY 28R at CMH. Pilots reported seeing 3 birds on
37	Pilot reported possible strike to tower upon landing runway 32. Ops inspected the runway and found remains of
38	

Figure 12.6 – Examples of remarks from the FAA Wildlife Strike database

You will notice that the remarks have a great deal of variability in the format of the content, the length of the content, and the acronyms that were used. Testing one of the entries by simply adding a statement at the beginning to `Summarize the following:` yields the following result:

Summarize the following: eReport ID: RBIRD10-23Description: At approximately 100 kts on the take off roll on runway 08L, we saw a large bird (appeared to be a large owl) cross our windshield from left to right. Bird most likely struck the right wing or was ingested into the right engine. We experienced no adverse engine indications or smells. Aircraft flew and performed normally. We advised CDG departure about the probable strike and discussed the event with maintenance personnel upon arrival in Cologne. DATABASE NOTE: ASSUME WING STRUCK, ASSUME NO DAMAGE

 The report, identified by eReport ID RBIRD10-23, recounts an incident in which a large bird, possibly an owl, was observed crossing the windshield during takeoff at approximately 100 kts on runway 08L. It is suspected that the bird collided with the right wing or engine, though no adverse indications or smells were experienced, and the aircraft operated normally. The incident was reported to CDG departure and discussed with maintenance personnel upon arrival in Cologne, with the database assuming that the wing was struck and no damage was sustained.

Figure 12.7 – Summarization of the remarks for a single incident using ChatGPT

Summarizing data for a less detailed **Remarks** field yields the following result:

 Summarize the following: Model737-8H4, Engine ManufacturerCFM INTLClassificationStandardEngine ModelCFM56-7B27E

 This is information about the engine and model classification for a Boeing 737-8H4 aircraft. The engine is manufactured by CFM International and the engine model is CFM56-7B27E.

Figure 12.8 – Summarization of a sparsely populated results field

In order to obtain uniform summaries from the FAA Wildlife Strike data's **Remarks** field, one must consider entries that vary in robustness, sparsity, completeness of sentences, and the presence of acronyms and quick notes. The workshop accompanying this technical book is your chance to experiment with various data fields and explore diverse outcomes. Both the book and the Packt GitHub site will utilize a standardized format as input to a GPT model that can incorporate event data and produce a consistent summary for each row. An example of the format is as follows:

```
Summarize the following in three sentences: A [Operator] [Aircraft]
struck a [Species]. Remarks on the FAA report were: [Remarks].
```

Using data from an FAA Wildlife Strike database event to test this approach in OpenAI ChatGPT is shown in the following screenshot:

 Summarize the following in three sentences: A SOUTHWEST AIRLINES B-737-7 struck a Turkey vulture. Remarks on the FAA report were: Model737-7H4, Engine ManufacturerCFM INTL.ClassificationStandardEngine ModelCFM56 SERIESJust under CA windshieldContinued to destination (BNA)

 During flight, a Southwest Airlines Boeing 737-7 aircraft collided with a turkey vulture near the captain's windshield. The aircraft was able to continue its journey to its destination at BNA airport. The incident was reported to the FAA and documented in their report, which includes information on the aircraft model, engine manufacturer, and classification.

Figure 12.9 – OpenAI ChatGPT testing a summarization of the Remarks field

Next, you test another scenario that had more robust text in the **Remarks** field:

 Summarize the following in three sentences: A UPS AIRLINES B-747-8 SERIES struck a Unknown bird - medium. Remarks on the FAA report were: eReport ID: RBIRD2-23Description: Shortly after takeoff at approximately 2000 ft we experienced a bird strike to the radome. All aircraft indications were normal. We continued to clean up and climbed to altitude. After top of climb all indications were still normal. We sent an ACARS to maintenance and dispatch informing them of the bird strike and that we were continuing to SDF. We also entered the bird strike in the logbook. On post flight there was bloody evidence of two medium size impacts to the radome. There did not appear to be any physical damage to the radome. TWO BIRD STRUCK. Model747-8F. Engine ManufacturerGEClassificationStandardEngine ModelGENX-2B67/P

 A UPS Airlines Boeing 747-8 aircraft encountered a medium-sized bird strike to the radome shortly after takeoff at around 2000 ft. However, all aircraft indications remained normal, and the aircraft continued to climb to its cruising altitude. Upon post-flight inspection, there were two medium-sized bloody impacts to the radome, but no visible physical damage. The incident was reported to the FAA and documented in their report, which includes information on the aircraft model, engine manufacturer, and classification.

Figure 12.10 – Another scenario with robust remarks tested using OpenAI ChatGPT

Based upon the results of your preliminary testing using OpenAI ChatGPT, you decide to move forward with both the text generation and summarization use cases used previously. First, you will get approval from your stakeholders, and then you will begin development. Before you begin developing the use cases in Power BI, you'll need to decide upon the GPT models for your API calls. Both OpenAI and Azure OpenAI support the use of REST APIs to call GPT models. These APIs will be used to generate text for each row of data that you want to use for description generations and summarizations.

Choosing GPT models for your use cases

OpenAI and Azure OpenAI offer several different GPT models that can be called iteratively using an API. At the time of writing this book, there is limited availability of the new GPT-4 models, which are the latest and greatest releases. The GPT-3.5 models are available in both OpenAI and Azure OpenAI, with a few different options. The following information was referenced on March 26, 2023, from the OpenAI website at this link: `https://platform.openai.com/docs/models/gpt-4`.

Latest model	Description	Max tokens	Training data
gpt-3.5-turbo	Most capable GPT-3.5 model and optimized for chat at one-tenth the cost of text-davinci-003. Will be updated with our latest model iteration.	4,096 tokens	Up to September 2021
gpt-3.5-turbo-0301	Snapshot of gpt-3.5-turbo from March 1, 2023. Unlike gpt-3.5-turbo, this model will not receive updates, and will only be supported for a 3-month period ending on June 1, 2023.	4,096 tokens	Up to September 2021
text-davinci-003	Can do any language task with better quality, longer output, and more consistent instruction-following than the Curie, Babbage, or Ada models. Also supports inserting completions within text.	4,097 tokens	Up to June 2021
text-davinci-002	Similar capabilities to text-davinci-003 but trained with supervised fine-tuning instead of reinforcement learning.	4,097 tokens	Up to June 2021
code-davinci-002	Optimized for code-completion tasks.	8,001 tokens	Up to June 2021

Figure 12.11 – GPT-3.5 models available from OpenAI on March 26, 2023 (information taken from the OpenAI website)

GPT-3.5 models will be used for this book and workshop as readers may not have access to GPT-4 models. When considering the models and matching them to your use cases, consider the following:

Latest model	Considerations
gpt-3.5-turbo	Most recent addition, built for speed and low cost
gpt-3.5-turbo-0301	Previous version of GPT-3.5-turbo
text-davinci-003	Versatile text model, more expensive and slower than gpt-3.5-turbo
text-davinci-002	Similar to text-davinci-003 but with less sophisticated results
code-davinci-002	Optimized for writing code

Figure 12.12 – Considerations for choosing a GPT model

Based upon your research at this time, gpt-3.5-turbo appears to be the best choice for testing your use cases, but text-davinci-003 has been around longer at the time of writing this book and has better reference literature. Your use cases are to do the following:

- Provide additional information about airplanes from an individually reported wildlife strike incident

- Summarize information from a use case

Swapping out different GPT models is a fairly simple process of redirecting the API calls. For your own projects, you should test all of the options to determine the best GPT model for your use case.

For the next chapter in the book, you decide to use text-davinci-003 to generate new descriptions about airplanes and summarizing remarks about wildlife strike incidents. Is it the best choice? You would need to do extensive testing and also choose specific criteria for what is best, and these are brand-new technologies without a historical body of standards from which to set baselines. For this book and workshop, you will make this choice to keep things moving along with a GPT model that should provide reasonable results.

The API calls can also be configured using additional settings. Settings such as temperature and top_p can change the results from leaning toward simplicity and straight fact to more creative answers. Be careful with these settings, as creativity in results can cause incorrect answers, which are referred to as **hallucinations**.

> Using the OpenAI API
>
> More information from OpenAI about temperature, top_p settings, and hallucinations can be found at this link: https://platform.openai.com/docs/api-reference/completions/create#completions/create-temperature.

This book and workshop will not dig into the specifics of these settings or do a comparison but instead will focus on the technical implementation of these GPT models within Power BI.

Summary

In this chapter, you have delved into the fundamental concepts associated with OpenAI and Microsoft Azure OpenAI, and how these platforms can be employed to generate and summarize text. Moreover, you have explored several options for integrating GPT models from both OpenAI and Azure OpenAI into your Power BI solution using FAA Wildlife Strike data. Following a careful evaluation process, it has been determined that the `text-davinci-003` GPT model will be utilized for the summarization of remarks present in FAA Wildlife Strike data reports, and for generating novel descriptive information about airplanes within the reports.

Chapter 13 will be dedicated to the implementation of functions within Power BI dataflows, enabling the seamless calling of OpenAI and Azure OpenAI REST APIs for data. These APIs will facilitate the successful implementation of your summarization and descriptive generation use cases, thereby providing new capabilities for your solution to address the challenges posed by FAA Wildlife Strike data. With these advanced features in place, your dataflows will be able to call upon OpenAI or Azure OpenAI with ease and efficiency each time they are refreshed.

This integration of cutting-edge functionalities within your project will undoubtedly bolster its efficacy, providing a streamlined and optimized approach to data summarization and descriptive generation.

13

Using OpenAI and Azure OpenAI in Power BI Dataflows

Chapter 12 of this book provided an overview of the OpenAI and Azure OpenAI technologies. The chapter also explored methods to incorporate these cutting-edge AI technologies into your use case using FAA Wildlife Strike data. To enhance the quality of the content in *Chapter 12*, OpenAI ChatGPT was utilized to generate better text. Moving forward, ChatGPT will continue to be used on occasion as a tool to improve the writing quality of the rest of the book.

Furthermore, there are two use cases for OpenAI and Azure OpenAI technologies that are discussed in detail in this chapter. Specifically, you will focus on their applications in summarization and descriptive content generation, as discussed in *Chapter 12*. To illustrate these use cases, a project is included in this chapter.

In this chapter, you will see how to integrate OpenAI (or Azure OpenAI) into your Power BI solution for FAA Wildlife Strike data. Through this integration, you will be able to leverage GPT model APIs by adding new functions to Power BI dataflows. These functions will enable the generation of new content for each row of data in your solution. You will also use **Cognitive Services** in Power BI, which is an AI capability that has existed in Power Query and dataflows for a few years.

By the end of this chapter, you will have gained the knowledge necessary to apply GPT REST APIs in either OpenAI or Azure OpenAI to Power BI dataflows. These dataflows can then be refreshed on a predefined schedule. This capability will provide you with a powerful toolset for generating new content and insights from your data with minimal effort. The step-by-step instructions and examples provided in this chapter will equip you with the necessary skills to implement this solution in your own projects.

Technical requirements

For this chapter, you'll need the following:

- An account with the original open source OpenAI: `https://openai.com/`.

- Optional – Azure OpenAI as part of your Azure subscription: `https://azure.microsoft.com/en-us/products/cognitive-services/openai-service`. The book is written so that this is optional since it is not available to everyone at the time of publication.

- FAA Wildlife Strike data files from either the FAA website or the Packt GitHub site.

- A Power BI Pro license.

- One of the following Power BI licensing options for access to Power BI dataflows:

  - Power BI Premium

  - Power BI Premium Per User

- One of the following options for getting data into the Power BI cloud service:

  - Microsoft OneDrive (with connectivity to the Power BI cloud service)

  - Microsoft Access + Power BI Gateway

  - Azure Data Lake (with connectivity to the Power BI cloud service)

Configuring OpenAI and Azure OpenAI for use in your Power BI solution

Prior to proceeding with the configuration of OpenAI and Azure OpenAI, it is important to note that OpenAI is still a nascent technology at the time of writing this book. In the future, the integration of OpenAI with Power BI may become less technical, as advancements in the technology continue to be made. However, the use cases that will be demonstrated in this chapter will remain applicable.

As such, the instructions provided in this chapter will showcase how this integration can be used to enhance your data analytics capabilities in the context of Power BI.

Configuring OpenAI

You can create an account in OpenAI (if you do not have one already) from this link: `https://chat.openai.com/auth/login`. At the time of writing, new accounts are granted trial credits to begin using OpenAI. If you run out of trial credits, or if the trial is no longer offered after this book has been written, you may need to pay for the use of OpenAI. Pricing details can be found at this link: `https://openai.com/pricing`.

Once you have an OpenAI account, you will need to create an API key that will be used to authenticate your API calls. An API key can be easily created at this link: `https://platform.openai.com/account/api-keys`. Clicking on **Create new secret key** will allow you to create a new key for API calls that you make later in this chapter. This book will use `abc123xyz` as an example key for the sample code. Be sure to use the actual **Key** from OpenAI, and not the **Key Name**.

Once you have an account and an API key, you are ready to go with OpenAI for this book!

Configuring Microsoft Azure OpenAI

OpenAI is also available as a service in Microsoft Azure. By using the Microsoft Azure OpenAI Service, users can leverage large-scale AI models with the benefits of Azure, such as role-based access security, private networks, and comprehensive security tools that integrate with other Microsoft tools in Azure. Billing and governance can be centralized for large organizations to help ensure the responsible use of AI.

For the purposes of this book, Azure OpenAI is optional as an alternative to the original OpenAI. Azure OpenAI may not be available to everyone since it is a new technology with high demand. All of the content for the workshop can be done with either OpenAI or Azure OpenAI.

Instructions for setting up Azure OpenAI can be found at this link: `https://learn.microsoft.com/en-us/azure/cognitive-services/openai/how-to/create-resource/`. Once you've created a resource, you can also deploy a model per the instructions at that link. As noted in *Chapter 12*, you will be using the `text-davinci-003` model for the workshop associated with this chapter. OpenAI is evolving rapidly, and you may be able to choose different models at the time you are reading this book. Take note of the following values when walking through these steps; they will be needed later in this chapter:

- **Resource name**: Note the name of your Azure OpenAI resource in your subscription. This book will use `PBI_OpenAI_project` for the examples in this chapter.

- **Deployment name**: This is the name of the resource for the `text-davinci-003` model deployment. This book will use `davinci-PBIML` for names of deployments in examples of code.

Next, you'll need to create a key for your Azure OpenAI API calls. From your Azure OpenAI resource, named `PBI_OpenAI_project` for this book, go to **Resource management | Keys and endpoint**, and your keys will be on that page. This book will use `abc123xyz` as an example key for the sample code.

Once you have either OpenAI or Azure OpenAI set up and ready to go, you can add some new generative text capabilities to your project using FAA Wildlife Strike data!

Preparing a Power BI dataflow for OpenAI and Azure OpenAI

In *Chapter 12*, you decided to use OpenAI for two use cases with your FAA Wildlife Strike database project:

- Generating descriptions of airplane models and the operator of the aircraft, for each incident
- Summarizing the free text remarks provided in the report for each incident

Since OpenAI is still new at the time of writing this book, Power BI does not yet have connectors built into the product. But you can still call OpenAI and Azure OpenAI APIs from both Power Query and Power BI dataflows using custom M scripts. Let's get started!

First, you will create a new dataflow for use with OpenAI and Cognitive Services in Power BI:

1. From your Power BI workspace, on the ribbon, select **New | Dataflow**.
2. Select **Define new tables | Link tables from other dataflows**.
3. Sign in and click **Next**.
4. Expand your workspace.
5. Expand the **Strike Reports** dataflow and check **Strike Reports Curated New**.
6. Click **Transform Data**.
7. Create a group named **Sources** and move **Strike Reports Curated New** into that group.
8. Right-click **Strike Reports Curated New** and unselect **Enable load**.

Next, you will create a version of the query that will be used with OpenAI and Cognitive Services:

1. Right-click on **Strike Reports Curated New** and select **Reference**.
2. Rename the new query `Strike Reports Curated New OpenAI`.
3. Create a group named **OpenAI** and move **Strike Reports Curated New OpenAI** into the group.

In *Chapter 12*, you decided to use the FAA Wildlife Strike **Operator**, **Aircraft**, **Species**, and **Remarks** database columns as part of your OpenAI prompts. Filtering out blank and unknown values from **Strike Reports Curated New OpenAI** will help produce better results for your testing. Note that you may need to select **Load more...** if the values all come up empty or UNKNOWN:

1. For the **Operator** column, filter out the UNKNOWN, UNKNOWN COMMERCIAL, BUSINESS, and PRIVATELY OWNED values.
2. For the **Aircraft** column, filter out UNKNOWN.
3. For the **Species** column, filter out Unknown bird, Unknown bird - large, Unknown bird - medium, Unknown bird - small, and Unknown bird or bat.

For the **Remarks** column, filter out (`blank`).

Finally – this step is optional – you can filter the number of rows for testing purposes. Both OpenAI and Azure OpenAI can run up a bill, so limiting the number of calls for this workshop makes sense. For the example in this book, the **Strike Reports Curated New OpenAI** table will be filtered to events happening in or after December 2022, which can be filtered using the **Incident Date** column.

Now you are ready to add OpenAI and Cognitive Services content to your data!

Creating OpenAI and Azure OpenAI functions in Power BI dataflows

As noted earlier, integrating OpenAI and Azure OpenAI with Power Query or dataflows currently requires custom M code. To facilitate this process, we have provided M code for both OpenAI and Azure OpenAI, giving you the flexibility to choose which version to use based on your specific needs and requirements.

By leveraging this provided M code, you can seamlessly integrate OpenAI or Azure OpenAI with your existing Power BI solutions. This will allow you to take advantage of the unique features and capabilities offered by these powerful AI technologies, while also gaining insights and generating new content from your data with ease.

OpenAI and Azure OpenAI functions

OpenAI offers a user-friendly API that can be easily accessed and utilized from within Power Query or dataflows in Power BI. For further information regarding the specifics of the API, we refer you to the official OpenAI documentation, available at this link: `https://platform.openai.com/docs/introduction/overview`.

It is worth noting that optimizing and tuning the OpenAI API will likely be a popular topic in the coming year. Various concepts, including **prompt engineering**, **optimal token usage**, fine-tuning, embeddings, plugins, and parameters that modify response creativity (such as temperature and top *p*), can all be tested and fine-tuned for optimal results.

While these topics are complex and may be explored in greater detail in future works, this book will focus primarily on establishing connectivity between OpenAI and Power BI. Specifically, we will explore prompt engineering and token limits, which are key considerations that will be incorporated into the API call to ensure optimal performance:

- **Prompts**: Prompt engineering, in basic terms, is the English-language text that will be used to preface every API call. For example, instead of sending [`Operator`] and [`Airplane`] as values without context, text was added to the request in the previous chapter such that the API will receive `Tell me about the airplane model [Aircraft] operated by [Operator] in three sentences:`. The prompt adds context to the values passed to the OpenAI model.

- **Tokens**: Words sent to the OpenAI model get broken into chunks called tokens. Per the OpenAI website, a token contains about four English language characters. Reviewing the **Remarks** column in the Power BI dataset reveals that most entries have up to 2,000 characters. (2000 / 4) = 500, so you will specify 500 as the token limit. Is that the right number? You'd need to do extensive testing to answer that question, which goes beyond the scope of this book.

Let's get started with building your OpenAI and Azure OpenAI API calls for Power BI dataflows!

Creating OpenAI and Azure OpenAI functions for Power BI dataflows

You will create two functions for OpenAI in your dataflow named **OpenAI**. The only difference between the two will be the token limits. The purpose of having different token limits is primarily cost savings, since larger token limits could potentially run up a bigger bill. Follow these steps to create a new function named **OpenAIshort**:

1. Select **Get data | Blank query**.

2. Paste in the following M code and select **Next**. Be sure to replace abc123xyz with your OpenAI API key.

   Here is the code for the function. The code can also be found as 01 OpenAIshortFunction.M in the Packt GitHub repository at https://github.com/PacktPublishing/ Unleashing-Your-Data-with-Power-BI-Machine-Learning-and-OpenAI/ tree/main/Chapter-13:

```
let
    callOpenAI = (prompt as text) as text =>
        let
            jsonPayload = "{""prompt"": """ & prompt & """,
            ""max_tokens"": " & Text.From(120) & "}",
            url = "https://api.openai.com/v1/engines/
            text-davinci-003/completions",
            headers = [#"Content-Type"="application/json",
            #"Authorization"="Bearer abc123xyz"],
            response = Web.Contents(url, [Headers=headers,
            Content=Text.ToBinary(jsonPayload)]),
            jsonResponse = Json.Document(response),
            choices = jsonResponse[choices],
            text = choices{0}[text]
        in
            text
    in
        callOpenAI
```

3. Now, you can rename the function `OpenAIshort`. Right-click on the function in the **Queries** panel and duplicate it. The new function will have a larger token limit.

4. Rename this new function `OpenAIlong`.

5. Right-click on **OpenAIlong** and select **Advanced editor**.

6. Change the section of code reading `Text.From(120)` to `Text.From(500)`.

7. Click **OK**.

Your screen should now look like this:

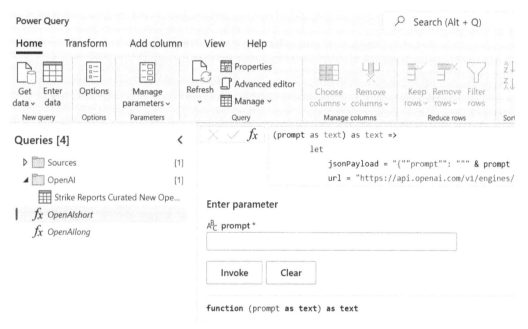

Figure 13.1 – OpenAI functions added to a Power BI dataflow

These two functions can be used to complete the workshop for the remainder of this chapter. If you'd prefer to use Azure OpenAI, the M code for **OpenAIshort** would be as follows. Remember to replace `PBI_OpenAI_project` with your Azure resource name, `davinci-PBIML` with your deployment name, and `abc123xyz` with your API key:

```
let
    callAzureOpenAI = (prompt as text) as text =>
        let
            jsonPayload = "{""prompt"": """ & prompt & """,
            ""max_tokens"": " & Text.From(120) & "}"
            url = "https://" & "PBI_OpenAI_project" & ".openai.azure.
            com" & "/openai/deployments/" & "davinci-PBIML" & "/
            completions?api-version=2022-12-01",
```

```
            headers = [#"Content-Type"="application/json",
            #"api-key"="abc123xyz"],
            response = Web.Contents(url, [Headers=headers,
            Content=Text.ToBinary(jsonPayload)]),
            jsonResponse = Json.Document(response),
            choices = jsonResponse[choices],
            text = choices{0}[text]
        in
            text
    in
        callAzureOpenAI
```

As with the previous example, changing the token limit for Text.From(120) to Text.From(500) is all you need to do to create an Azure OpenAI function for 500 tokens instead of 120. The M code to create the dataflows for your OpenAI functions can also be found on the Packt GitHub site at this link: https://github.com/PacktPublishing/Unleashing-Your-Data-with-Power-BI-Machine-Learning-and-OpenAI/tree/main/Chapter-13.

Now that you have your OpenAI and Azure OpenAI functions ready to go in a Power BI dataflow, you can test them out on the FAA Wildlife Strike data!

Using OpenAI and Azure OpenAI functions in Power BI dataflows

Your next step is to prep the FAA Wildlife Strike data for the OpenAI or Azure OpenAI functions to do content generation and summarization. As discussed previously, you'll need to build effective prompts to provide context for the OpenAI models to process. The completed query for **Reports Curated New OpenAI**, which can be copied and pasted into Power BI, is also available from the Packt GitHub repository: https://github.com/PacktPublishing/Unleashing-Your-Data-with-Power-BI-Machine-Learning-and-OpenAI/tree/main/Chapter-13.

Looking back to *Chapter 12*, you decided upon the following combinations of new text with row-level content from the FAA Wildlife Strike database:

- Generating new information about airplanes and the carriers: Tell me about the airplane model [Aircraft] operated by [Operator] in three sentences:

- Summarizing the remarks from each report, including the operator, aircraft, and species: Summarize the following: A [Operator] [Aircraft] struck a [Species]. Remarks on the FAA report were: [Remarks]

You can now add two new columns to the **Strike Reports Curated New OpenAI** query. First, you add a column to prompt text generation:

1. Select **Add column | Custom Column**.

2. Set **New column name** to Text Generation Prompt.

3. Paste in the following text: "Tell me about the airplane model " & [Aircraft] &" operated by " & [Operator] & " in three sentences:". Then, select **OK**.

4. Change the data type to Text.

5. Validate that the new column creates text to be used as information with built-in prompts that look like this:

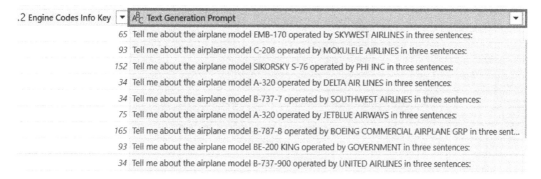

.2 Engine Codes Info Key ▼	A^BC Text Generation Prompt
65	Tell me about the airplane model EMB-170 operated by SKYWEST AIRLINES in three sentences:
93	Tell me about the airplane model C-208 operated by MOKULELE AIRLINES in three sentences:
152	Tell me about the airplane model SIKORSKY S-76 operated by PHI INC in three sentences:
34	Tell me about the airplane model A-320 operated by DELTA AIR LINES in three sentences:
34	Tell me about the airplane model B-737-7 operated by SOUTHWEST AIRLINES in three sentences:
75	Tell me about the airplane model A-320 operated by JETBLUE AIRWAYS in three sentences:
165	Tell me about the airplane model B-787-8 operated by BOEING COMMERCIAL AIRPLANE GRP in three sent...
93	Tell me about the airplane model BE-200 KING operated by GOVERNMENT in three sentences:
34	Tell me about the airplane model B-737-900 operated by UNITED AIRLINES in three sentences:

Figure 13.2 – New column to be used with OpenAI

Now create a second column that will be used for text summarization that also contains built-in prompts:

1. Select **Add column | Custom Column**.

2. Set **New column name** to Text Summarization Prompt.

3. Paste in the following text: "Summarize the following: A " & [Operator] & " " & [Aircraft] & " struck a " & [Species] & ". Remarks on the FAA report were: " & [Remarks].

4. Change the data type to Text.

5.   Validate that the new column for summarization, with a built-in prompt, looks like this:

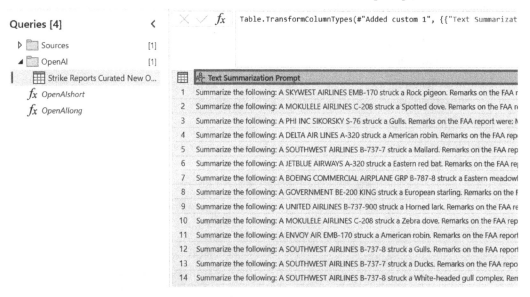

Figure 13.3 – New column for summarizations with built-in prompt

Now you've created two columns in your Power BI dataflow query that are ready for OpenAI functions! Start by calling OpenAI using the `OpenAIshort` function for text generation:

1.   Select **Add column | Custom Column**.

2.   Set **New column name** to `OpenAI Aircraft Description`.

3.   Paste the following text into **Custom column formula**: `OpenAIshort([Text Generation Prompt])`.

4.   Click **OK**.

5.   Validate that OpenAI generated text for the new column. You can hover over a field in the new column to read the full text:

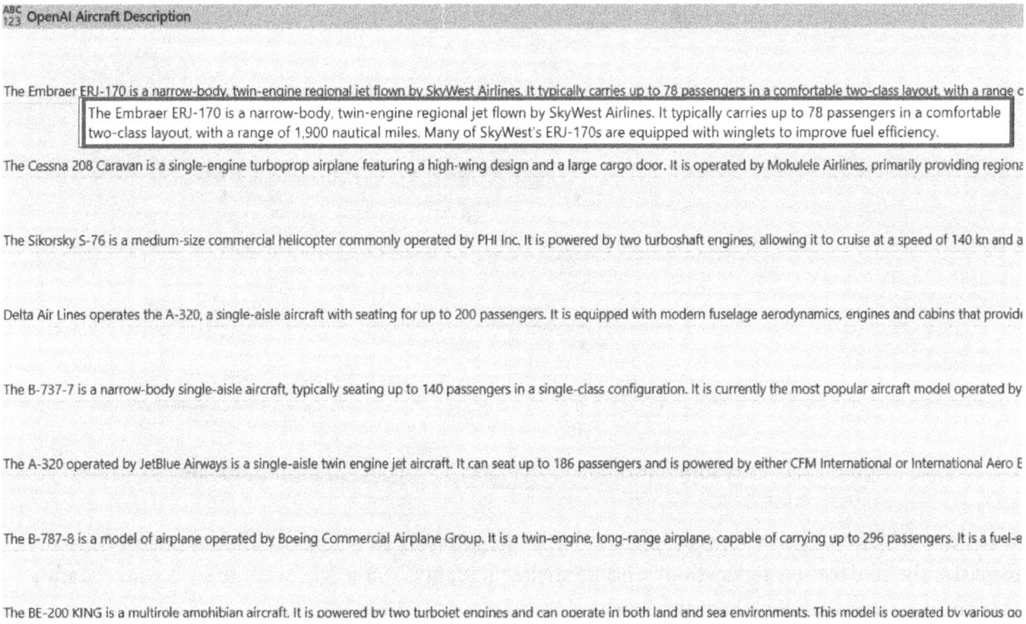

ABC 123 **OpenAI Aircraft Description**

The Embraer ERJ-170 is a narrow-body, twin-engine regional jet flown by SkyWest Airlines. It typically carries up to 78 passengers in a comfortable two-class layout, with a range c

> The Embraer ERJ-170 is a narrow-body, twin-engine regional jet flown by SkyWest Airlines. It typically carries up to 78 passengers in a comfortable two-class layout, with a range of 1,900 nautical miles. Many of SkyWest's ERJ-170s are equipped with winglets to improve fuel efficiency.

The Cessna 208 Caravan is a single-engine turboprop airplane featuring a high-wing design and a large cargo door. It is operated by Mokulele Airlines, primarily providing regiona

The Sikorsky S-76 is a medium-size commercial helicopter commonly operated by PHI Inc. It is powered by two turboshaft engines, allowing it to cruise at a speed of 140 kn and a

Delta Air Lines operates the A-320, a single-aisle aircraft with seating for up to 200 passengers. It is equipped with modern fuselage aerodynamics, engines and cabins that provide

The B-737-7 is a narrow-body single-aisle aircraft, typically seating up to 140 passengers in a single-class configuration. It is currently the most popular aircraft model operated by

The A-320 operated by JetBlue Airways is a single-aisle twin engine jet aircraft. It can seat up to 186 passengers and is powered by either CFM International or International Aero E

The B-787-8 is a model of airplane operated by Boeing Commercial Airplane Group. It is a twin-engine, long-range airplane, capable of carrying up to 296 passengers. It is a fuel-e

The BE-200 KING is a multirole amphibian aircraft. It is powered by two turbojet engines and can operate in both land and sea environments. This model is operated by various op

Figure 13.4 – OpenAI generated a description of the aircraft for that operator
with new data from outside the FAA Wildlife Strike database

Repeating the preceding steps for text summarization of the **Remarks** column is next using the `OpenAIlong` function:

1. Select **Add column | Custom Column**.

2. Set **New column name** to `OpenAI Remarks Summarization`.

3. Paste the following text into **Custom column formula**: `OpenAIlong([Text Summarization Prompt])`.

4. Click **OK**.

5. Validate that OpenAI generated text for the new column, and again you can hover over a field to view the full summarization:

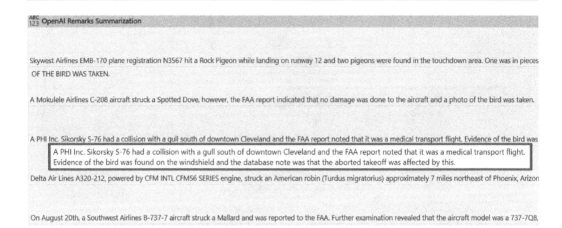

Figure 13.5 – Text summarization for remarks about aircraft hitting wildlife

You've done it! OpenAI was successfully used to both generate new information about aircraft and summarize the free text remarks about wildlife strike incidents. You might want to save your dataflow at this point so that you don't lose any work.

Adding a Cognitive Services function to the solution

Finally, you decide to add more value to the deliverables by showcasing the Cognitive Services capabilities in Power BI. In both Power BI Desktop and Power BI dataflows, Cognitive Services is built in as part of the SaaS tool. Details about using Cognitive Services in Power BI can be found at this link: `https://learn.microsoft.com/en-us/power-bi/connect-data/service-tutorial-use-cognitive-services`.

Cognitive Services refers to Azure services that can be called using APIs to score data with standard ML models. These tools can score the sentiment of text, identify images, extract key phrases, detect emotion in pictures, and more. The following Cognitive Services features are native to Power BI at the time of writing this book:

- **Detect Language**
- **Tag Images**
- **Score Sentiment**
- **Extract Key Phrases**

For this final addition to the project, you will use the Score Sentiment function on the **Remarks** column of the FAA Wildlife Strike database. The scores typically range from 0 to 1, with 0 being negative, 0.5 being neutral, and 1 being positive.

Opening back up your **OpenAI** dataflow, navigate to the query for **Strike Reports Curated New OpenAI** and follow these steps:

1. Highlight the **Remarks** column.

2. Navigate to **Home | Insights | AI Insights**.

3. Sign in and an **AI Insights** window will pop up.

4. Notice that Cognitive Services is available, along with the Power BI ML models that you created! You can also use this capability to reuse your Power BI ML models to score multiple columns of data in different dataflows.

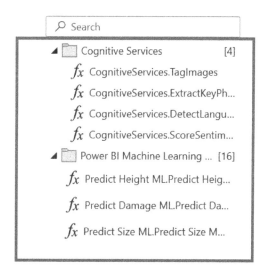

Figure 13.6 – Cognitive Services and Power BI ML models can be called as functions

5. Select **CognitiveServices.ScoreSentiment**.

6. Select the **Remarks** column from the dropdown and hit **Apply**.

7. Change the data type to `decimal number`.

8. Validate that the sentiment was scored and added as a new column:

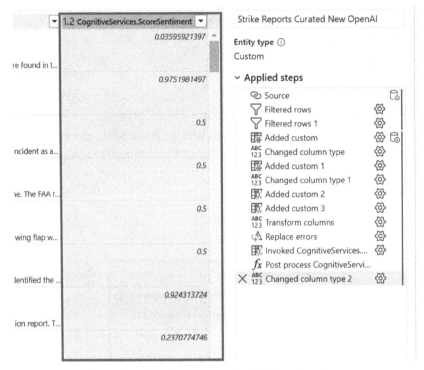

Figure 13.7 – Sentiment scores for the Remarks column

You can now save and refresh your dataflow, and you're done! When the dataflow has refreshed, you can connect from Power BI Desktop and browse the results of your work:

Aircraft	Operator	Species	OpenAI Aircraft Description	OpenAI Remarks Summarization	Sentiment
A-319	AMERICAN AIRLINES	Barn swallow	The Airbus A-319 operated by American Airlines is a two-engine, narrow-body commercial airliner. It has a maximum range of approximately 3,650 nautical miles and a seating capacity of 124-156 passengers. The A-319 is primarily used for short-haul domestic and international flights.	An American Airlines A-319 aircraft struck a Barn swallow during takeoff from TLPL. The aircraft continued to its destination KCLT without incident and a tissue sample from the remains was sent to the Smithsonian for analysis. No damage was found on the aircraft and inspection of the arrival runway showed no other remains/evidence. The airline informed local CLT Airside Ops of the strike.	0.50
A-319	AMERICAN AIRLINES	Cedar waxwing	The Airbus A-319 operated by American Airlines is a two-engine, narrow-body commercial airliner. It has a maximum range of approximately 3,650 nautical miles and a seating capacity of 124-156 passengers. The A-319 is primarily used for short-haul domestic and international flights.	Evidence of the strike was found by post-flight inspection on the windshield. A tissue sample of the remains was sent to the Smithsonian for analysis and it was identified as a Cedar waxwing. No other remains or evidence were found after inspection of the runway.	0.92
A-319	AMERICAN AIRLINES	Chipping sparrow	The Airbus A-319 operated by American Airlines is a two-engine, narrow-body commercial airliner. It has a maximum range of approximately 3,650 nautical miles and a seating capacity of 124-156 passengers. The A-319 is primarily used for short-haul domestic and international flights.	American Airlines flight A-319 struck a Chipping Sparrow while departing runway 24 at KILM. The flight continued without incident and no damage was found on the aircraft. A tissue sample from the remains was collected by CLT Airside Ops personnel and sent to the Smithsonian for analysis, identifying the bird species as the Chipping Sparrow (Spizella passerina).	0.09

Figure 13.8 – Results of OpenAI and Cognitive Services viewed in Power BI

To make it easier to read, *Figure 13.8* is split into two images. *Figure 13.9* shows the left hand columns.

Aircraft	Operator	Species	OpenAI Aircraft Description	OpenAI Ren
A-319	AMERICAN AIRLINES	Barn swallow	The Airbus A-319 operated by American Airlines is a two-engine, narrow-body commercial airliner. It has a maximum range of approximately 3,650 nautical miles and a seating capacity of 124-156 passengers. The A-319 is primarily used for short-haul domestic and international flights.	An America continued t Smithsoniar showed no
A-319	AMERICAN AIRLINES	Cedar waxwing	The Airbus A-319 operated by American Airlines is a two-engine, narrow-body commercial airliner. It has a maximum range of approximately 3,650 nautical miles and a seating capacity of 124-156 passengers. The A-319 is primarily used for short-haul domestic and international flights.	Evidence of remains wa remains or
A-319	AMERICAN AIRLINES	Chipping sparrow	The Airbus A-319 operated by American Airlines is a two-engine, narrow-body commercial airliner. It has a maximum range of approximately 3,650 nautical miles and a seating capacity of 124-156 passengers. The A-319 is primarily used for short-haul domestic and international flights.	American A continued was collect bird specie

Figure 13.9 – Results of OpenAI and Cognitive Services viewed in Power BI

The right-hand column is shown in *Figure 13.10*.

otion	OpenAI Remarks Summarization	Sentiment
		0.50
ated by American Airlines is a dy commercial airliner. It has pproximately 3,650 nautical acity of 124-156 passengers. used for short-haul domestic s.	An American Airlines A-319 aircraft struck a Barn swallow during takeoff from TLPL. The aircraft continued to its destination KCLT without incident and a tissue sample from the remains was sent to the Smithsonian for analysis. No damage was found on the aircraft and inspection of the arrival runway showed no other remains/evidence. The airline informed local CLT Airside Ops of the strike.	
	Evidence of the strike was found by post-flight inspection on the windshield. A tissue sample of the remains was sent to the Smithsonian for analysis and it was identified as a Cedar waxwing. No other remains or evidence were found after inspection of the runway.	0.92
ated by American Airlines is a dy commercial airliner. It has pproximately 3,650 nautical bacity of 124-156 passengers. used for short-haul domestic s.		
		0.09
ated by American Airlines is a dy commercial airliner. It has pproximately 3,650 nautical acity of 124-156 passengers. used for short-haul domestic s.	American Airlines flight A-319 struck a Chipping Sparrow while departing runway 24 at KILM. The flight continued without incident and no damage was found on the aircraft. A tissue sample from the remains was collected by CLT Airside Ops personnel and sent to the Smithsonian for analysis, identifying the bird species as the Chipping Sparrow (Spizella passerina).	

Figure 13.10 – Results of OpenAI and Cognitive Services viewed in Power BI

Once you have gained a solid understanding of how to implement various tools and services within Power BI, such as Cognitive Services provided by OpenAI or Azure OpenAI, you can experiment with different prompt strategies and explore a wide range of additional capabilities.

By leveraging the knowledge and skills gained from this book, you will be equipped to test new ideas, fine-tune your approaches, and optimize the performance of your solutions. With these tools at your disposal, the possibilities for enhancing your data analytics and content generation capabilities within Power BI are virtually limitless. So, don't be afraid to dive in and explore all that these powerful technologies have to offer!

Summary

This chapter covered the integration of OpenAI or Azure OpenAI with Power BI, along with a use case for Power BI Cognitive Services. By leveraging these advanced tools, you were able to generate new descriptions of airplanes using external data and GPT models, summarize remarks about wildlife strikes, and even score the remarks for sentiment analysis.

Moving forward, the next and final chapter will provide an opportunity to review and reflect on the work accomplished throughout this book and the accompanying workshop. We will also begin to explore new strategies for enhancing and expanding upon the existing project, as we recognize that projects are never truly complete if there is still potential for additional value to be achieved.

14

Project Review and Looking Forward

Chapter 13 of this book was an adventure to the cutting edge of technology, as you integrated OpenAI and Azure OpenAI into your Power BI project using the FAA Wildlife Strike data. Over the course of this book, you have walked through a project for ingesting raw data, transforming and prepping the data, building a BI solution for analytics, using analytics to discover data features for predictive ML models, building those ML models, scoring new data with the ML models, and adding new, robust descriptive and summarization capabilities to the solution using LLMs from OpenAI and Azure OpenAI. In *Chapters 12* and *13*, you augmented and improved text using OpenAI, too. All of this was accomplished, from end to end, using Power BI.

In this chapter, you will review what you have accomplished throughout the book and project, revise important key concepts, and then discover some suggestions for future iterations of the project and your career as a data professional. In the real world, most projects are never truly complete. At some point, they may end, but more often than not, there is the opportunity to improve upon the existing solution or expand the scope of the solution to provide more value. Understanding and articulating the outstanding value that can be captured by new iterations of work and communicating that message to stakeholders, along with estimates of the required investments, is key to building your projects to be bigger, better, and more impactful.

Unlike the previous two chapters, this chapter is not written with the assistance of OpenAI, but in the authentic voice of the author (with assistance from human editors and reviewers).

Lessons learned from the book and workshop

At the beginning of this book, you started with the objective to provide your leadership with tools to enable interactive analysis of the FAA Wildlife Strike data, in order to find insights about factors that influence incidents and make predictions about future possible wildlife strike incidents and associated costs. The primary goal of your project, predicting the future impact of FAA Wildlife Strikes, required building out Power BI ML models. Through the chapters of this book, you walked through the process, using content from the Packt GitHub repository, to plan out and implement an end-to-end project. Everything in this project was achieved using tools within Power BI or that were integrated with Power BI. A high-level summary of the artifacts you created in Power BI is shown in *Figure 14.1*:

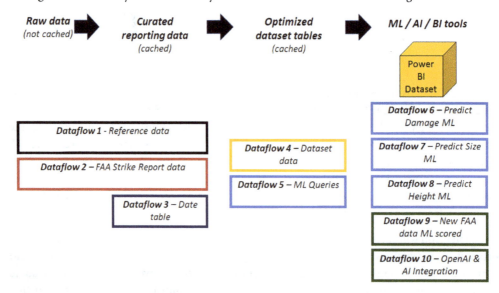

Figure 14.1 – Summary of the artifacts created in Power BI in this book

The primary technical training for this book revolved around ML in Power BI, but several other concepts were interwoven with the end-to-end workshop. If you have taken Microsoft's **Power BI Dashboard in a Day** course (`https://aka.ms/diad`), you probably will have found some style similarities between that course and this book, but with ML, AI, and OpenAI added as the pivotal capstone deliverables while also using FAA Wildlife Strike data from the real world.

Exploring the intersection of BI, ML, AI, and OpenAI

BI, ML, AI, and OpenAI encompass tools and solution architectures methodologies that overlap with one another but can also be approached as separate disciplines. Within the context of Power BI, many different tools have been combined under the umbrella of a single SaaS platform. Over the years, Power BI has evolved from a data visualization tool to SaaS-ify many different Microsoft tools, as per *Figure 14.2*:

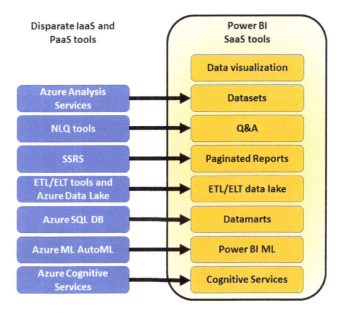

Figure 14.2 – Power BI consists of many tools within a SaaS platform

Within the context of the Power BI SaaS toolset, you walked through the following exercises, which provided a baseline conceptual understanding of when and where to use ML, AI, and OpenAI:

- *Chapter 1*: You reviewed the use case, browsed the data, and planned your data model to account for a BI design that facilitated data exploration and feature discovery, while also planning for a design that will work with ML.

- *Chapters 2* and *3*: You transformed data and created a baseline design for a BI dataset in Power BI. You modeled the data in a way that provided a strong foundation for the future.

- *Chapter 4*: You designed tables of data to be used for ML. These tables were flattened, with each row representing a unique incident with features describing that incident.

- *Chapter 5*: You explored the dataset to find features for ML using the BI tools along with AI visuals. New features were then added to the ML queries.

- *Chapter 6*: You found new features using R and Python visuals. These features were also added to the queries for Power BI ML.

- *Chapter 7*: You migrated your work from Power BI Desktop to the Power BI cloud service. After this chapter, all of your work was done in the Power BI cloud service.

- *Chapters 8 to 11*: You built and improved your ML models. You ran the flattened ML queries through Power BI ML for three separate predictive models, reviewed the training and testing results, and then iterated upon the ML models to improve the predictive capabilities.

- *Chapters 12 and 13*: You added OpenAI and Cognitive Services to the solution for even more value. OpenAI was used to summarize and generate data in readable language.

A visual representation of your efforts is displayed in *Figure 14.3*. Other than the OpenAI integration, everything was done completely within the Power BI SaaS set of tools:

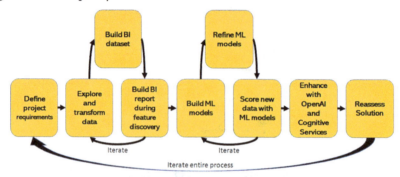

Figure 14.3 – Project methodology integrating BI, ML, AI, and
OpenAI tools within the Power BI SaaS platform

In summary, you walked through the process of an entire project that started with raw FAA Wildlife Strike data and ended with ML models – all within the SaaS tools of Power BI.

ML within Power BI

Since the name of this book is *Power BI Machine Learning and OpenAI*, the Power BI ML tool is obviously the capstone component of the workshop and story adventure you have completed. There are a few reasons why the entire book was not based on Power BI ML:

- Power BI ML is extremely easy to use, when used properly. It is a version of AutoML, and prepping the data properly can be very difficult.

- Many BI experts have never designed and prepped data for ML. The intersection of these skills is the hardest part of using Power BI ML for a BI professional.

- The end-to-end workshop affiliated with this book was designed to represent real-world projects as closely as possible. If you completed the workshop, even if you took shortcuts by cutting and pasting scripts and content from GitHub, you should be able to repeat a variation of the process for your own future projects.

- At the end of this book, you should now have a very strong understanding of how, when, and why to use ML in Power BI.

You have now built, assessed, deployed, and re-trained binary prediction, general classification, and regression ML models in Power BI. Not only did you accomplish this feat, but you did it with real data from the FAA Wildlife Strike database. The data was not artificially curated or synthesized to improve your results or make the process easy. As an added bonus, you added some OpenAI and Cognitive Services integration to the project for added value. You should be proud of yourself!

But now the real test begins! How do you ensure that your stakeholders appreciate the results of the project? Is the project done or can you do more to make it better? How can you translate these lessons to your future career plans?

Looking forward

Now that you've progressed from defining requirements, to transforming and exploring raw source data from the FAA Wildlife Strike database, to building ML models, to working with OpenAI and Cognitive Services, what's next? Do you publish the solution for your stakeholders and users, give yourself a high five, and move on to the next project? Do you continue to iterate on this project for added value? Do you build upon the lessons from this book and dive deeper into ML and OpenAI?

Next steps for the FAA Wildlife Strike data solution

The examples used in this book only scratch the surface of the different use cases that could be built out using the FAA Wildlife Strike database. In your real-world work, most people will never need to use FAA Wildlife Strike data. Even so, there is value in brainstorming possible next steps so that you can incorporate such thinking into your solutions. Without adding new data, a few examples might include, but not be limited to, the following:

- Predicting the height of different bird species, at different times of the year, at different locations

- Predicting the damage likelihood for different types of aircraft

- Predicting seasonal risk rates for wildlife strikes

- Evaluating the impact of Covid on wildlife strikes (fewer flights during the pandemic)

- Assessing differences in wildlife strikes on aircraft with tail-mounted versus wing-mounted engines

Bringing in external data might provide opportunities to enrich your solution, too:

- Weather data could be used as a factor for predicting different types of wildlife strike criteria

- Data for all airline flights (most don't have wildlife strikes) could be used to determine the rates of wildlife strikes and add more robust information about flights

- Data about wildlife and bird deterrents (fences, decoys of predators, and so on) at airports could be added to assess the effectiveness

Iterating upon your existing ML models will most likely give you better results than those in the workshop, as will testing different features, evaluating different ranges of dates, bringing in newer data, testing new filter criteria. With Power BI, new tests are only a few clicks away. If you are able to get better results than the workshop, please share them! The ML models in this book were not intended to be perfect, but rather to give you a launching pad for getting started with the technology.

Next steps with Power BI and ML

Now that you've built and deployed ML models in Power BI, what do you do next? Hopefully, this book has been a learning experience that not only enriched your skills with the Power BI toolset but also helped you learn the conceptual intersection of BI, ML, and AI (including OpenAI). In the modern era, tools such as Power BI will continue to evolve and improve over time. How should you plan to use Power BI ML moving forward? What other considerations might be good ideas to consider?

As shown back in *Figure 14.2*, Power BI is a suite of SaaS tools that are constantly evolving and improving. Power BI ML will inevitably evolve, too. The tools and techniques covered in this book should give you a foundation for understanding and adjusting to future changes to the product suite. You've hopefully learned a methodology to reveal use cases for ML, discover features to build ML models, and assess the possible utility of ML for those use cases within the context of Power BI.

Will Power BI ML be the right tool for the next iteration of this project or for your next ML project? Maybe, maybe not! As discussed in previous chapters, the use cases for ML models developed in this book might be more impactful if the next round of improvements is done with the help of a data science team with enterprise-grade ML capabilities that go beyond the AutoML capabilities in Power BI ML. Or, perhaps a few more rounds of iterations in Power BI ML could also result in a better end product. In the long term, the design and architectural concepts from this book will hopefully provide longer-lasting value than the technical trainings for Power BI ML.

Next steps for your career

Having completed this book and the affiliated workshop using FAA Wildlife Strike data, hopefully you are excited about considering ML and AI as components for future projects. On your journey through this book, you started with raw data and built up to Power BI ML with OpenAI integration. The data that you used was not curated or optimized for this project but represented real data from the real world. What now? Well, hopefully, this experience can help you find new pathways to enhance your career!

If you are a Power BI and analytics enthusiast, you can now add ML as a new tool to your war chest. You can now leverage Power BI ML to do the following:

- Assess new ideas for solving problems for existing projects using ML models

- Scope out the utility of data for larger ML projects

- Use Power BI ML as a way to rapidly prototype ML models before sending the project along to a data science team

- Impatiently await updates and new capabilities from Microsoft for ML in Power BI

If you have aspirations to become a data science professional, or if you already work in data science, you can use your learnings to do the following:

- Gain a better understanding of how to work with BI teams to collaborate and solve problems

- Build out BI components of your solutions in Power BI

- Assess the pros and cons of AutoML tools versus your traditional data science toolbox

- Dive deeper into OpenAI and Azure OpenAI integration for your projects

For a passionate architect, a solution is never complete and there are always opportunities to add new data, approach problems from a new perspective, test new AI and ML tools, and improve upon the end user experience.

Summary

In this chapter, you reviewed all of the lessons from the book and the affiliated workshop. Over the course of 13 chapters, you have traversed the intersection of BI, ML, AI, and OpenAI by way of a single use case. Beginning with raw FAA Wildlife Strike data, you built an end-to-end workshop using the affiliated Packt GitHub repository. Particular attention was given to Power BI ML, and then integration with OpenAI and Azure OpenAI. The next steps and options for working with the FAA data were discussed. Options for future career plans were then covered in the context of the content in this book. In an age of rapid technological evolution, hopefully the architectural design process and strategies covered in this book will help you long after these tools have evolved beyond the state in which they were covered in this book.

Learning about Power BI ML in this book will hopefully open the door for you to find whatever is next in your career. It may be as a Power BI professional, a future data scientist, an industry analyst, or as a project manager. If nothing else, you will have a different perspective of your surrounding landscape the next time you gaze upon the world from a window seat on your next airline flight.

Index

T

U

W

Packtpub.com

Subscribe to our online digital library for full access to over 7,000 books and videos, as well as industry leading tools to help you plan your personal development and advance your career. For more information, please visit our website.

Why subscribe?

- Spend less time learning and more time coding with practical eBooks and Videos from over 4,000 industry professionals

- Improve your learning with Skill Plans built especially for you

- Get a free eBook or video every month

- Fully searchable for easy access to vital information

- Copy and paste, print, and bookmark content

Did you know that Packt offers eBook versions of every book published, with PDF and ePub files available? You can upgrade to the eBook version at packtpub.com and as a print book customer, you are entitled to a discount on the eBook copy. Get in touch with us at customercare@packtpub.com for more details.

At www.packtpub.com, you can also read a collection of free technical articles, sign up for a range of free newsletters, and receive exclusive discounts and offers on Packt books and eBooks.

Other Books You May Enjoy

If you enjoyed this book, you may be interested in these other books by Packt:

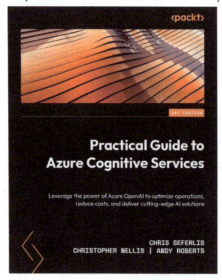

Practical Guide to Azure Cognitive Services

Chris Seferlis, Christopher Nellis, Andy Roberts

ISBN: 9781801812917

- Master cost-effective deployment of Azure Cognitive Services
- Develop proven solutions from an architecture and development standpoint
- Understand how Cognitive Services are deployed and customized
- Evaluate various uses of Cognitive Services with different mediums
- Disseminate Azure costs for Cognitive Services workloads smoothly
- Deploy next-generation Knowledge Mining solutions with Cognitive Search
- Explore the current and future journey of OpenAI
- Understand the value proposition of different AI projects

Azure Machine Learning Engineering

Sina Fakhraee, Balamurugan Balakreshnan, Megan Masanz

ISBN: 9781803239309

- Train ML models in the Azure Machine Learning service
- Build end-to-end ML pipelines
- Host ML models on real-time scoring endpoints
- Mitigate bias in ML models
- Get the hang of using an MLOps framework to productionize models
- Simplify ML model explainability using the Azure Machine Learning service and Azure Interpret

Packt is searching for authors like you

If you're interested in becoming an author for Packt, please visit `authors.packtpub.com` and apply today. We have worked with thousands of developers and tech professionals, just like you, to help them share their insight with the global tech community. You can make a general application, apply for a specific hot topic that we are recruiting an author for, or submit your own idea.

Share Your Thoughts

Now you've finished *Power BI Machine Learning and OpenAI*, we'd love to hear your thoughts! Scan the QR code below to go straight to the Amazon review page for this book and share your feedback or leave a review on the site that you purchased it from.

`https://packt.link/r/1-837-63615-X`

Your review is important to us and the tech community and will help us make sure we're delivering excellent quality content.

Download a free PDF copy of this book

Thanks for purchasing this book!

Do you like to read on the go but are unable to carry your print books everywhere?

Is your eBook purchase not compatible with the device of your choice?

Don't worry, now with every Packt book you get a DRM-free PDF version of that book at no cost.

Read anywhere, any place, on any device. Search, copy, and paste code from your favorite technical books directly into your application.

The perks don't stop there, you can get exclusive access to discounts, newsletters, and great free content in your inbox daily

Follow these simple steps to get the benefits:

1. Scan the QR code or visit the link below

https://packt.link/free-ebook/9781837636150

2. Submit your proof of purchase
3. That's it! We'll send your free PDF and other benefits to your email directly